D0650963

REFORMING
JOURNALISM

PREVIOUS BOOKS BY MARVIN OLASKY

On Journalism

Prodigal Press
Telling the Truth
Central Ideas in the Development of American Journalism
The Press and Abortion, 1838–1988

On American History

The Tragedy of American Compassion
Fighting for Liberty and Virtue: Political and Cultural Wars in Eighteenth-Century America
The American Leadership Tradition: Moral Vision from Washington to Clinton
Philanthropically Correct: The Story of the Council on Foundations
Abortion Rites: A Social History of Abortion in America
Corporate Public Relations: A New Historical Perspective
Monkey Business: The True Story of the Scopes Trial (with John Perry)

On American Society

Renewing American Compassion
Compassionate Conservatism
Patterns of Corporate Philanthropy
The Politics of Disaster
More Than Kindness (with Susan Olasky)

Understanding the World

World View: Seeking Grace and Truth in Our Common Life
The Religions Next Door
Whirled Views (with Joel Belz)
Freedom, Justice, and Hope (with Herbert Schlossberg)
Turning Point: A Christian Worldview Declaration
(with Herbert Schlossberg)

Fiction and Memoir

Scimitar's Edge
2048: A Story of America's Future
Echoes of Eden
Unmerited Mercy: A Memoir, 1968–1996

REFORMING
JOURNALISM

Marvin Olasky

P&R
PUBLISHING
P.O. BOX 817 • PHILLIPSBURG • NEW JERSEY 08865-0817

© 2019 by Marvin Olasky

All rights reserved. No part of this book may be reproduced, stored in a retrieval system, or transmitted in any form or by any means—electronic, mechanical, photocopy, recording, or otherwise—except for brief quotations for the purpose of review or comment, without the prior permission of the publisher, P&R Publishing Company, P.O. Box 817, Phillipsburg, New Jersey 08865–0817.

Scripture quotations are from the ESV® Bible (The Holy Bible, English Standard Version®), copyright © 2001 by Crossway, a publishing ministry of Good News Publishers. Used by permission. All rights reserved.

Printed in the United States of America

ISBN: 978-1-62995-667-1 (pbk)
ISBN: 978-1-62995-668-8 (ePub)
ISBN: 978-1-62995-669-5 (Mobi)

Library of Congress Cataloging-in-Publication Data

Names: Olasky, Marvin N., author.
Title: Reforming journalism / Marvin Olasky.
Description: Phillipsburg, NJ : P&R Publishing, [2019] | Includes index.
Identifiers: LCCN 2019010059| ISBN 9781629956671 (pbk.) | ISBN 9781629956688 (epub) | ISBN 9781629956695 (mobi)
Subjects: LCSH: Protestant press--History. | Journalism, Religious--Methodology. | Journalism, Religious--Philosophy.
Classification: LCC PN4888.R4 O42 2019 | DDC 070.4/492--dc23
LC record available at https://lccn.loc.gov/2019010059

For courageous Chinese Christian journalists,
and for my grandchildren.
I hope they will also be bold for Christ

Contents

Foreword

I WAS WORKING as a reporter for Marvin Olasky when a Baptist preacher threatened to cut off my hands.

That Saturday, I had interviewed the pastor about allegations that he had sexually abused women who came to him for counseling. I cited witnesses and court documents, but the pastor denied it all. The following morning, I sat in on his Sunday sermon. His subject was spiritual warfare, and he had titled his message "Let's Pick a Fight." With the gathering momentum of a locomotive, amid a congregational soundtrack of hallelujahs and amens, the preacher was thundering about principalities and powers and demonic attacks when he slipped in his threat.

"Anybody wanna write something bad about me?" he cried. "They got children? They got a family? Anybody wanna write something bad about me? They must not like having hands!"

"Amen!" the congregation said.

The pastor then let it be known that he had posted several men around the sanctuary, all of whom were carrying guns. When a preacher starts talking guns and dismemberment, it's a good bet that you're getting too close to the truth.

Telling the truth has been Marvin Olasky's professional calling for the twenty years I've known him as editor, wise mentor, and friend. Yet he has not, as is the habit of some Christian editors, shied away from ugly stories like the one above, stories that would seem to cast the Christian church in a negative light. Marvin taught me that telling the truth as Christian journalists means hard-nosed reporting, not producing thumb-sucking PR for God.

What does that mean? How should Christian writers approach journalism in a fundamentally different way from our secular colleagues? Marvin advocates *biblical objectivity*, a view of people, places, and events as seen through a biblical lens. It does not pretend omniscience, but shows that some things are right, others are wrong, and Scripture is the measure we use to determine which is which. Mainstream reporters also make judgments—they just use different scriptures. Some have faith in scientism, others secular humanism. Still others surf the zeitgeist, buffeted along in the cultural winds. The problem they all face is that those "truth" paradigms change as reliably as weather.

An example: When Marvin released in 1996 a previous book about journalism, *Telling the Truth*, an overwhelmingly bipartisan majority of Congress passed the Defense of Marriage Act, which recognized marriage as an institution reserved to one man and one woman. Gender dysphoria was a known pathology, but women were generally understood to possess twin chromosomes—XX—while men were understood to have the DNA imprint XY. Abortion had been legal for more than two decades, but based on advances in ultrasound technology, a growing number of people had become pro-life, and overall abortion numbers were in decline.

That was just over twenty years ago, barely a generation. Today, people who hold a traditional view of marriage are fired, sued, decried as bigots, and barred from government contracting—with their businesses and reputations destroyed. Biologically determined sex now gives way to gender, a construct of the mind. And abortion? New York state legislators literally danced in the aisles after legalizing abortion through all nine months of pregnancy, shrinking the margin between life and death for a full-term infant to the length of a birth canal.

It is into this churning river of changing "truth" that Marvin has heaved the immovable rock called Scripture. His concept of biblical objectivity acknowledges that in order for truth to be true a priori, it cannot, by definition, change. Biblical objectivity acknowledges that God has established a moral universe with unchanging principles, and that by those lights we must report if we and our readers are to apprehend and understand the world.

I was introduced to biblical objectivity in 1998 when I became a reporter for *World* magazine, where Marvin is still editor-in-chief. From him, I learned much that you will find in this book: the big picture on news-gathering, the rewarding grind of street-level reporting, the virtues of specific detail over bland generalities, the balancing of tough-minded analysis and compassion.

I learned that God is not surprised by the failings of either believers or unbelievers, and is in fact glorified when we drag evil and injustice into the light—even when doing so offends readers. And I learned that biblically directed reporting is not the application of dogma to interpreting world events. Rather, it is a way of contextualizing events according to a moral framework that has served humanity well for millennia, forming the foundation of Western law and government, which have produced the most good for the most people in the history of the world.

Contrast that with the shape-shifting moral framework now fashionable in newsrooms. Everywhere that we see progressives unraveling biblical principles such as hard work, self-sufficiency, the role of fathers, the value of traditional marriage, the sanctity of human life, and the rule of law, we see alarming pathologies tearing the fabric of American culture. Rising rates of poverty, divorce, sexual abuse, addiction, incarceration, and suicide have occurred in lockstep with the rise of progressivism and the American abandonment of the Judeo-Christian worldview.

Critics will object: How dare Marvin Olasky suggest that journalists heed a dusty, outmoded book when gathering and analyzing the news? How dare he conflate reporting with *religion*? What is he, some kind of bumpkin?

Actually, he's a revolutionary. And his views, once establishment, are now courageously countercultural.

A capital-C, card-carrying Communist in the early 1970s, Marvin was once steeped in the very worldview that governs today's mainstream reporting. In this view, journalists should frame people and events in terms of political and class warfare. Marvin did that as a *Boston Globe* correspondent, but in 1974 Marvin was reading the New Testament in Russian—he had studied that language to improve his communication with Soviet big brothers—when the words of Christ ripped the veil off his eyes.

For that, I am grateful. Had God not intervened, I, too, might have fallen under the spell of what I'll call today's *zeitgeist objectivity*, in which editors designate victims according to the whims of culture, and reporters crusade against the evil du jour.

The hard truth is that there will always be evil until Christ returns—not because of an oppressive bourgeoisie, but because of the fallen nature of man. And as Marvin observes, journalists are not saviors. We are only watchmen on the wall. As such, we would do well to examine in these pages his well-reasoned framework for discerning truth—a framework that has stood the test of time.

Lynn Vincent
June 2019
San Diego, California

Acknowledgments

This book exists through grace times three.

First comes the grace of Christ. He turned around my life, and— the Heidelberg Catechism says it better than I could— "with his precious blood has fully satisfied for all my sins. He delivered me from all the power of the devil, and so preserves me that without the will of my heavenly Father, not a hair can fall from my head."

Second is the grace of my wife, Susan. Some novelists turn marital misery into pressure-filled plots, but nonfiction writing comes easiest in a nonfriction household. That's one of the benefits Susan has provided during forty-three years of marriage. Her love shows me how to live.

Third is the grace of my mentor, Joel Belz. He founded *World* and altered my career by inviting me onto the *World* board thirty years ago, and then into the *World* editorship. His Christlike combination of fortitude and gentleness continues to inform, educate, and inspire me.

I am also indebted to all the Worldlings who have put up with me for so long. I've made it hard for our advertising, marketing, and fundraising folks by insisting on a wall of separation between our editorial and business sides: Given financial pressures, that's increasingly rare in journalism. I've made it hard on our reporters by aggressively editing their stories at times.

Particular thanks to Nick Eicher, Mindy Belz, and Tim Lamer, fellow editors since the twentieth century, and to CEO Kevin Martin, who has repeatedly protected my blind side. I've learned from the hundreds of World Journalism Institute mid-career and college students who have studied in my living room and in Asheville, New York City, Iowa, and Shanghai classrooms.

Finally, I appreciate the work of John Hughes and others at P&R who regularly publish good books and are a bit like the Holy Spirit, that shy member of the Trinity. Authors, like reporters, enjoy spotlights only because of off-stage labors. Thank you.

Introduction

IN 1987 AND 1994, I wrote *Prodigal Press* and *Telling the Truth*, two mostly theoretical books about journalism. Since then, I've spent more time doing journalism as chief editor of *World*, a biweekly American news magazine from a Christian perspective. I've had the pleasure of seeing theory turn into successful practice.

Reforming Journalism incorporates material from *Telling the Truth* and from my editing experience over the years. It consists of three parts with ten chapters each and includes stories about China, plus an appendix by *World*'s China bureau chief on the history and current challenges of Chinese journalism. That's because the courage of Chinese Christian journalists impresses me, so I've written this book in a way that I hope will be helpful in both America and China. Christians have translated it into Chinese and are passing it around.

Part 1 of *Reforming Journalism* is about foundational principles, such as biblical objectivity, directed reporting, biblical sensationalism, storytelling, and staying low on the ladder of abstraction by practicing street-level rather than suite-level journalism. It also discusses how reporters should act in countries where Christians are a minority, explains why journalists should not think and act like either the younger or the elder brother in the parable of the prodigal son, and proposes humble sowing.

Part 2 offers how-tos and why-tos: how to conduct interviews and write profiles; how and why to investigate Christian groups and government bodies; how to structure chronological, circular, linear, parallel, and multigrain stories; and how to construct leads, nut grafs, and endings. It also includes tips for better writing, careful word use, and responding to complaints. While American and Chinese cultures are vastly different, the fundamentals of asking questions and telling stories are universal.

Part 3, largely on the history of American journalism, exists because of a surprise. I thought Chinese Christian journalists would not be interested in doings from a long time ago on the other side of the world from them. I was wrong: they now face some of the same issues regarding government control that subjects of the British Empire faced centuries ago. They want to understand how Americans gained press liberty, how they might gain it as well, and how they might avoid some of the trends that now threaten American journalism.

Guess whether the following regulations emanated from British colonial authorities three hundred years ago or from current Beijing authorities:

> No one may establish an entity whose primary purpose is to transmit news information and engage in other news publishing activities without permission from the press and publication administration agency. The nation implements a licensing system for the printing industry. Units or individuals may not engage in printing activities unless they have obtained a Printer Operating License. . . . Enterprises engaging in publication printing activities may not print publications that the government has ordered censored.
>
> News activities shall conform to national regulations and policies, and shall make social benefit their priority. Non-news publishing organs may not engage in news activities without permission from the State agency administering news and publishing. . . . Rumormongering or defamation or other means to incite subversion of the national regime or the overthrow of the socialist system shall be punished. . . .

The reference to "socialist system" gives away the answer, of course, but those statements show why it's worthwhile for Chinese

Christians to learn a little about Western journalism. In the sixteenth century, Britain's structure of government was in some ways similar to China's today. The state, with its official church, was at the center. It gave orders to other social institutions, as do China's government and its Communist Party today.

Protestant Reformation leaders, such as Martin Luther and John Calvin, though, did not equate the kingdom of God with state interests. They believed that God reigns everywhere, and that people can serve God directly in every area of life—government, journalism, education, business, wherever. They placed God's laws above those of the state or any other institution.

Reformers did not advocate extremist intransigence or overturning of governmental authority. Scotland's John Knox, for instance, appealed for moderation and compromise whenever truly fundamental issues were not at stake. Reformers read and believed what the apostle Paul wrote to the Christians in Rome long ago: "Let every person be subject to the governing authorities. For there is no authority except from God, and those that exist have been instituted by God" (Rom. 13:1).

But an emphasis on God's sovereignty also gave journalists an independent authority. They had printing presses and the talent to write because God had given them those material and intellectual advantages. They had a calling to tell the truth and apply biblical principles when officials tried to shackle them. They had the life of Christ to imitate, the Bible to read, and the hope that more and more people would stand firm against religious and governmental tyranny.

Gaining freedom of religion and freedom of the press was not easy. Part 3 describes the last minutes in this life of Pastor John Hooper, tied to a stake and praying. Executioners lit a fire under him, but the green wood was slow to burn. An official handed Hooper a box and told him it contained his pardon—if only he would give in. "Away with it!" Hooper cried. As the fire reached Hooper's legs a gust of wind blew it out. A second fire then slowly burned up Hooper's legs, as he said repeatedly, "Lord Jesus, have mercy upon me. Lord Jesus, receive my spirit!"

Fear of the flames pushed Thomas Cranmer, archbishop of Canterbury, to write a recantation and apology in return for a pardon, only to hear that he would have to burn anyway. Cranmer then resolved to go out boldly. He declared in one final statement that his recantation was "written with my hand contrary to the truth. . . . Therefore my hand shall first be punished; for when I come to the fire, it shall be first burned." Cranmer made good on that promise. Sent to the stake, he placed his right hand firmly in the fire crawling up his legs and held it steadily there until it appeared like a coal to observers.

The last words of another Protestant, Hugh Latimer, were, "We shall this day light such a candle, by God's grace, in England, as I trust shall never be put out." Other protesters also left brave legacies. When John Stubbes wrote a pamphlet in 1579 criticizing Queen Elizabeth, officials cut off his right hand. A contemporary account described his amazing response: "John Stubbes, so soon as his right hand was off, put off his hat with the left, and cried aloud, 'God save the Queen.'" Stubbes, under such duress, set the pattern of respecting those in authority over us, while exposing their unbiblical actions.

For two centuries, the battle went on in England and then America. The breakthrough did not come until 1735, after editor John Peter Zenger, in jail for exposing the corruption of New York royal governor William Cosby, faced a trail for seditious libel. Zenger said he was following the Bible by telling the truth. Judges in red robes and white wigs were ready to convict him, but the jury included Christians who risked imprisonment themselves by declaring Zenger not guilty. Cosby, not wanting to have a revolt on his hands, let Zenger go free, with cheers resounding in his ears.

There's more about this in part 3—and more in China's future, by God's grace. But first, let's discuss the basic principles that should underlie Christian journalism.

PART 1

JOURNALISTIC FOUNDATIONS

1

Two Countries, One Hope

THE TWO COUNTRIES with the largest Christian populations are the United States and China. They are also the two countries that can work together for a peaceful world or plunge us into World War III several decades from now. In both countries, journalism has become part of the problem, rather than part of the solution.

In the United States, a Pew Foundation survey found eight out of ten Americans believe journalists are not independent and are "often influenced by powerful people and organizations." Seven out of ten say "stories are often inaccurate" and journalists "try to cover up their mistakes." Six out of ten say journalists "don't care about the people they report on." Other surveys show nine out of ten Americans distrust reporters.

China has not had similar polling on attitudes toward journalists, but it seems Central Television reporter/producer Wang Qinglei spoke for many in December 2013, when he resigned, saying journalists had become "manipulated clowns" and had lost "credibility and influence." Chinese reporters have a partial excuse: if they do not satisfy officials, prison terms await them. American reporters very rarely go to jail, but if they don't satisfy those with political power, unemployment might be around the corner.

How did we get to this point? The United States and China have very different journalistic traditions, but in both countries reporters often do public relations for those who say they are fighting oppression, but in practice oppress those without political power. The deeper question is why. Certainly, individual journalists seek influence, but what are the justifications for doing so?

Materialist journalists in both the United States and China have no belief in absolute truth. They believe man is mammal or machine, but certainly not made in God's image. The logical end of such thinking in the United States is the belief that (within minimal legal structures) we should be free to do whatever we feel like doing at the moment—whether or not that creates long-term happiness for us or misery for others. The logical end of such thinking within communism is that all truth is class truth, and we should obey the vanguard of the working class to achieve economic progress and social cohesion.

Most reporters do not argue for those propositions; they assume them. That's the nature of a worldview: we wear glasses with lenses that help us to see in particular ways that then seem natural and even unquestionable. Academics use the word *metanarrative* to describe these big understandings that form the basis for framing individual stories. I've called them macro-stories, since they provide a grounding for smaller stories.

We'll look first at the United States. Through most of the eighteenth century, newspapers in America—then ruled by the king of England—usually printed the macro-story I've called "the official story." The job of a journalist was to trust the king and his royal governors, print what officials wanted printed, and not print anything that would hurt the officials' reputation. The big idea was that if people lose confidence in officials, anarchy will result and everyone will be hurt.

Late in the century, most of the founders of the new United States and most of the editors were Christians. They believed the Bible's teaching about creation, fall, and redemption. They understood from the apostle Paul's letter to the Romans that all people "have sinned and fall short of the glory of God." They also knew Christ redeems many and allows us to live better lives and build a better society.

American journalists favored a system of checks and balances. They did not like monarchy, because it could lead to tyranny. They did not like aristocracy, because it could result in feudalism. They also didn't want democracy by itself, because it could lead to "mobocracy," rule by crowd psychology and the passions of the moment. They criticized those who would make idols out of any person or institution.

American political leaders and journalists created a mixed government, featuring a separation of powers. They made the president an executive with only a four-year term. They created a Senate they hoped would be an aristocracy of experience and wisdom. They created the House of Representatives as the voice of democracy. They foresaw a time when the executive and the legislative branches might join forces to expand their own power, at the expense of liberty, so they created a Supreme Court that would prevent or at least curtail such power grabbing.

Political leaders also supported one more check on corruption: journalism. As Thomas Jefferson, author of the U.S. Declaration of Independence in 1776, said a decade later, "Were it left to me to decide whether we should have a government without newspapers or newspapers without a government, I should not hesitate a moment to prefer the latter." Journalists were the last line of defense against tyranny.

During much of the nineteenth century, many American journalists proceeded boldly because they embraced the Bible's news story of God saving sinners through Christ's sacrifice. They saw themselves as representatives of the people generally. They gained their education at street level, rather than in classrooms or at suite level. They listened skeptically to the words of the powerful and often produced stories about corruption, based on their understanding of universal sin affecting the ruled and rulers alike.

In twentieth-century America, though, more journalists started to disbelieve in the good news of Christ redeeming us. They saw man as naturally good, not corrupt. They asked: if we're good, what makes us bad? Many started writing about "oppression." The villains were external influences, such as corporations or churches or schools or guns or meat or something. Within the oppression macro-story, liberal and radical heroes led the way in overturning barriers, such as tradition or property or bourgeois consciousness. They fought "reactionaries" who opposed change. They idolized "progressive" elements and demonized others.

In the twenty-first century, a strange phenomenon has emerged: the official and oppression stories have merged. The original impetus for O&O (official and oppression) late in the twentieth century was the civil rights movement, in which the federal government (prodded by journalists) overturned centuries of oppression and helped to bring about equal rights for African-Americans. That was good, but many journalists went from that triumph to seeing officials such as President Barack Obama as the great helmsmen who would create a radically new and wonderful America.

O&O journalists praised officials who fought a war on poverty by giving people money, whether they worked or not. They praised officials who expanded secular and often atheistic schools and colleges. They praised officials who promoted abortion. O&O journalists attacked those who got in the way of "progress." They placed most Christians in that category.

Many American journalists are now "establishment revolutionaries"—enjoying affluence, but feeling radical as they criticize American traditions. Some others, including those at *World*, challenge them, but Christian journalists are very much a minority.

That's certainly the case in China as well. China's journalistic history is much longer than America's. China had news written on bones or rocks more than two thousand years ago. Chinese reporters recorded King Xuan's death in 782 B.C. and the political successes of Qin Shi Huang in 219 B.C.

The earliest newspaper in world history, the *Kaiyuan Gazette*, appeared in China between A.D. 713 and 742. Others, during the Tang and Song dynasties (618–1279), also presented good news from the imperial standpoint: nothing about mutinies and peasant uprisings. Floods, droughts, and locust plagues also went unreported because these signs of heaven's disappointment could weaken the emperor.

During the Ming dynasty (1368–1644), every Chinese province had a provincial courier officer whose task was to transmit military news and distribute imperial gazettes and notices that contained edicts, news of appointments, imperial examination results, punishments and imprisonments, and attempts to fight corruption—such as the "Ban on Acceptance of Advantages," the "Ban on Fixed Rice Price," and the "Ban on Revenge."

Freedom of the press? No. Penalties were severe for "giving inappropriate comments on current affairs, writing misleading books, spreading fallacies," and passing along any information the emperor deemed secret. The emperor's office could publish notices on big sheets of yellow paper, but all others had to use a lesser size of white paper. Peasants who rebelled could not afford to produce newspapers, but they reported war news and political declarations on wooden boards and pieces of bamboo.

During China's last dynasty, the Qing (1644–1911), a literary inquisition sometimes sentenced to death those who referred negatively to rulers. Toward the end of that era, Christian journalism appeared in China. British Protestant missionary Robert Morrison started China's first modern periodical, the *Chinese Monthly Magazine*, in 1815. Articles on Christianity made up about 85 percent of the magazine, with the rest covering technology, history, poetry, and current events. Although the publication lasted only six years, other missionaries also started Chinese-language magazines and newspapers, which slowly shifted toward a stronger focus on news.

The most influential Christian publication was *A Review of the Times*, by American missionary Young John Allen. It ran from 1868 to 1907 and sold up to fifty thousand copies each week. With a focus on Western ideas of economics, politics, international relations, and religious freedom, the publication had a big impact on leading reformers in the late Qing dynasty. Missionaries also contributed to printing press technologies, and after the Chinese empire fell in 1911, more Chinese started their own publications.

Early in the twentieth century, though, Vladimir Lenin wrote vigorous critiques of capitalist publications. He believed under capitalism only the wealthy could publish newspapers, and they would report and analyze the news in ways that furthered their class interests. Along with other Marxists, he said the economic base of a society determines its superstructure, including its social, political, and religious understandings. He saw mass media as devoted to disseminating bourgeois worldviews and defusing alternative understandings.

Lenin hoped to overthrow bourgeois press freedoms and in so doing kill capitalism's key ideological weapon. When the Communist Party (CP) succeeded in leading a revolution, it would make sure mass media disseminate only proletarian worldviews. The autocrats whom Lenin fought and defeated in Russia had not allowed press freedom. He thought it foolhardy for victorious Communists to allow opposition publications that would threaten revolutionary gains.

China followed Lenin's prescriptions. In 1981, China's CP, in its "Current Propaganda Regulations for Print and Broadcast Media," declared "professionals in publishing, news, radio and television must uphold the spirit of the Communist Party." Deng Xiaoping said, "Party newspapers and periodicals must be sure to publicize the opinions of the Party." President Xi Jinping says reporters should be "disseminators of the Party's policies and propositions, recorders of the time, promoters of social advancement and watchers of equality and justice."

Xi has called the management of journalism "crucial for the Party's path, the implementation of Party theories and policies, the development of various Party and state causes, the unity of the Party, the country and people of all ethnic groups, as well as the future and fate of the Party and the country." Christians favor social advancement and the furthering of equality before God, but also seek press freedom.

Over the centuries, many Christians have fought slavery, ethnic discrimination, and the oppression of women. Many have promoted literacy and social advance, particularly for the poor. Christians have also been loyal citizens under all kinds of political systems. We do not make politics our god, and we follow the prophet Jeremiah's instructions to pray for the peace of the cities in which God has placed us.

American Christians a century ago popularized "The Journalist's Creed," written by Walter Williams, dean from 1908 to 1931 of the first journalism school in the United States and probably the world, at the University of Missouri. Williams in 1921 lectured in Beijing and Shanghai, and created a department of journalism at China's

Yenching University in 1928. His creed emphasized placing the public good above private satisfaction, and noted that "the public journal is a public trust; that all connected with it are, to the full measure of their responsibility, trustees for the public." Williams called for reporting that "fears God and honors man . . . self-controlled, patient, always respectful of its readers."

All Chinese journalists are now supposed to pass a multiple-choice test that includes questions like this one: "What is the most important difference between our news ethics and that of Western developed countries?" The correct answer: "The most basic principle of our news ethics is wholeheartedly serve the people; the most basic principle of news ethics of Western developed countries is freedom of the press." Williams would have embraced both principles, in the belief that freedom of the press, understood not as personal glorification but as a search for truth, does serve the people.

Americans sometimes lecture Chinese about press freedom, but we are really in no position to do so. Journalism in both countries falls short of the Christian ideal.

Sadly, in the United States at least, so do many evangelical publications. Many are content to print public relations releases. Too often they fall from a proper seriousness of purpose into solemnity, so readers who page through them do so out of duty rather than pleasure—and many who want hard-hitting news do not bother to read Christian publications.

The rarity of strong Christian journalism represents both a crisis of entrepreneurship and a faltering of applied faith. Many aspiring Christian journalists know the Bible, but do not know how to apply biblical wisdom to problems of writing and editing. Many editors fill their pages with warmed-over sermons, rather than realistic reporting. Some that do speak up often communicate in a tone so screeching as to be useless in building coalitions.

Is the struggle for strong Christian journalism worth it? I still remember a conference held at Wheaton College thirty years ago, in part because the scheduling of concurrent sessions bothered me. The great theologian J. I. Packer was scheduled to speak in one room. Conference organizers placed me in the next room. I knew Packer's words would be more valuable than mine. I wondered whether attendees would—or should—come to a session on ephemeral journalism, when they could hear a fine lecture on eternal verities.

Providentially, I was staying in a dorm room that shared a bathroom with another dorm room. As I brushed my teeth, who should come in to brush his teeth but Packer himself! He kindly showed God's grace. When I apologetically stammered that I was, in comparison to him, talking trivia, he said in his resonant British accent,

> Nonsense. Think of what revitalizing journalism would do for the cause of Christ in America! It is the most needed sort of pre-evangelism. It is training in Christian worldview. It is an aid to sanctification, and you need to teach people how to do it.

For my nearly three decades with *World*, I've tried to keep his pep talk in mind. Pre-evangelism. Aid to sanctification. I've also remembered Packer's succinct definition of biblical faith: "God saves sinners." Our holy God saves. Man cannot save himself. Neither government nor any other institution can save us. Our righteous God saves through his sovereign grace, not because of anything we do, but out of love for those he calls and covers over with Christ's blood. Our compassionate God saves sinners. We are not essentially good and brought down by a flawed social environment; rather, we are sinners.

Christian journalists vary on some doctrinal matters, but all who wish to be Bible-based editors or reporters must understand that sinful people—that's all of us—need Christ as Savior and also as Lord. Christian publications lose their punch when journalists forget the Bible is useful not only for salvation, but also for application to all aspects of current events. Bible-based magazines and newspapers, like individual Christians, witness to God's saving power, but also to ways in which transformed sinners can exercise Christ-centered dominion over parts of God's creation.

Some people and publications, however, praise Christ as Savior, but trust in worldly rather than biblical wisdom to live their lives and cover the news. They emphasize moments of justification, but pay less attention to years of perseverance. Others emphasize the Lord's rules but not his saving grace, and thus practice a disciplined but joyless Christianity that rapidly becomes legalistic.

This book is addressed to those who want to trust fully in Christ and no one else.

Some hard-edged reporters might contend that ideas do not have practical consequences. They do: biblical commitment or lack of it radically affects a publication's posture in every area. Some evangelicals have tended to become otherworldly. Many in recent years have compromised with secular and atheistic ideas. Courageous Christian journalists, however, need a biblical understanding of this world. Only then can their analysis go far beyond the conventional wisdom.

An understanding of sin should leave journalists skeptical about sweeping claims we can rapidly achieve the "Great Society" that some American politicians once advocated or the "Great Leap Forward" that some Chinese leaders pushed. Many limitations on human progress come out of human nature, not from external forces. People who emphasize unbounded human potential see problems and solutions differently from those who understand the limitations of sinful man. Those who rely on the Bible have views different from those who rely on man's wisdom.

To understand the full need for Christ's sacrifice, we must grasp the depth of sin's ravages. If man is essentially good, then Jesus did not have to die—but an understanding that God saves sinners pushes us toward biblical compassion, which means suffering with those in need and offering a Christ-based challenge to sinful practices. (True compassion is very different from the variety that assumes natural goodness and thus offers merely a pat on the back and coins in the pocket.) A stress on biblical compassion also separates Christians from those secular conservatives who twist the biblical understanding of man's limitations into scorn for tender mercies.

I hope Christians both in the United States and in China can develop and support Bible-based publications that couple an understanding of man's limitations with a concern for others based on God's holy compassion. Our goal should not be the creation of a new Israel or the winning of total victory, for we know God has placed us in Babylon and Christian triumph will come only when Christ returns.

Our goal should be faithful perseverance in the containment of evil. We cannot destroy sin—Christ will take care of that when he comes again—but through God's grace we can contain it, and regain lost ground when possible.

Nearly two thousand years ago, the apostle Paul told oppressed Christians they should still respect rulers. In God's timing, regimes will change as more persons become Christians, but government wields the sword, and those who wield swords against it are likely to perish. Eighteenth-century Americans understood that and did not pick up the sword until local government clashed with the imperial government: then they had to choose. Twenty-first-century Chinese Christians also practice patience, so they give patriotic respect to the Beijing government and the Communist Party, while pushing for greater religious freedom.

Journalists in our two countries can strive for one goal: to tell the truth by providing salt, not sugar, as we report good news without making it sticky sweet, and bad news that shows us our desperate need for Christ. In the United States, China, and other countries, powerful forces push reporters to issue propaganda rather than the honest truth. Some of those pressures are internal, but if we do not lie to support a political faction, we also should not lie because someone thinks it will help God's cause. We believe in a God who tells the truth and wants us to do the same.

KEY TERMS

macro-story
official story
corruption story
oppression story
O&O

STUDY QUESTIONS

1. How have worldviews affected journalism in the United States and China over the centuries?

2. To what extent does O&O journalism embody a false gospel?

3. By better applying their faith to their work, how could Christian journalists help those in other vocations?

4. What examples of journalism have you read/heard/seen that served as pre-evangelism, training in a Christian worldview, and an aid to sanctification?

5. What should be the goals of a Christian journalist, whether in the United States, China, or any other country?

6. Given the distrust that most Americans and Chinese feel toward journalists, how can Christian journalists win back their trust?

FOR FURTHER READING

Ronald T. Farrar, *A Creed for My Profession* (University of Missouri Press, 2013).

Yutang Lin, *A History of the Press and Public Opinion in China* (University of Chicago Press, 1936).

John Blanchard, *Does God Believe in Atheists?* (Evangelical Press, 2000).

2

Why Be a Journalist?

CHAPTER 1 NOTED the pressures journalists face in both the United States and China. Why, then, do some Christians in each country become journalists?

It couldn't be the money: some journalists in the United States and China become rich, but not many. It couldn't be the prestige; Americans on surveys place journalists near the bottom of the barrel, alongside politicians and funeral directors. In China, parents also warn their children against entering a profession rife with problems.

Some negative reasons could drive us: Ego, including the pleasure of seeing our words and bylines on paper and online, and our faces on television and in pixels. Power, the opportunity to make or break some careers. Biblically, we are all fallen sinners: even when God has forgiven us, we are not above responding to some unholy appeals.

Positive reasons also have an impact. Journalists have fun at odd events and meet extraordinary people, instead of sitting behind a desk all day. We can also enjoy using God-given talents to serve and alert others. One American journalist in the 1830s who was also a minister, John McDowall, said reporters were the modern version of the watchmen Ezekiel wrote about. When we see "the sword coming upon the land," we are to blow trumpets and warn the people.

The Bible is full of trumpet-blowing. Genesis 4 quotes the first violent news headlines: Cain killing his brother, and Lamech boasting he killed a man for wounding him. Later chapters in Genesis report God punishing sin by the worst flood in history. He also responds to selfishness and sodomy by destroying Sodom and Gomorrah. The incest of Lot and his daughters immediately follows that disaster.

The book of Judges is certainly full of tough reporting. When Ehud plunged his sword into the belly of the king of Moab, "the hilt also went in after the blade, and the fat closed over the blade, for he did not pull the sword out of his belly" (3:22). When Jael assassinated Sisera, a reporter described the deed in five graphic ways, almost like a repeated slow-motion replay. Abimelech murdered his seventy brothers. Residents of one town gang-raped and killed a woman, whose husband then cut her body into twelve pieces and sent them throughout Israel.

Journalists report bad news, but also help us to honor Paul's injunction to the residents of an immoral city, Philippi: "Whatever is true, whatever is honorable, whatever is just, whatever is pure, whatever is lovely, whatever is commendable, if there is any excellence, if there is anything worthy of praise, think about these things" (Phil. 4:8). One attribute worthy of praise is a willingness to make sacrifices for others, following the example of Christ, who, while we were yet sinners, died for us.

The Gospels are news stories, not an instructional manual, and Luke almost two thousand years ago began his account by saying his purpose was to write an orderly history that would give us certainty concerning what we had heard. Luke knew and we know particular events are important because the world is important, but particular events are not ultimate. They are part of a bigger story of God accomplishing his will, and journalists can help Christians to avoid panic even amid gloom.

Such a crucial calling means Christian journalists should bake cakes with three layers. We report events, provide interpretations of events, and probe for deeper meaning—and in the process show people who overcome their circumstances because Christ gives us hope. Some journalists have contempt for ordinary folks who supposedly lack imagination, but Jesus turned Simon, who dreamed of fish, into Peter, a fisher of men. He can do that to anyone anywhere in the world, from any background, race, class, or ethnicity. Because of our sin and God's mercy, we can be fully realistic, but also fully optimistic.

In short, a Christian journalist, through his work, answers each day a simple but crucial question: whose world is this? Abraham Kuyper, a Dutch editor who was also a theologian and even served as prime minister of the Netherlands, answered that question this way: "Every square inch of creation belongs to Christ." Let's think about that. What if every square inch is truly God's? What if every person is made in God's image? What if every moment is within God's providence? How do our answers to those questions affect the way we report the news?

Naturally, officials in both the United States and China like journalistic accounts that praise them. They discourage stories investigating their malfeasance. Christian reporters in both countries have to be bold and courageous (particularly in China) to go crosswise against those in power, and that means sometimes being foolish in the eyes of the world (see Paul's teaching in 1 Corinthians 4).

The heavens declare the glory of God, as Psalm 19 tells us, but the streets declare the sinfulness of man. Sadly, Christian reporters need to cover sorrow, tragedy, and even evil. The Bible teaches that when man turns away from God, he acts like a beast, and that beastliness will show itself sometimes in awful crimes. We do not want to dwell on them, but if we ignore them, we're ignoring evidence for the understanding of man's sinfulness that is essential to Christianity—for if man without God is not a beast, then Christ's sacrifice for us was unnecessary.

A Christian journalist is one who not only goes to church on Sunday, but believes that Christ rules 24/7. A Christian journalist trusts the biblical message that God created the world and is active in the life of his creation. Christian journalists know God created a good world, but Adam and Eve fell, and the whole creation with them. Christian journalists see evidence of that fall—the sin and misery— all around us. Yet we also know the Bible is a story of redemption. We report on brokenness and renewal in culture and education, in communities and families, in church and state.

At *World*, we have wondered at times whether to avoid writing stories on miserable evils such as clergy sexual abuse, but what Paul wrote to the Ephesians heartens us: "Take no part in the unfruitful works of darkness, but instead expose them" (Eph. 5:11). It's sad we have to do this, but actions exposed by the light become visible, and that's how evildoers are pushed to change their lives. As commentator Matthew Henry wrote three centuries ago, evil acts should "be made to appear in their proper colors to the sinners themselves, by the light of doctrine or of God's word in your mouths, as faithful reprovers."

John Calvin, commenting on that Ephesians passage, asked whether evildoers would "lay aside all shame, and give loose reins to their passions, if darkness did not give them courage, if they did not entertain the hope that what is hidden will pass unpunished?" His following words speak to us: "You, by reproving them, bring forward the light, that they may be ashamed of their own baseness. Such shame, arising from an acknowledgment of baseness, is the first step to repentance."

We have decided not to pamper adults or unduly shelter children. Ann Voskamp, in *One Thousand Gifts* (2010), wrote about chaperoning her church's youth group, made up of farm kids, through Toronto's mean streets. She was scared when a man with a wild mane of graying hair put on a clown's mask and started yelling at the children: "I'm masking the real me! Know what I mean? . . . I'm messed up, man. Look at me! . . . Fried my brain on crack, know what I mean? . . . Don't do crack, know what I mean?"

Voskamp wrote,

> He steps into the company of young people. Some look away.
> . . . His rage shakes us. Shakes the drowsy, shakes the slumbering,
> shakes us to look at what we really came to see, to look straightway
> into it and really open the soul wide *to see* and it terrifies.

She thanked the wild man for shaking her and them.

World has covered ugly examples of sin, such as prostitution and sexual molestation in schools, importation of prostitutes and slaves, and partial-birth abortion. Some people cancel subscriptions when we run such stories. But here's the type of letter we now receive frequently: "My heart was broken by your article. Thanks for printing this 'hard-to-read' information. Because of it, God has called me to prayer and action like never before."

To summarize, most religions are predictable in their philosophy of exchange: you do something nice for a god; the god in return does something for you. The gospel, though, is sensational: while we were yet sinners, Christ died for us. Biblical journalism is Christ-oriented, covering both crucifixion and resurrection. Our articles should suggest CFR—creation, fall, redemption—by showing how terrible man is, yet how wonderful, created in God's image and worth dying for.

It's not easy to be a Christian journalist. Public relations is an easier pursuit. But one of my favorite movies, *The Right Stuff*, has an official telling pilot Alan Shepard, who became the first American in space, that the work of an astronaut is "dangerous. Very dangerous." Shepard's instant response: "Count me in." That's what prospective Christian journalists should say. We can learn from a secular journalist, David Halberstam, who said,

> The legwork of reporting is critical and most of the fun. Think of it as part of a continuing education; we're paid to learn. It isn't just getting a byline that drives you; it isn't just where the story lands in the paper. Fifty-two years later, I still like what I do.

Christian journalists especially should have that attitude. We know human interest is important because every human is created in God's image. Over three thousand years ago, the Egyptian Ptahhotep gave career advice: "Be a scribe! You sit grandly in your house, beer is poured copiously. All who see you rejoice in good cheer. . . . Happy is the heart of him who writes; he is young each day." Many media organizations, sadly, include journalists bored with life, which they see as purposeless, but Christians especially should relish the joy of journalism, making it part of life's goal. As the Westminster Shorter Catechism states, our chief end is "to glorify God, and to enjoy him forever"—and forever begins right now.

To enjoy our craft fully, Christian journalists need to realize the children's song "It's a Small World (after All)" is dumb. It's not a small world. It's a large one, with millions of nooks and crannies and opportunities for adventure. In Robert Boynton's book *The New New Journalism*, writer Susan Orlean recalls with excitement an article she wrote about a gospel singing group: "It was astonishing for me to glimpse a world that was so fully developed—with its own stars, sagas, myths, history, millions of devotees—that I, in my narrow life, I had no idea existed."

Christian journalists hate atrocities, including abortion—the killing of babies, sometimes behind the curtains and sometimes right before our eyes. Still, we try to keep calm by reporting sensational facts with understated prose. We try to have an accurate self-image. An excellent secular reporter, Richard Ben Cramer, said of himself,

> I'm a smith. I occupy the position in our society that a good wheelwright would have occupied in his. Making wheels is a highly specialized skill. I don't consider myself to be an artist. I consider myself to be a skilled workman.

That's how we as Christian journalists should see ourselves. We are not saviors. We are watchmen on the walls. We are creatures in a great big world, but creatures with a great opportunity to glorify God and enjoy him immediately. As John Piper notes, "Every joy that does not have God as its central gladness is a hollow joy and in the end will burst like a bubble." Christian journalists can have great joy by discovering and communicating the reasons that exist for honoring Christ in all things and above all things.

Piper points out that we should aspire "to study reality as a manifestation of God's glory, to speak and write about it with accuracy, and to savor the beauty of God in it." The Bible teaches us that God created this world to be his theater, so the more we report accurately what happens in it, the more we will praise him. A Christian journalist who highlights good news is praising God. Our natural selfishness means that what is good comes from him. A Christian journalist who reports bad news, showing the results of sin, is praising God because the bad shows how desperately we need him.

Zeal for God's glory should characterize all of a Christian journalist's editorial decisions. We should praise marriage and hate abortion in the realization that our natural tendencies are toward selfishness. When a mom sacrifices her freedom to care for a child, and when a dad sacrifices his freedom to provide for his family, that glorifies God. We should cover compassionate ministries because God showed his glory the most when Christ lowered himself to live among us and then suffer and die for us. Since Christ so amply displayed compassion, our attempts to follow in some of his steps is another way of glorifying God.

All journalists can have the joy of writing provocative and evocative news stories that come out of pavement-pounding rather than thumb-sucking. Christian journalists can have greater joy by standing not only for factual accuracy, but also for biblical objectivity, which means trying to see the world as best we can in the way the Bible depicts it—we'll discuss this at greater length shortly. Christian journalists can be humble by presenting not our own opinions, but God's perspective from the Bible, distinguishing between issues on which the Bible is clear and those on which it isn't.

Christian journalists, in short, can have the joy of offering salt, not sugar and not acid. We can publish what we believe to be true, not what we or someone else would like to be true. Christian journalists can have the joy of speaking up for those it's convenient to forget: the unborn, the unemployed, the uneducated victimized by poor schools, and the politically unfashionable. We can know that we are fallen sinners, but sinners who look upward and create a no-scream zone within a high-decibel society.

We will encounter opposition, but—as the writer of Hebrews begins chapter 12,

> Since we are surrounded by so great a cloud of witnesses, let us also lay aside every weight, and sin which clings so closely, and let us run with endurance the race that is set before us, looking to Jesus, the founder and perfecter of our faith, who for the joy that was set before him endured the cross, despising the shame, and is seated at the right hand of the throne of God.

KEY TERMS

exchange religion
Christian religion
compassion
salt

STUDY QUESTIONS

1. If the heavens declare the glory of God, what do the streets declare?
2. What are the limitations of amoral journalism and journalistic moralism?
3. Should Christian journalists emphasize reporting on brokenness or reporting on renewal—and if we do both, should it be 50/50? 90/10?
4. While following the emphasis of Ephesians on exposing the "works of darkness," how can journalists avoid sowing despair?
5. When should journalists head into dangerous places or situations, and what precautions should they take in doing so?
6. How and why should Christians find joy in being journalists— and what can disrupt or steal that joy?

FOR FURTHER READING

Robert Boynton, *The New New Journalism* (Vintage, 2005).
Randy Alcorn, *The Grace and Truth Paradox* (Multnomah, 2003).

3

Biblical Objectivity

LET'S HEAD TO the central concept of Christian journalism: biblical objectivity. It may seem strange to those who have accepted secular definitions of objectivity, so after laying out the basics, we'll look into those definitions and how they have ruled different periods of American journalism. We'll also contrast biblical objectivity with Marxist views of class objectivity.

Let's start with some basic dictionary definitions of "objective": "existing independent of mind; emphasizing or expressing the nature of reality as it is apart from personal reflections or feelings." An objective report, therefore, is one "stressing objective reality as distinguished from subjective experience or appearance." But what is reality? Can we perceive it? As human beings, we can perceive it in part, but always through our own perspectives. Marx emphasized class, some emphasize race, and others stress an existential subjectivity.

How do we get accurate information? The person who understands not just the appearance of a building, but every cubic foot of its innards, is often the builder. How much more does God, the builder and sustainer of this world, know every atom of his creation? This means only God knows the true, objective nature of things. Happily, he hasn't kept it to himself. He gave us the Bible, which, since it comes from him, is the only completely objective and accurate view of the world. Given our human limitations and sinfulness, we can never achieve God's perspective, but by following the Bible's teachings we try to come as close as we can. The only true objectivity is biblical objectivity.

Since we are fallen sinners, it's hard to practice biblical objectivity. We can easily fall into amoral journalism, journalistic moralism, or existential subjectivity. Amoral journalism emphasizes all the sound and fury in the world and presents people's lives as tales told by idiots, signifying nothing. It is not the same as sensationalism, which the Oxford English Dictionary defines as "a condition of excited feeling produced in a community by some occurrence." The Bible is often sensational as it wakes up the sleeping and reminds us of the nature of God and man. But amoral journalism is sensationalism that does not point us to God.

We can also fall into journalistic moralism, which emphasizes the good and uplifting parts of life so people can feel better about themselves. The churchy form of journalistic moralism presents happy, smiling church people, removed from the sinful world and moving from one triumph to the next—and it thus seems unrealistic. Existential subjectivity, where every person becomes a god in his own eyes and decides for himself what is right and wrong, is also a danger. The Christian goal is to reflect biblical thinking as well as we can.

Biblical objectivity, in contrast to these other emphases, shows how humans are both terrible and yet wonderful, created in God's image and worth dying for. It is Christ-oriented, covering both crucifixion and resurrection. That gives Christian reporters a license to cover sorrow, tragedy, and even evil. The Bible teaches that when man turns away from God, he acts like a beast. That beastliness will show itself sometimes in awful crimes. We do not want to dwell on them, but if we ignore them, we're ignoring evidence for the understanding of man's sinfulness that is essential to Christianity—for if man without God is not a beast, then Christ's sacrifice for us was unnecessary.

One other element needs emphasis: Christians have the opportunity to get things right by looking to the Bible, but Christians are not immune to the temptations and pressures that affect other journalists. Since we are far from godly, we will get things wrong. Our goal is to take strong stands when the Bible is clear, and to avoid doing so when the Bible is not. Taking a strong position does not mean that we ignore unbiblical positions, misquote or ridicule opponents, or give up reporting to engage in propaganda.

To deepen this discussion of objectivity, we have to understand how it has gone through four definitions in American journalism. In phase one, many early American journalists assumed God is objectively real, with an existence independent of our minds. In 1690, the first American newspaper, *Publick Occurrences Both Forreign and Domestick*, noted God's "Merciful Providence" as fact, not opinion. Editor Benjamin Harris reported that Plymouth residents "have newly appointed a day of Thanksgiving to God for his Mercy in supplying their extreme and pinching Necessities under their late want of Corn, & for his giving them now a prospect of a very Comfortable Harvest."

Although no one in early American journalism used the term "objective reporting," some editors obviously understood that factuality demanded taking into account the spiritual. They reported recoveries from illness as acts of God. A *Boston Recorder* story began with a note that when a ship sank "by the will of Providence" and a merchant lost all he had, his wife "was rendered altogether insane, and that to such a degree, that it was necessary to confine her in order to prevent her from doing herself and others harm."

The wife's insanity continued until her father, who lived one hundred miles away, received a letter describing what had happened, and immediately "gathered together at his house many of the brethren of the Church for the purpose of pleading with God on her behalf. It was a solemn season of united and earnest supplication to the Lord." A few days later, the father received a letter saying his daughter had suddenly "sat up in bed . . . in an instant restored to her usual health." The story concluded:

> Here we cannot but notice, in grateful acknowledgements, the goodness and mercy, compassion and faithfulness of that God who has said, "Call upon me in the day of trouble, I will deliver thee, and thou shalt glorify me," for that evening and that hour of

restoration, were the *same evening* and the *same hour* when many were gathered together, and prayer was made unto God for her.

Recorder editors knew that many individuals recover after prayer, but many others die. There is a problem when Christians want so much for God to "do justice" right away that they exaggerate reports of his intervention. God does not need public relations help. But when truly miraculous cures do occur, a *Recorder* editorial writer asked, "Can you rationally draw any other inference" than that of God's sovereignty?

Many early American journalists would have been amazed to hear that anyone who ignores the spiritual would consider himself objective. Then, those who ignored the spiritual were considered subjective atheists, allowing their own feelings to overcome what really exists. Paul's epistle to the Colossians notes that Christ "is before all things, and in him all things hold together" (1:17). How then could a reporter, in describing reality, not refer to God, the Creator of reality?

Starting midway through the nineteenth century, though, a new phase in the understanding of objectivity took hold among American journalists. They began to see "fact" only as that which was scientifically measurable. As photographs began to provide a record of the visible, many journalists equated the visible with the real and began seeing the world as largely non-mysterious. They did not use the term "objectivity," but they made their own eyes the standard of authority: they were human cameras. This represented a considerable departure from biblical notions of fallen man and a complicated world—and, as Paul wrote, one we could see only through a dark window. The metaphor also became limited as reporters saw that stories changed when they pointed cameras in a different direction and changed film or filters.

Early in the twentieth century, the concept of reporter as camera began to fall apart theoretically and practically. Some journalists also rebelled against the idea of camera objectivity, not because of questions brought forward by Christians, but because of the impact of Marxism and Freudianism. We'll explain this more in chapter 27, but the result was a third phase in the definition of journalistic objectivity.

Previously, journalists had redefined it to mean an ignoring of the spiritual. Now they could ignore part of the material that journalists themselves observed, for that part might be gained through bias. They thought reporters should forgo some of their own reporting, so as to assemble as many reports from others as they could.

Objectivity could be reached, they thought, only through a balancing of multiple subjectivities. The outcome might be neither truthful nor accurate, but who knew what accuracy, let alone truth, really was? The triumph of theological liberalism in major Protestant denominations in the United States occurred at the same time as the development of phase three objectivity. This was no coincidence, since the balancing-of-subjectivities mode often suggests right or wrong does not exist—just opinion.

Soon, instead of reporting both material and spiritual considerations, or reporting the material only, journalists began to report what a variety of observers thought about things. Instead of holding up a mirror to society, they urged others to hold up their own mirrors, so reporters could then describe the funny shapes each mirror produced.

In practice, this kind of objectivity has limitations. Reporters have never felt the need to balance anti-cancer statements with pro-cancer statements. In recent practice, secular-liberal reporters have seen pro-life concerns or "homophobia" as cancerous, and many other Christian beliefs as similarly harmful. Objectivity was a reporting of multiple subjectivities, and truth was out there at a constantly receding horizon. If journalists in phase two happily saw themselves as cameras, journalists in phase three unhappily started to see themselves as stenographers or tape recorders.

Many journalists found the balancing of subjectivities to be a boring exercise—occasionally demeaning, and generally purposeless. Boredom tended to set in because the reporters, to be evenhanded in reporting subjectivities, had to tell much less than they knew. Specific details might be damning to one side or the other, but the reporter's task was to quote a variety of positions while keeping the more interesting but biased story buried in his notebook.

Some famous American journalists became acerbic about objectivity. Former *New York Times* reporter David Halberstam complained that "objectivity was prized and if objectivity in no way conformed to reality, than all the worse for reality." Douglas Cater put it succinctly: the straight reporter is a "straight-jacket reporter." Politicians often treated reporters as delivery boys, using them to carry their messages.

Late in the twentieth century, some well-known American television journalists attacked the entire concept of objectivity. Robert Bazell said, "Objectivity is a fallacy. . . . There are different opinions, but you don't have to give them equal weight." Linda Ellerbee wrote, "There is no such thing as objectivity. Any reporter who tells you he's objective is lying to you." In the United States, some writers argued for a "new journalism," in which reporters emphasized their own subjective impressions.

Chinese Marxist journalists also objected to any definition of objectivity that did not take into account class perspectives, but they did not emphasize subjectivity. They desired to cover news from the perspective of the workers, and argued that reporting should present the views of the vanguard of the workers, the Communist Party.

Discomfort in the U.S. led to a fourth phase: disguised subjectivity, sometimes called "strategic ritual" (pseudo-objectivity that provides defense against criticism). A key aspect of strategic ritual is choice of sources and selection of quotations. With half a dozen legitimate spokesmen on a particular issue, reporters can readily play journalistic ventriloquism by using the one who expresses their own position. As NBC reporter Norma Quarles acknowledged, "If I get the sense that things are boiling over, l can't really say it. I have to get somebody else to say it."

Similarly, of the many statements an opponent may make during an interview, reporters can play up one that will make that opponent look foolish. The upshot is that, once again, a reporter often makes a story conform to the "pictures in his head," just as in the era of straightforward materialism. ABC executive producer Av Westin acknowledged how strategic ritual helped him to sell abortion to the American public a half-century ago. He showed dramatic photos of bruised, "unwanted" babies, and shots of "a silhouetted woman telling how she nearly died after an illegal abortion." Then, "with the case for legalized abortion powerfully presented, an opponent of abortion would be given a chance to make the pro-life side of the case, usually without dramatic pictures, inserted merely as a 'talking head.'"

Furthermore, American newspapers until the 1960s referred to creatures in women's wombs as "babies" or "unborn children." Then they switched to "fetus," which is technically correct but linguistically distancing—and inconsistent, since they didn't also use Latin by calling the pregnant mom a *gravida* or having their crime reporters write about the *corpus mortuum*. Now, the term used—fetus or unborn child—quickly types a person as favoring or opposing abortion. New Orleans residents refer to their boulevard median strips as "neutral ground," but we lack neutral nomenclature on abortion.

Strategic ritual is now giving way to social radicalism. For example, when an internal Associated Press (AP) memo expressed concern about reporting two husbands or two wives within a "marriage," former *USA Today* reporter Janet Kornblum complained in mock horror, "Surely the straightlaced AP wasn't saying that husbands are not husbands and wives are not wives—unless they are heterosexual." Kornblum noted that if AP did not use terms like "his husband" or "her wife," it was basically siding with people who opposed same-sex marriage.

AP leaders briefly took some heat and then flipped. The *Los Angeles Times* declared a victory for homosexuality and stated, "Those who get married have already decided about terminology. AP's job is to reflect this reality without hesitation." That summarizes a major tenet of much nonbiblical philosophy: we create our reality—in this case, by endorsing "same-sex marriage."

The Bible offers a different understanding of the nature of man, the nature of God, the nature of man's tasks and man's hopes, the nature of reality. Christians don't have great confidence in man's wisdom. We assume that fallen man naturally distorts and lies. We suspect that fallen man's wisdom will slide us even deeper into sin and misery. Former *Louisville Courier-Journal* editor James Pope once declared, "Objectivity is a compass for fair reporting, a gyroscope, a little secret radar beam that stabs you when you start twisting news to your own fancy." But, given man's nature, is journalistic goodwill a major check on pernicious news twisting?

Instead, a Christian solution starts with confidence in God's objectivity. God alone, the Christian knows, has given us a biblical measuring rod built of true, godly objectivity. As the prophet Amos saw, "The Lord was standing beside a wall built with a plumb line." God then told Amos that he was "setting a plumb line in the midst of my people Israel" (Amos 7:7–8). We have that plumb line today, the Bible. Thus, we know what man should do.

A Christian solution is based on man's limited ability, with God's grace, to study God's objectivity and apply it to everyday situations. We do not think we arrive at truth by wiping our minds clean, because then we are at the mercy of our fallen vision. Our hope relies on filling our fallen minds with God's vision. Walter Cronkite, the most trusted U.S. broadcast journalist from the 1960s through the 1980s, once called himself a liberal, defined as one "not bound by doctrines or committed to a point of view in advance." But, given our fallen natures, we are all captive to sin, unless we commit to Christ.

Christians are skeptical of self-generated conclusions, but sure of God's. As we study the Bible and try to apply biblical principles, we go beyond subjectivity by responding to problems with God's Word, which is objective. Since the Christian presuppositional structure is closer to reality than competing frameworks are, biblical Christians can explain more accurately how the world truly works.

That's what biblical objectivity is. God created the world—that's biblically objective fact. He created human beings male and female—that's biblically objective fact. He created Adam and Eve and made their union "marriage"—that's biblically objective fact.

What is not biblically objective? Ignoring or misquoting opponents is not biblically right. Second Kings 18:32 (and Isaiah 36:17) quote the blandishments of a blaspheming Assyrian general who demanded surrender and promised exile to "a land of grain and wine, a land of bread and vineyards, a land of olive trees and honey." The general was saying that Assyria would give the Israelites what God had promised but failed to do—and God's inspired writers quoted that lie.

Biblical objectivity is not a claim that we have answers to all policy questions. The next chapter will show how we can be certain about an issue when the Bible is clear, and how we should balance diverse positions when the Bible is not. Nor does biblical objectivity mean disregarding the specific detail of stories. Chapter 5 will emphasize the importance of street-level reporting that's low on the ladder of abstraction.

Biblical objectivity means that we report accurately only when we realize this is the world the Lord has made, and only he understands it fully. Objectivity is the God's-eye view. We acknowledge our inability to be fully objective since we are sinners with fallen wills and very limited understanding. Nevertheless, we do not give up. The Koran calls Allah "inscrutable," but the Bible shows that God reveals his thoughts to man.

Much remains hidden, as Job learned, and much we see darkly, as the apostle Paul pointed out. Still, we do have some sight, and when we study the Bible to see what God says about issues, we can come closer to that God's-eye view. Therefore, a solidly Christian news publication should not be conventionally balanced. It should offer provocative and evocative, colorful and gripping, Bible-based news analysis.

Biblical objectivity emphasizes not a technique, but a plumb line. Stories that end in sadness often teach the wages of sin. Those that end well may emphasize the wages of piety. Those that are unclear teach us that much of life is unpredictable and often confusing. Immediate justice often is not forthcoming, except in poetry. Poetic justice tells us what heaven will be like, but an undue emphasis on good guys always winning might make us believe, falsely, that the present, shattered earth is our real home. Biblical objectivity means having both eyes focused on God.

Biblical objectivity is of course hateful to atheists, who say its practitioners are being subjective by reporting God as reality, since God is merely an object of the Christian's consciousness—but atheists are assuming, without proof, that atheism is true. Christians see atheists as leaving out basic fact due to spiritual blindness. No easy compromise is possible when such fundamental presuppositions battle each other.

Atheists argue that God, as a product of imagination, has no real place in an objective news report. Christians argue that God's existence and sovereignty are objective truth, regardless of an atheist's personal belief in God's nonexistence. Is an objective reporter supposed to treat God as a matter of fact (in which case he is joining the theistic side) or as a matter of opinion (in which case he has assumed the truth of atheism)? That's the question for journalists of this age or any age.

God shows Christians he exists independently of our minds by acting on our minds from outside. Yet if a person who has not had that experience is unwilling to accept the testimony of others, and thus sees internally generated psychological change rather than God's grace, he will see Christian fact as imagination and Christian objectivity as subjectivity.

The Bible shows the importance of making choices. First Kings 18:21 says, "Elijah came near to all the people and said, 'How long will you go limping between two different opinions? If the LORD is God, follow him; but if Baal, then follow him.'" In the long run, journalistic differences between followers of God and agnostics or atheists (including those who are nominally Christian, but practically indistinguishable from non-Christians) are inevitable. There is no neutrality: we are either God-centered or man-centered.

KEY TERMS

> objective report
> biblical objectivity
> class objectivity
> conventional objectivity (late twentieth century): a balancing of
subjectivities
> sensationalism
> biblical sensationalism

STUDY QUESTIONS

1. How can secular journalists write objectively?
2. How did Darwin's *On the Origin of Species*, published in 1859, affect journalism?

3. Might the "strategic ritual" of pseudo-objectivity be a tactically helpful approach at times even for a publication that stands solidly on a foundation of biblical truth?
4. Can you give an example of a news story you have read/heard/seen that overused the Bible? Underused it?
5. Suppose a candidate running for office has been involved in adultery. He has made a public confession, but is not withdrawing from the race. How might four reporters coming from different perspectives cover this story?

FOR FURTHER READING

James Anderson, *What's Your Worldview?* (Crossway, 2014).
Jeff Baldwin, *The Deadliest Monster: A Christian Introduction to Worldviews* (Coffee House, 1998).
Darrow Miller, *LifeWork: A Biblical Theology for What You Do Every Day* (YWAM Publishing, 2009).

4

Navigating the Rapids

THE FIRST DECISION journalists make is not how to write about particular issues and questions, but which topics to cover. The world is vast, resources are limited, and we always make choices. Even a local publication has more shoveled onto its plate than it can consume. An editor who simply says, "We'll cover the news," is not being honest with others and perhaps himself as well, for "the news" does not just happen. Some stories are obligatory for publications to report, but more often editors have considerable discretionary choice over which events to cover.

Agenda-setting is inevitable. Print publications have limited space. The internet has given journalists greater flexibility than we used to have, but we still have limited time. A lengthy examination of one issue may mean no time spent on another. Every editor who assigns a reporter to a story is thereby not assigning the reporter to another. Virtually every experienced reporter has some idea about a story line before reporting begins. Honest reporters have to be willing to change story lines when facts on the ground confound expectations—but each fact has a context.

Journalists emerge from the early reporting and interviewing process with a thesis—an idea of what the story is all about—either supported or changed. With a thesis in mind, reporters look for ways to tell a lot with a little. We train ourselves to observe and record the details that help to characterize a person, a meeting, and so forth. At a certain point, a thesis solidifies and reporters are no longer looking for evidence that disproves it (although we should take into account any that emerges). Instead, journalists from that point on are building a case as an honest lawyer would, bringing out supporting evidence and refuting what appears to undermine the thesis but actually does not.

In this sense, all reporting is directed reporting, directed by some worldview. Many stories feature a protagonist who faces an antagonist and perseveres in his mission while overcoming obstacles—PAMO, for short. A normal template for a story is that the protagonist wants to do X as part of his mission, but Y (the antagonist) and Z (obstacles) are in his way. The protagonist may be an organization, rather than an individual, and the antagonist may be a worldview.

For example, here's a paragraph from *World* (with names omitted):

> On July 4 six women arrived at the top prosecutor's office in Beijing with the names of their detained husbands pasted onto their summer dresses with messages like "I support you" and "Waiting for you." The wives, joined by lawyers and several Western diplomats, came to raise their frustrations that authorities in the neighboring city of Tianjing had barred them from contacting their husbands, whom authorities arrested last year in a nationwide roundup of human rights lawyers and activists.

In that paragraph, the six women are the protagonists and their mission is to express their frustrations, so as to support their husbands. Their antagonists are government officials, and one of the obstacles is the order than bars them from contacting their husbands. *World* is sympathetic to those women and their husbands. The story could be written from a different perspective that would have the authorities as protagonists with the mission of preserving law and order, and the wives, lawyers, and Western diplomats as antagonists ignorantly or maliciously wasting everyone's time.

Even the simplest spot news story has a protagonist, mission, antagonist, and barriers. Here's one:

Firefighters [protagonist] last night battled a blaze [antagonist]. Because of high winds and low water pressure [barriers], it took two hours to extinguish the flames [mission].

Or another:

Police [protagonist] yesterday took a bite out of crime [mission] by arresting the East Side cat burglar [antagonist]. He surrendered only after he fired two shots [obstacle] and yelled, "You'll never take me alive."

Because only arsonists cheer for the fire, the choice of protagonist—firefighter or fire—is clear. The choice is not clear to all reporters covering abortion. Christian reporters normally see the unborn baby as the protagonist, since the baby's life is at stake. Those who would kill the baby are antagonists. Other reporters make legislators or a particular reading of the Constitution the antagonists.

Compelling stories have a protagonist or protagonists on a mission, one or more antagonists, and obstacles to success. For example, in the United States children learn about the three little pigs: One who works hard takes the time to build his house out of bricks. The other two choose a faster alternative and build their houses out of straw or sticks. The three pigs are our protagonists. Their mission is building houses. The barrier to success for two of them is laziness—they don't want to spend the time to build a strong house. They have an antagonist: a big bad wolf who huffs and puffs and blows down the houses made of straw or sticks.

Good stories have strong, vigorous antagonists. If the wolf's problem was just big teeth and a pointy nose, officials could give him free orthodontist visits and free plastic surgery—but the wolf's murderous disposition is integral to a gripping story. Communist Party stories, if true, are compelling. The protagonists are workers and peasants and their vanguard, committed CP members. They are on a mission to raise standards of living and free a nation from bourgeois or aristocratic restraints. Their antagonist is the ruling class or, once Communists take power, reactionaries who sabotage efforts to make sure all are well fed, housed, clad, and cared for. Obstacles include independent media, businesses, and churches.

The Bible has a complicated structure, but it is essentially a story of creation, fall, and redemption. God's mission is to rescue his people and save them from sin. Christ is the protagonist, and Satan is the antagonist who seems to win in the garden of Eden, seems to win often throughout the history of Israel, and seems to win on Good Friday—but loses in the end. Each book of the Bible, sometimes each chapter, has its own drama. In Genesis 3, for example, Adam and Eve are the protagonists with the mission of continuing to be able to walk with God in the garden of Eden. Satan, in the form of a serpent, is the antagonist, tempting the first couple to sin. The fruit of the two trees are the obstacles to mission fulfillment, which occurs through obedience. When Adam and Eve disobey, they are cast out.

PAMO analysis is also useful when looking at other chapters of the Bible. For example, Ezekiel 33 portrays watchers on the wall who have a calling like that of journalists. The protagonist is the watchman, and the antagonist is a literal enemy bringing a sword to the land—or a metaphorical enemy, sin. The watchman's goal is to warn the people when a threat appears. Barriers to successful fulfillment of the mission include laziness (the watchman sleeping at his post), blindness (not seeing the threat), cowardice (fear that warning the wicked will bring retribution from them), and wickedness (siding with evil).

After I visited China and saw with my own eyes the burgeoning house churches movement, I wrote, "With house churches multiplying in cities and influential executives coming to faith, Christianity is growing so fast in China that Communist officials are having a hard time keeping up." In that story, Chinese Christians are the protagonists, with a mission of spreading the gospel, and Communist officials are the antagonists. The protagonists face barriers: harassment, sometimes persecution, and their own fear and desires.

Near the end of a story with the literal headline "Dead ends in Darfur," *World* reported that janjaweed ("armed horsemen") were raiding Sudanese villages, raping women, killing children, and torching property. The protagonists are innocent people, their mission is to raise crops and children, and their biggest obstacle is the lack of any obstacles in the way of their antagonists, the janjaweed.

Other stories aren't as clear-cut. A *World* article about the effect of soaring food prices on the poor concluded, "Many forces are at work in bringing about higher food prices. One of these forces—the diversion of land and crops to biofuel production at the expense of food production—is unlike the others: Congress has the power to change it." Here the protagonists are poor people with the mission of obtaining less expensive food, the antagonist is biofuel production that raises prices, and the obstacle is a Congress providing biofuel incentives and thus indirectly raising the price of food.

Journalists write feature stories, in short, from a variety of viewpoints, but most have protagonists and antagonists, missions and obstacles. Stories don't write themselves. Some journalists say, "I just report the facts," but it's important to understand that facts by themselves sit like lumps of coal. Those lumps provide warmth only when placed in a furnace. Facts heat our minds only when placed within stories. Authorities regularly try to get us to place facts within stories in ways that please them and solidify their power. Some push hard on this, using state power to imprison, torture, or even kill those who disagree.

Sometimes officials use social pressure. Alexis de Tocqueville, a French traveler to the United States in the 1830s, wrote *Democracy in America*, a book still studied in American universities. He praised American freedom, but saw a potential problem, soft despotism:

> The will of man is not shattered, but softened, bent, and guided; men are seldom forced by it to act, but they are constantly restrained from acting. Such a power does not destroy, but it prevents existence. It does not tyrannize, but it compresses, enervates, extinguishes, and stupefies a people, till each nation is reduced to nothing better than a flock of timid and industrious animals.

Journalists in China often face what Spanish speakers call *dictadura*, a hard dictatorship. Journalists in America face *dictablanda*, a soft dictatorship. Officials do not tell reporters what they must write, but most journalists at influential media outlets enthusiastically partic-ipate in groupthink. They embraced "progressive" concepts in college and have reinforced those ideas since then by living and working in echo chambers where seldom is heard a contrary word. The few who read more widely and think more broadly learn to self-censor their work if they wish to rise. Governments prefer *dictablanda* to *dictadura*: there is no need to pay overtime to jailers, if journalists will imprison themselves.

That's why consciousness of the Bible is so important. Psalm 19:1–2 tells us, "The heavens declare the glory of God, and the sky above proclaims his handiwork. Day to day pours out speech, and night to night reveals knowledge." But once the heavens and Christ's coming to earth declare God's glory, what then? Christian journalism is worth pursuing only if we value God's counsel highly enough to live by it, even when it hurts, and to interpret the world in accordance with it.

A biblically objective reporter confidently knows that God's rev-elation in the Bible is relevant to our daily lives. A convinced Marxist reporter is confident that the Bible is not our instructor and Karl Marx's revelation is. Other nonbiblical reporters follow their own scriptures or at least their own instincts. Everyone worships something and tries to live by some code, whether written or not.

That distinction does not mean that a Christian reporter automat-ically knows how to report every story. We should live by the doctrine that became central in the Protestant Reformation five centuries ago: *sola scriptura*, the Bible only. Applied properly, the doctrine helps us to avoid overusing or underusing the Bible. If we overuse it by assert-ing that the Bible says certain things that it does not say, we feed our human tendency to make up rules that purportedly will help us save ourselves, or at least allow us to think ourselves better than others. Overassertiveness feeds the legalism that has pushed many Christian students I've taught into animosity toward the denominations of their youth.

Underuse is also a problem. When we say the Bible is not clear on a subject when it actually is, that feeds into antinomianism, the belief (particularly familiar today) that we make up our own rules. In the

United States, legalistic overuse harms some conservative Christians, and antinomian underuse is rampant among some modern Christians who prefer to say, "I read the Bible and decide what it says to me. No one has the right to tell me I'm wrong, and I don't have the right to tell someone else—it's between him and God."

Overuse and underuse are the Scylla and Charybdis of biblical application. Three millennia ago, Homer wrote about those two mythical sea monsters, and Greeks said they were on opposite sides of the Strait of Messina between the island of Sicily and the Italian mainland. Few sailors could survive the passage. At *World*, we've tried to navigate our way through during the past two decades with the help of another watery metaphor based on whitewater rafting. Going down rocky streams in a rubber raft is a popular American activity, and experts talk of six classes of rapids where the water runs swiftly, from class one (easy enough for a novice) to class six (death with a roar).

A class one rapids issue is one on which the Bible is explicit. Murder, adultery, theft, and other sins clearly and specifically identified as such in the Bible are wrong. In reporting such issues, Christian journalists should be careful to describe non-Christian views accurately and refrain from caricaturing opponents, but we should not feel any need to give equal time or space to ungodly views or to pretend we don't know right from wrong.

For example, when *World* praises long-term marriages, we don't balance reportage with scorn for golden anniversaries. Similarly, Bible-oriented reporters describing the sad consequences of heterosexual adultery or homosexuality do not need to balance anti-sin and pro-sin perspectives. The Bible is also clear on abortion, although clarity requires combining "You shall not murder" with the explicit recognition that unborn babies are human beings "fearfully and wonderfully made" and knit together in our mothers' wombs, as Psalm 139 declares.

Here's an example from a *World* story about abortion in China:

> The smell of steamed rice and stir-fried beef wafted into the simple warehouse converted into a church in northern China. Fans mounted on the walls breathe air into the warm room, as gracious

hosts hand visitors cups of boiling water, the drink of choice no matter the weather. As two pastors—one American, one Chinese—finished teaching on the sanctity of life, women and men of all ages stood up, sobbing and praying for repentance: "Lord, forgive me for aborting my child; I didn't know it was murder. Lord, forgive me for shedding innocent blood."

Here's more:

> For most in the room, this was the first time they had seen photos of fetal development, learned about what abortion entails, and studied what the Bible says about the sanctity of life. A middle-aged Chinese woman with cropped hair approached me with a nervous smile afterward. "Where do the aborted babies go?" she asked, eyes watering. "I've had it done before and was wondering if I'd ever see them again."

Reporter June Cheng then contrasted this scene with the insides of an abortion center in southwest China:

> Next to a room lined with thin, musty cots and IV stands, a stout female doctor sits behind her desk, bragging to me about her experience performing abortions for 40 years. She's done them both at a hospital and at the clinic (where she makes much more money) and promises patients a simple "operation"—one girl had eight abortions done, and "she's doing fine."
>
> She then showed me where the operation is performed, a locked back room that reeked of chemicals and death. In one corner stood a rusting operating chair with stirrups, which the doctor quickly walked toward to toss out blood-stained tissues from her last operation, an 18-year-old who was five months pregnant. . . . While the government counts 13 million abortions a year, the actual number including unreported abortions could be as high as 30 million.

The specific detail about the abortion business—musty cots, reeking chemicals, rusted operating chair, blood-stained tissues—is accurate, based on Cheng's eyewitness visit to this killing field. But Cheng also deliberately evoked a feeling of misery and horror, and was free to do that because she is humbly confident in the knowledge that abortion is wrong. Tone is important: ranting is far less effective than concrete reporting.

Christians battle abortion in different ways. Some emphasize compassionate alternatives such as adoption, others counsel pregnant women and help them access resources, and still others picket abortion businesses, elect pro-life candidates, pass legislation, fight court battles, and so forth. Some push for personhood laws, others for abortion prohibition after the first trimester, and still others for laws based on feeling pain. Biblical objectivity suggests sympathy for all these efforts.

A class one rapids story is not a paint-by-numbers exercise. Journalists must show discernment in exploring nuances, but it's easier in some ways than higher rapids stories because the overall perspective is clear.

Clarity is not as great on class two issues. For example, the Bible (Deut. 6:7) says Christian parents are responsible for teaching their children about God's love and commands: "You shall teach them diligently to your children, and shall talk of them when you sit in your house, and when you walk by the way, and when you lie down, and when you rise." Does this mean that parents must homeschool their children or send them to Christian schools?

It is clearly wrong for parents to abdicate, and *World* is positive about Christian schools and home schools, but they are not problem-free. *World* does not say it is sinful for parents ever to send sons and daughters to government schools, as long as they find ways to counter the propaganda their children are likely to hear. We do report on the difficulties, including the puzzlement when first graders are told that boys may be girls and vice versa.

With some American Christians lax in diligent teaching, a *World* reporter found the commitment of some Chinese Christians inspiring:

> I visited six church schools and three teacher training centers where I interviewed principals, teachers, students, and parents who were part

of the fledgling Chinese Christian school movement. I met parents desperate to give their children a God-centered education, and saw scrappy schools with limited funding and inexperienced teachers. I sensed the palpable excitement of starting an indigenous Christian school movement, the uncertainty of students' future prospects, and the determination to follow God's calling in a hostile environment.

Class three stories are those in which partisans on both sides can quote Bible verses, but careful study results in definite conclusions. For example, a biblical understanding of helping the poor means an emphasis on generosity, but not the kind that just makes the giver feel good. The goal should be challenging, personal, and spiritual care for widows, orphans, aliens, prisoners, and others among the unemployed, uneducated, or unwanted. Since the apostle Paul wrote that even widows are not automatically entitled to aid, broad entitlement programs are suspect, and all who are able to work should do so.

Still, applying this principle in modern society is not easy. Should we give to all who ask on a city sidewalk or at the entrance to a freeway? Jesus in John 5 asked the key question to a man who had been lying by the Bethesda pool for thirty-eight years: "Do you want to be healed?" I've interviewed several hundred homeless men and learned that many are sadly used to degradation and do not want help that pushes them to give up drinking and drug use. Peter in Acts 3 does not give silver or gold to a panhandler at the gate of the Jerusalem temple, but responds with a message of far deeper salvation.

I've written about this at length in *The Tragedy of American Compassion* and other books that show how Christians have shown biblical kindness by *suffering with* those in need. This literal meaning of compassion requires not only contributing money, but giving time, love, jobs, and housing—not on the other side of town, but sometimes in our own businesses and homes. Such biblical analysis strikes against both Chinese Communist doctrine—that the poor by their class position are more virtuous than the rich—and mainstream Chinese and American practice. Many within the skyscrapers of Shanghai's new Pudong district worship mammon as vigorously as their Social Darwinist counterparts on Wall Street.

But many who follow Christ are different, as the life of Yang Hui, 37, shows. She once stayed at a hotel by the railroad station in a small town in northwest China. A hotel clerk mentioned to her that several orphans were in a room upstairs. She looked for them and found behind a locked door four barely clothed children—one a tiny baby, the others one, three, and six years old—crying in a cold, moist, dark room featuring a floor streaked with feces.

Yang learned that the young children were stashed there until a government orphanage had room for them. The next morning, instead of taking the train home, she told the hotel clerk she wanted to clean up the room and the children. The baby had died during the night, but she worked on the other three, all of whom had cerebral palsy. When she was finished, they looked "angelic."

Yang stayed at the hotel for one month, until the government finally took the children. She returned home, but "couldn't forget those children." She volunteered at a government orphanage, yet she particularly wanted to help the children with cerebral palsy whom Chinese experts said had "no social value."

A Chinese woman who also wanted to aid disabled children eventually offered her life's savings, $30,000, to buy an apartment that could become a refuge for them. Yang became its director. When I visited, she and her assistants were caring for thirty-one children between the ages of five months and ten years—most with cerebral palsy, but others with autism and cleft palate.

On class four issues, we should humbly bring to bear the Bible's perspective on human nature. For example, biblical objectivity on international issues emphasizes striving for peace without appeasing aggressors. Those who believe peace is natural emphasize disarmament, but a biblical understanding of sin leads to some tough questions: What if war is the natural habit of sinful man? What if some leaders see war as a useful way to gain more power, believing they can achieve victory without overwhelming losses? History is full of mistaken calculations of that sort. Leaders have a tendency to overrate their own power, and so they may plunge ahead, unless restrained by the power of potential adversaries.

Another example: drugs. Many governmental anti-drug programs look at addiction as purely a physical problem, rather than a spiritual one as well. For a *World* story headlined "A Government Cure for Sin," our reporter interviewed former addicts who had been through secular American rehabilitation programs and found they rarely worked. They gained help from Victory Outreach, an inner-city ministry that promotes turning to Christ and rejecting former lifestyles. As one staff member, a former drug dealer, said about addiction, "It's not a disease. It's something you do to yourself. It's an action you take. It's sin."

Further testimony came from another former addict who had become a Christian and changed:

> I wasn't thinking about anything like my environment or peer pressure when I took a drug. I did it because I wanted to have everything—and I guess to some people, it would look like I did. I had my drugs, I had money from dealing drugs, I had my wife, I had my girlfriends, I had my gang around me. But I also had a void. I knew something was missing. I was trying to fill that void with drugs, with sex, with alcohol, but it wasn't working.

Since the Bible does not say explicitly that one kind of anti-addiction program will work and another won't, a *World* story about drug prevention programs is likely to report on a variety of proposals. We do know, though, that "the fear of the Lord is the beginning of wisdom," and any program that leaves out the spiritual is an incomplete program. This understanding undergirds our reporting on contemporary scourges.

We do not have clear biblical teaching regarding class five issues, but historical understanding can break us out of our natural tendencies toward thinking our side is right and others are wrong. For example, Western Christians should recognize that England sinned against China during the 1839–1842 Opium War that forced the country to allow opium imports from India. French troops joined in during a second Opium War from 1856 to 1860, and the United States took advantage of Chinese weakness later in the century.

Ironically, when Xi Jinping met with Donald Trump in December 2018, the U.S. president needed to ask for help in curbing the flow of fentanyl from China to the United States. Fentanyl is a synthetic opioid 50–100 times stronger than morphine. Opioid overdoses, often involving fentanyl, led to more than 70,000 American deaths in 2017.

Happily, China's president in this instance did not return evil for evil. He agreed to help. This may be difficult to do, and biblical objectivity means reporting the gesture while remaining skeptical about its practical application. *World* reported that Chinese websites advertise fentanyl to American clients, who have it shipped to their mailing addresses. Drug dealers also sell fentanyl-laced counterfeit pills or fentanyl mixed with heroin, leading to overdoses. Even though China has banned twenty-three fentanyl-type drugs, drugmakers can easily produce derivatives of fentanyl not yet banned.

Class six issues are those in which there is no clear biblical position nor other clear indications, so people equally well-versed in the Bible will often take diametrically opposed positions. Technical economic issues—whether to raise or lower interest rates, for example— are often of this nature, as are complex questions of international diplomacy. Biblical understandings will often help analysts in sorting out the relevant questions, but Christians should be careful not to state that there is one biblical position on these subjects to which all should ascribe, or else.

For example, the Bible doesn't provide much instruction regarding the trade relationship between China and Nigeria. A Christian journalist's story on that can be similar to a secular journalist's. *World* reported,

> China and Nigeria are 7,000 miles apart with a continent between them, but the two disparate cultures are mixing in the Lagos marketplace, in Beijing universities, and even on sweaty Nigerian dance floors. Part of the reason is China's drive to grow its influence in African countries like Nigeria with billion-dollar loans, infrastructure projects, and multinational state-owned enterprises. But another driving factor is the horde of Chinese businessmen acting independently of the Chinese government, eager to make money in an import-dependent country.

On an issue like Chinese claims to sovereignty over the South China Sea, through which a third of the world's trade passes, *World* tried to report both sides. On the one hand, "Southeast Asian countries feel bullied by their giant neighbor as it busily constructs artificial islands and patrols the waters, spraying water cannons at those who sail near." On the other hand, the coast is "critically important to China, as it provides economic and military access to the rest of the world: China's enormous wealth is contained largely in its coastal provinces, in big cities like Beijing, Shanghai, and Guangzhou." The Bible does not tell us what the Christian position on the South China Sea is, but it does tell us we should strive for peace.

The rapids metaphor suggests a framework for biblical objectivity that allows us to push hard, but avoid twisting Scripture. When we take a strong biblical stand on a class one issue, we are objective. When we take a balanced position on a class six issue by citing the views and approaches of a variety of informed sources, we are also biblically objective, because we cannot be sure about an issue when the Bible is not clear. Objectivity is a faithful reflection of the biblical view, as best we can discern it through God's Word. When we cannot discern a specific view, we cast about for wisdom where we can find it.

In summary, biblical objectivity—commitment to proclaiming God's objective truth as far as we know it—has different applications on different kinds of questions. Biblical objectivity does not fall into relativism or situational ethics, though, because its sole goal is to reflect biblical positions. Biblical objectivity's philosophical base is diametrically opposed to the prevailing liberal theory of objectivity, which assumes the absence of certain truth on any issue and suggests approaching every story as if it were a class six. Christ did not die for us so we would be captives of fear.

KEY TERMS

agenda-setting
thesis
directed reporting
PAMO

creation, fall, redemption, restoration
dictadura
dictablanda
antinomianism
rapids
class one rapids
class two rapids
class three rapids
class four rapids
class five rapids
class six rapids

STUDY QUESTIONS

1. When should Christian journalists claim biblical authority?
2. How should Christian journalists respond when told that biblical objectivity reflects bias rather than objectivity?
3. What safeguards assist a Christian journalist in keeping a class five or six issue from being treated as a class one or two issue?
4. Must a class six rapids story be balanced? Or might a Christian journalist or magazine push a preferred stance?
5. Can and should Chinese or American Christians pursue biblical objectivity while working in the secular media?
6. If Christian reporters within a news organization have very different views about a particular issue, what can they do to prevent or mitigate conflict?
7. How do Christian journalists fight the temptation to compress reality and tell a better story than one that would be true to reality?

FOR FURTHER READING

Cornelius Van Til, *The Defense of the Faith* (P&R Publishing, 1955).
Walter Lippmann, *Public Opinion* (Harcourt, Brace, 1922).
Edward L. Bernays, *Propaganda* (Liveright, 1928).

5

Street-Level Journalism and the Ladder of Abstraction

WE'VE DISCUSSED THE goal of biblical objectivity and the reality of directed reporting. Now we'll move on to how to find and hold an audience: Christian journalism that draws in readers and introduces them to places they probably haven't been, people they probably haven't encountered, and applications of biblical truth they may not have considered.

Here's a poor, but typical article from a Christian publication in the United States (with names removed):

> If you missed the Right to Life First Annual Fundraising banquet on October 9th, you missed history in the making. The Hyatt was pro-life headquarters for the evening, with hundreds filling the huge banquet room. As guests came from far and near, it was obvious from the start, this night belonged to the pro-life movement. Everywhere you turned there was this wonderful feeling of victory.
>
> As the festivities began, X dazzled the large audience with her wit and charm. Known for her dedication and sensitivity for the right to life, she generated an air of success for all present. State Representative Y showed why he was elected to the state legislature with his boyish smile and soft humor.

That's a suite-level, public relations story, told from the point of view of officials and instructing us to applaud. I've seen many similarly fawning stories about Chinese officials. But it's biblically wrong to treat anyone other than the real Messiah as a messiah. It is much better to leave the suites, go to the streets, and report on courageous people risking their freedom, as in this story:

> For about 10 minutes on Saturday, young men and women stood in front of major hospitals in Chengdu, China, holding up red pro-life banners and graphic photos of abortion. After snapping a few photos and capturing the attention of a few passersby, the groups quickly left to keep ahead of local police officers who likely would have arrested them.
>
> Their goal wasn't to hold the protest but to start a conversation on social media with photos of their activism. The signs read "Unborn children are children too," "Men don't take responsibility, so women abort," "If unborn children aren't human, then what is a human?" Other signs depicted the abortion process and images of aborted babies next to the words, "Is this your 'pain-free' abortion?" referring to a commonly advertised promise from Chinese hospitals and abortion centers.
>
> The public demonstration put on by Chengdu Early Rain Reformed Church is unprecedented in China, where abortions are common practice even among Christians and between 13 and 30 million babies are aborted each year. But . . . Early Rain, a 500-person house church, is no stranger to attracting attention on the topic of abortion. For the past few years, on the June 1 Children's Day holiday, [members of a house church] have bought ad space on buses and passed out brochures telling women not to abort.

Both positive and negative stories should generally be written from street level, based on accurate observation. Observing God's world lackadaisically shows disrespect for his creation. This is the world that God has made; rejoicing and being glad in it means not coveting an alternative world. An editor's demand for specific detail should also be more than a utilitarian cry to increase reader interest.

Just as Rembrandt, Franz Hals, and other great Dutch painters of their era showed Reformation understanding by painstakingly portraying humans on earth, not floating off the ground, so a search for descriptive material is moral as well as mechanical.

A lack of precise detail often reflects a murkiness of observation and thought, but it also contributes to a tendency to scream. Here's one lead paragraph from a Christian newspaper in America:

> Ordinary Americans are increasingly living in a fantasy world created by a mendacious and cavalier oligarchy of would-be rulers . . . a haughty association of self-proclaimed demigods whose control of great wealth has provided them the means to suborn, use and manipulate morally weak human beings. . . .

That is an extreme example, and *World* has never run anything loaded like that, but it is easy to fall into the trap of emphasizing hysteria rather than writing the first draft of history. When we research and write stories, we should ask whether we are teaching readers to be resolute in biblical application, but calm in the face of anti-Christian aggression—or are we fostering panic?

Showing the problem at street level is better than orating. When reporting from Havana, Cuba, I wrote:

> The rice ration is six pounds per person, which works out to be about three ounces per day. Beans are another staple, but a common complaint is that the *canasta basica* (ration book) includes less than ever. Nor are the rations free: Prices have increased in recent years but wages have not. . . .
>
> In a society long known for being child-friendly, the milk shortage greatly distresses Cubans. When a baby is born, parents get a card that is supposed to entitle them to a quart of milk per week until the child is seven years old. But Cubans regularly say that some milk never shows up and other portions are watery. They say the type of milk distributed to children aged from three to six is of such low quality that many children have stomach problems.

Telling readers about problems, or quoting people talking about them, would have been weaker than showing them:

> At a pharmacy that's supposed to be one of the best-stocked, since it's across the street from the Havana Children's Hospital, I flipped through one price list that hung next to the counter, not knowing that perusal of it is restricted to MDs. The impressive list even showed that 20 50-mg tabs of Vitamin E could be purchased for $1.20. The pharmacist, though, had no vitamins. "Luxuries" like coffee (ration: enough to make four to five cups once per month) or soap (one small bar per person per month, which is heaven for small boys but hard on others) are particularly hard to come by.

Good reporters try to be the eyes, ears, and pores of readers. Then writers can have fun making the metaphorical connections that readers will enjoy. God tells us to taste, eat, and see whether his provision is good, and that is what we should also do for our readers. We should give them sensational facts and understated prose—aromatic food, not just a descriptive menu—and then allow them to taste and eat.

For example, here's how *World* introduced the bravely pro-life Chinese church to an American audience:

> CHENGDU, China—The spicy smell of mouth-numbing Sichuan pepper permeates the air in Chengdu in southwest China, wafting out of restaurants selling wontons and noodles drenched in red chili oil.
>
> On one busy main street past a fruit stand advertising hand-squeezed orange juice, around the corner from a men's clothing store blaring Korean pop music, stands an unassuming low-rise office building that now houses one of the most influential house churches in China . . . , Chengdu Early Rain Reformed Church.
>
> On a sunny Sunday, about 700 congregants shuffled into the newly purchased office space that's been renovated into a spacious church auditorium. Accompanied by a piano and robe-clad choir, young and old sang the hymn "Whiter Than Snow" in Chinese, before listening to a sermon on God's design for marriage.

The search in directed reporting is always for specific detail. In a similar vein, we should not write that a basketball player is big: give us his specific height and weight. We should show him filling up an elevator or dancing with a relatively small girlfriend. We should not say that a politician is energetic; show him running to meetings or racing around with his children.

Staying low on "the ladder of abstraction" helps us *show* rather than *tell.* Here's a simple example inspired by my Ford Fiesta, a humble but good car. I could say, "I went to the office via transportation," but that's way up the ladder and does not help a reader to picture how I got there. Coming down the ladder, step by step: I use a vehicle, drive a car, drive a Ford, drive a Ford Fiesta, drive a silver Ford Fiesta. Each step down carries more specific detail and is more reader-friendly. In pushing for descriptive information, always ask for names, dates, times, colors, locations, ages, numbers: What exactly did you see? What did he look like?

Specificity is felicity. Where we are on the ladder of abstraction also makes a difference in covering key issues. A typical *Time* cover concerning abortion had a gavel on the cover—high on the ladder of abstraction. *World* covers on abortion have typically shown babies— low on the ladder. "Product of conception" or the Latin word *fetus*— high on the ladder. "Unborn baby"—low on the ladder. Every story has to include some higher-on-the-ladder material, but reporters should strive to go lower.

Here's an example of one paragraph low on the ladder that sets up the next paragraph that's higher:

CHINA—In a residential area on the outskirts of a large city, children in navy blazers and khaki skirts push open a bright yellow wrought iron gate. Inside sits a Christian school with classrooms displaying alphabet letters, caterpillar crafts, beanbag chairs, and Bible verses. Some kindergarten and elementary-age students squeal while grabbing their pint-sized red-and-white choir robes from student lockers for Monday morning chapel.

Second paragraph:

Not an unusual sight in the United States, right? But it's an amazing sight in China, where 300–500 Christian schools, most newly formed, officially do not exist. As these children practice speaking English with American teachers, read Chinese books in their well-stocked libraries, and learn traditional Chinese tea etiquette, in the government's eyes it's as though they never stepped inside a classroom.

Reporters should always be watching and listening—observing and recording details that help to characterize a person, a meeting, or a project. We accumulate specifics by pounding the pavement and always carrying a pen. We describe what we see, not what we infer. If we have seen the front of a house, we do not say, "The house is blue." We say, "The front of the house is blue."

When a massive trend is under way, we can portray it best by finding a "face," one person whose changed life can show what's happening with millions. For example, one *World* story noted:

> Pastor Wang, 42, speaks in a measured tone, peppering his speech with Chinese idioms and references to Reformed theologians. Most Chinese preachers are fiery, but Wang's quiet intensity reflects his past as a law professor. That's not to say he minces words: He calls the government-run Three-Self Patriotic Movement church a "movement of the Antichrist."

Philosophy is up the ladder: What's the meaning of life? What is man? What's my purpose? It's best to show philosophical changes by showing how one life changes:

> Wang grew up with no knowledge of Christianity. He was 29 before he met a Christian believer. Still, as a young man he rejected the materialism inherent in Communism and later became interested in Christianity while studying Western systems of government. Like many Chinese intellectuals in the 1990s, he became a "cultural Christian" who revered the values of Christianity from an academic standpoint but didn't make a personal confession of faith.

Telling a story is better than quoting an expert:

> In the early 2000s, the gospel started spreading from the country-side into urban centers, and these intellectuals started coming to a life-changing knowledge of Christ. . . . Yet Wang felt nervous as he watched congregants passionately singing and praying to their heavenly leader. That brought back memories of the leader-worship present in Communism: "Because in the past we worshipped a false god, now we feel scared to worship the real God."

Showing the steps by which a person slowly comes to belief makes conversion real:

> Over the next few years, God began changing Wang's mindset. He defended house churches persecuted by the government and found that these Christians possessed a true freedom that dwarfed his scholarly pursuit of "freedom." While investigating cases, he attended humble village churches, waking up at dawn for early morning prayer meetings. Slowly, the knowledge of Christianity trickled down to "faith for my life." A Christian co-worker started meeting weekly with Wang's wife to study the Bible, and soon a small group formed in his living room. He began to see the cracks in his self-righteous veneer as he realized he was only willing to help others as long as it didn't inconvenience him.

Staying low on the ladder of abstraction helps people to break free of some ideological clichés. For example, one year, when I taught big lecture classes, I surveyed one thousand University of Texas students and found that 74 percent said yes to this proposition: "There is no such thing as absolute truth: Two people could define what's right in totally conflicting ways, but both could still be correct."

That sounds like three-quarters of students are lost to any absolute, transcultural statements concerning right and wrong. And yet, 88 percent said rape and child abuse are "wrong everywhere," 86 percent said female circumcision is wrong even in West Africa, where some tribal traditions uphold it, and 80 percent said slavery in the Sudan is wrong, even if it is traditional in some cultures there.

Their answers to specific questions contradicted their answers to questions higher on the ladder of abstraction. Specific detail of right and wrong moved them to state that there is universal right and wrong. After big talk of "rights" had them identifying with secular left perspectives, specific detail had them affirming parts of what the Bible says. For example, 60 percent of the students agreed that "A woman should have a right to an abortion," but 75 percent said, "Unborn children should be protected."

Some theoreticians hate these tendencies to back away from grand statements when specific cases are examined—but reporters should love them. That's because stories that look one way at suite level, from the vantage point of executives or theoreticians, often look very different when we ask questions and see what's happening on the street. The essence of journalism is watching and listening, observing and recording details that help to characterize a person, a meeting, a movement.

One good story started with this look and listen:

> Near a grimy steel-welding factory on the outskirts of the Chinese city of Wenzhou, a six-story, 900-seat, modern gothic-style church looms overhead with its lancet windows, spires, and stained glass. A chorus of 300 voices singing hymns in a local dialect to an out-of-tune piano rises from the sanctuary, and school-aged children learn about Christ's ascension in Sunday school classes next door. Yet something feels amiss about the imposing building. An upward glance to the top of the church reveals nothing but gray sky and an empty steeple—the cross that once stood there, a symbol of God's reconciliation with man through Jesus, is gone.

Articles should inform readers, but people will keep reading when a street-level story has the action or description necessary for a story to come alive. For example, the *Washington Post*, a publication of the secular left, once sent reporter Walt Harrington to Alabama to do a story about what a fundamentalist Christian family was like. Harrington recalled,

I didn't know how to begin my interview, so I asked for a tour of their house. Mrs. Webster, a sweet woman, walked me through the house, full of tacky teddy bears and knickknacks. "Boy, these people have bad taste," I thought.

Prejudices sustained. Reporting over, right? Wrong. Harrington continued:

Then she made comments like, "This really ugly teddy bear was a gift from the thirteen-year-old girl who moved in with us after her mother kicked her out when she was two months pregnant. She stayed with us, and we took care of her through the pregnancy. And this silly little knickknack is from the eighty-four-year-old woman who my husband takes to the pool twice a week. He carries her out of her wheelchair and into the swimming pool so she can have some exercise."

KEY TERMS

suite-level journalism
street-level journalism
ladder of abstraction
high on the ladder
low on the ladder
face

STUDY QUESTIONS

1. Since street-level journalism draws on the power of anecdote, how should journalists avoid "sampling bias"?
2. In stories about abstract ideas such as postmodernism or central bank policy, how can a journalist stay low on the ladder of abstraction?
3. How can Christian journalists guard against moving up the ladder of abstraction too quickly as they go from specific detail to more general statements?

4. When journalists stay low on the ladder of abstraction, what place is there for statistics and expert witnesses?
5. Can a journalist go too low on the ladder of abstraction—and what does that look like?

FOR FURTHER READING

Mark Kramer and Wendy Call, eds., *Telling True Stories* (Plume, 2007).

6

Eyes, Ears, Noses

ESSAYISTS OFTEN GET information from books or in other ways that don't require leaving the office. Experienced journalists like books, but often learn the most by pounding the pavement. Journalists are the eyes, ears, and noses of readers. We provide vicarious experience, going places the readers do not or could not visit. To give readers the sense of being on the scene, we dump vagueness: "Eric Liddell ran a brave race, astounding observers by brilliantly recovering from an early disaster" is inferior to "Eric Liddell, knocked down by another runner, got up and saw he trailed by 30 yards, but sprinted in pursuit. Gasping for breath, he somehow accelerated to the tape, won the race, then collapsed."

Another example: one church in the U.S. decided not to install air conditioning and instead give money to create an orphanage in Namibia. Was that a good decision? Instead of offering a general conclusion, we described in *World* a day at the orphanage:

> Early in the morning seven boys in the Micah room are sleeping within mosquito nets. Others sleep in rooms named David, Timothy, Job, and so on. They (and girls in the other wing of the orphanage) will soon awake and wash up in the Sea of Galilee room: Their dirty clothes will go to the Jonah room with its washing machines.

All the children (except the very youngest) go to their daily farm chores. One week the job of 11-year-old Albert, the formerly enslaved boy who had lived in a tire, was to milk a goat—but one day he forgot to take in the milk. The next day he discovered the spoilage and wanted to cover it up by dumping the new milk on top of it. Another boy, though, said he should ask someone, and—filled with fear about the consequences of honesty—Albert finally agreed to do so. He received an admonition about responsibility but also praise for telling the truth.

After breakfast, American and African staff members sit on couches and chairs in the dining room for devotions. The loudest voices for a praise chorus come from the Americans, but when the singing turns to "Amazing Grace," the African voices take over, adding wonderful harmonies. On the walls banners proclaim that "Jesus is King of Kings and Lord of Lords (Rev. 19:16)" and depict "Fruits of the Spirit (Galatians 5:22)."

Many of the kids had never been to school before they came to the home because they couldn't afford the fees (five dollars per term) or uniforms (the same amount). All classes are in English: In one classroom, 14 children crowd around two tables to study the difference between possessive and personal pronouns. When the teaching turns to geography one boy, Martin, can name all seven continents and all four oceans.

In another room, volunteer teacher Jessica Schwartz pulls rhythm sticks from a cloth bag and hands them to the four 3- and 4-year-old girls arranged in a circle around her. "Put them in the rest position," she says, setting an example by laying her own sticks down to form the top two sides of a triangle. The little girls lay theirs down also. "Okay, ready position." She picks up her sticks and the little girls do the same. "Play." Jessica and the girls hit their sticks together. "Rest." They lay them down. "Ready." They pick them up. "Play." They hit them together. "Rest. Ready. Play." Jessica picks up the pace, and the little girls laugh as they try to keep up.

School ends at noon. After lunch another volunteer teacher, Lydia Alder, sits on the sandy ground outside the home while two almost-teenaged girls painstakingly plait her long blonde hair into tiny braids. They've been working on it during recess and free time for several days. The 3- and 4-year-olds try to braid another volunteer's hair. Since they haven't yet mastered braiding, they twist and tug at it, managing to tie some of it in knots.

At mid-afternoon an African vet wearing a lab coat cuts into a goat that died from unknown causes. He suspects tick fever. Older children stare as the vet skins and beheads the animal, draping the skin over a wheelbarrow and painstakingly explaining his actions. An assistant sorts through the pile of guts to produce stomach, kidneys, heart and intestines. The vet cuts open each organ, using his scalpel to point out signs of disease.

Late in the afternoon Mark Chiyuka, a Namibian auto mechanic, teaches bicycle repair to five boys in the shade near a sandy drive. On a tarp are a few bicycle frames, flat tires, and a box of parts. Each afternoon the boys come and learn how to straighten fenders, adjust seats, tighten chains, and repair wheels. Chiyuka and the boys work side-by-side. He often pauses from his own work to answer their questions and resolve disputes. When two boys start to fight over a wrench, he says, "Don't fight. Why should you fight?"

Details like the ones above make a story real and help readers conclude that giving up air conditioning was worth it. When an American football team playing at home is ahead, its fans near the end of a game hear the crowd chanting, "Defense. Defense." When we sit at our computers, we should hear in our minds calls for "Describe. Be specific. Show, don't tell." Instead of summarizing scenes, we should recreate them. Instead of saying, "It was a Christian environment," we should show the readers what made it so.

In American writer Mark Twain's words, "Don't say the old lady screamed—bring her on and let her scream."

Every generalization should be followed by specific detail to indicate the truth of the generalization. Better yet, skip the generalization, give the detail, and most readers will come up with the generalization themselves. Good descriptive material should be spread throughout the story. When we're reporting, we should use all our senses, not just our ears. Some articles are not show but show-off. For example, the reporter is proud that he has interviewed someone important and has compiled many quotations. But missing in the torrent of words is a word picture: mannerisms, gestures, habits, chin strokings, and leaning back in the chair.

Our goal should be pavement-pounding reporting. For example, to write a story about homelessness, we should eat with homeless folks at a shelter—doing so sometimes as a reporter, but in other shelters dressed as a homeless person. To write about the impact of federal environmental laws on workers in the timber industry, we should visit the home of a logger who lost his job: "Mrs. Lynch home-schools her children in a modest sky-blue house with a For Sale sign in the small front yard." Wherever we go, we should sit and listen.

Experienced reporters collect, collect, collect. We always want more in our notebooks than we can use. Some journalists complain of "writing blocks," but they almost always occur because we do not have good material. Some people try to write around holes in their research, and some get away with it for a while, but the common denominator of good stories is tenacious research. Writers who do not have adequate material, and try to make up for that by adding rhetoric, need to follow *World*'s motto: "Sensational Facts, Understated Prose."

Journalists, when visiting organizations, should watch, describe, and never settle for lengthy discourses from a guide. Quotations should be short and rare, because the goal is to concentrate on action, not words. In writing, we should use nouns and strong verbs, and minimize adjectives and adverbs. In describing ministries, we should be aware of the danger of doing public relations for the ministry, or appearing to do so. Yes, we're sympathetic to most of the Christian ministries we encounter, but unless we eyeball a group's activities, we should not assume we're getting an accurate description of what occurs.

Knowing that every ministry has problems, we should press for information: What's the biggest difficulty you have? How are you dealing with it? Tell me about a situation that almost sunk this organization. When visiting a ministry, good reporters do not rely on the officials giving tours or those they want you to meet. It's important to talk with clients—and not just those handpicked by the organization. It's important to talk with folks in the waiting room, or hanging around outside, or others in a community who have had dealings with the ministry. It's also important to request financial documents or obtain them online.

Some journalists do sit-down interviews in offices, but it's much better to shadow a person for a day. One street-level reporter, Katherine Boo, is fine with an interviewee saying, "I've got to go and pick up my kids from day care and go to the grocery store." She seizes the opportunity to go along and see, not just how a subject talks, but how she lives. Reporter Lane DeGregory asks interviewees, "Can I go along for a ride or take a walk or be at a meeting, a trial, or a funeral? Can I be a fly on the wall at an already scheduled event?" She writes, "If my subject has a regular routine, I go along."

The reporter's goal at that point is to learn, not what a subject says about himself or his views, but how he relates to others and puts beliefs into practice. Following a person around allows a street-level look at life. For example,

> Liao Zhi, 29, craned her neck in the dance studio to watch as a group of Shanghai women in long dresses rhythmically stomped their heeled feet on the 12-count, following the instructions of the flamenco dance instructor. Subconsciously, the petite Liao found herself following along, turning to her husband Charles Wang to note that this was just the class she was looking for.

Then the surprise:

> With Liao's constant smile and breezy personality, it's easy to miss that under the dancer's long skirt are two prosthetic legs, complete with high heels. Liao's life story is known throughout China—how the small-town dance instructor lost her legs and her baby in the 2008 Sichuan earthquake, yet managed to return to dancing, even competing on China's version of *Dancing with the Stars*.

If we can't walk around with an official or leader, and can only interview him in his office, at least we can get there early and observe the office. For example, to give an impression of a congressman who did not give in to government-expanding political pressure, I noted that "Henry Hyde's office also has room for the two bulldog book-ends of twentieth-century British politics, Winston Churchill and Margaret Thatcher, and a portrait of Thomas More, the sixteenth-century English lord chancellor. . . . Hyde has a bust of More as well: 'He gave his life for a principle.'"

Hyde, the leading pro-life congressman in the late twentieth century, also had three Don Quixote statuettes in his office, indicating his realization that he knew he was unlikely to succeed. A brave Christian leader in Havana outdid him:

> Leoncio Veguilla, president of the Baptist Convention of Western Cuba, sits in an office decorated with, among other items, 18 Don Quixote statuettes. The kindly 73-year-old did hard labor in prison from 1965 to 1970 for not toeing the Party line. He spent time in a forced labor camp, cutting sugar cane alongside criminals and other religious prisoners labeled by the government as "social scum." He looks back on that time as "very difficult, but an opportunity to preach the gospel to prisoners," many of whom became Christians. Released and told not to preach again, he started up immediately and recently celebrated his 50th anniversary as a preacher.

Reporters, while observing, should automatically start counting, whether statuettes or chairs:

> Efrain Paz, some 20 years younger than Rev. Veguilla, wears a baseball cap and rides a 1963 Czech motorcycle. An Assemblies of God church group used to crowd into his living room, but the government gave him permission to put a covering over his backyard so members could gather there. Instead of a patio, though, they built four years ago a stand-alone sanctuary, which has room for 84 battered folding chairs, 12 white plastic porch chairs, 28 wooden seats from a movie theater, and a pulpit.

Numbers add credibility:

At one prayer meeting at the home, 16 elderly women, bright-eyed and alert, some holding Bibles, asked God for wisdom in using their time and for His mercy in the lives of each other's children and grandchildren. . . . Only three of the 46 persons at the home are Salvation Army (SA) members, and one resident who died recently was a Communist Party member. The government pays for the salaries of not only the one doctor and three nurses but some attendants as well, all of whom the SA can choose.

Given suspicions that some charity workers collect donations for their own benefit, it's important to show details of poverty:

Walk up two flights of dark and narrow stairs, enter a small room with cracked vinyl couches and an artificial Christmas tree on one desk: Welcome to the office of 3-year-old MANA, an interdenominational Ministerio de Ayuda a Necesitados y Ancianos (help for the needy and the elderly). Director Dulce Montalvan says, "I don't have a budget. I scrounge. I go to this house and ask for lemons. . . . A non-Christian who worked in a bar gave me part of his tips. He had been very critical of Christianity, but then he saw that we try to put it into practice. Now he goes to church, and he and his friends find milk for distribution to children."

Once we've situated the subject of the story in her present conditions, readers will be curious about her past:

Montalvan was in desperate need. Her husband escaped to Miami, leaving her alone with an 8-month-old daughter. With neighbors yelling in bullhorns that she was a traitor and family members "not helping because they would also be judged, [she] met people who were going to church, so I went there also, I felt at home there. Pastors prayed for me. I became a different woman."

When Christian reporters travel and spend time with people from different worldviews, the goal should be to make them as individuals real to our readers, who will then be able to feel their pain, even as they disagree with their conclusions. For example, *World* ran these mini-profiles of Buddhists I encountered during travel in Japan:

Yamamoto Maya is a Japanese woman in her 40s with a mottled, taut face and some bruising under one eye. She smiles but seems sad, and when she talks she is intense, as befits a person who has had a hard life. Her parents divorced when she was young, and neither wanted to take care of her. She was the fifth and youngest child, with grown-up brothers and sisters who also abandoned her. She was sent around to the homes of various relatives as half maid, half slave.

As Yamamoto grew older she tried to have herself committed to an orphanage, but those who mistreated her would not allow an action that would bring public shame to the family that was acting shamefully. Finally she married, only to find that her husband beat her, broke her bones and teeth, and put her in the hospital. She and her husband had one child, but that did not improve their marriage. A decade ago, with her son a toddler, she began coming to a Shingon Buddhist temple on Mount Koya-san, a two-hour drive south from the crowded streets of Osaka.

To find new relief, Yamamoto at 10:20 on a cool Saturday evening waited on steps leading down to a cold river, her hands clasped before her. It was dark, with incense burning so that for those more than ten yards away smell had to replace sight. She wore a white robe, indicating purity, and threw handfuls of salt into the water, as another purifying gesture. She began chanting the names of Buddha, very fast, very loud, without seemingly stopping for breath. She let out an animal-sounding scream ("VEE-AYE"), entered the water, and knelt chanting for ten minutes. She later said during that time she felt Buddha enter her body.

And:

Takagi Kinho, 22, comes from a family of Shingon priests and wants to carry on the tradition. To do so he must serve an apprenticeship: last year he was finishing his third year of serving on

Mount Kyosan by getting up each morning at 5 A.M., often after only three hours sleep, and going through *kugyo*, which consists of ascetic austerities such as sitting with his legs tucked under himself for 3–4 hours, or holding a book of sutras at arm's length for 3–4 hours. The only food he received during his initial year of training was rice and a little tofu, so he had lost 20 pounds. (One beefier fellow trainee lost 88 pounds and "looked like an African refugee at the end.")

Takagi did not drop out as many did, but at the end of the first year, "I couldn't stop crying." He was resigned to the practice—"To become a priest, you have to do it"—but was skeptical about the spiritual benefits he had derived: "I don't buy the idea that I will reach *satori* [a state of illumination]. The belief is that you call on a Buddha so many times you change places with him. I've called many times and it hasn't happened. But something *shimpi*—spiritually mysterious—is going on here."

Honda Yoshinari has turned his back on part of that mystery. Born in Hiroshima in 1943, at age two he had to help dispose of atom-bomb-blasted bodies, and is now the priest at a small Jodo Shinshu temple that sits amid the hubbub of Yao, an Osaka exurb that is one of Japan's fastest growing cities. Wearing a black robe and white socks, he pads around on short red carpet during the traditional sutra-chanting service every morning at 6 A.M., but keeps a blackboard and folding chairs to use during "evangelizing" services that include piano and congregational singing. For Honda, salvation comes not through meditation and strenuous exercises but only through faith in the power of a Buddha manifestation who (in an echo of Christianity) sacrifices himself for others.

We also wrote about Buddhists who had become Christians:

Junko Blockson grew up in a small Buddhist temple run by her family—both of her grandfathers were Buddhist priests—but then came to believe in Christ and joined the church at age 20. Why? Now in her late 30s and married to a professor at Kyoto International University, a Christian school, she recalls that "I knew all the do's and don'ts, but not how and why to lead a good life. Out of curiosity I started coming to a chapel; I heard a sermon and believed."

That change was dramatic, and so were the consequences. When Junko said Christianity is the only way and stopped bowing before the family altar, her father said she was breaking *wa*, harmony. Her father shaved off his hair and apologized to all his relatives for not having raised his daughter rightly. And yet, her father, who along with performing his priestly duties works in a government social welfare department, has told her that Christians do best at helping handicapped children, because they see meaning in the existence of those children.

KEY TERMS

pounding the pavement
writing block
sensational facts, understated prose

STUDY QUESTIONS

1. How should a reporter decide on a "face" for a story—and how can we know that the chosen face truly represents a major trend?

2. Sometimes the drive to present specific and evocative details lures "journalists" into becoming short-story writers who blend details of settings or meld descriptions of subjects to present a "composite" picture. What standards should Christian journalists apply in telling a story that's both accurate and compelling?

3. When and how much should a journalist's first-person responses (emotional, physical, etc.) enter the story? At what point does the pursuit of detail get tedious for the reader?

4. How should journalists avoid moving from reporting to public relations?

FOR FURTHER READING

Angela Hunt, *Writing Lessons from the Front* (Hunt Haven, 2014).

Marvin Olasky, ed., *Salt [Not Sugar]: Twenty Years of World-Class Reporting* (World Magazine, 2006).

Matthew Robinson, *Mobocracy* (Prima, 2002).

7

Biblical Sensationalism

THEOLOGIAN-PASTOR JOHN PIPER has restored to honor a word often used as a slur: *hedonist*. Piper defines *Christian hedonism* as "the massive role joy plays not only in the Christian life, but in all of creation and God's purposes in it. . . . *God is most glorified in us when we are most satisfied in him.*"

Sensationalism has been within journalism a similarly abused word, but Christian publications have an opportunity to follow the Bible in recognizing the importance of sensations. The Oxford English Dictionary defines *sensation* as "a condition of excited feeling produced in a community by some occurrence." One of the hard questions for a Christian magazine is how to report bad news that, when reported, will cause a sensation. Observers for two centuries have condemned sensational stories that emphasize death and destruction—and yet, if the goal is to avoid any sensation-causing news, we should indict the Bible itself.

Let's start with Moses' history book, Genesis. He quotes the first news report, Lamech's announcement in chapter 4 that he killed a man who had wounded him. Later in Genesis comes the original tale of sodomy, leading to the destruction of Sodom and Gomorrah, followed immediately by the story of the incest of Lot and his daughters (chapter 19).

Many more sensational events fill the pages of Genesis and

the four following books of Moses. That part of the Bible culmi-
nates in the blessings for obedience and curses for disobedience in
Deuteronomy 28. The culmination of the curses is especially vivid,
with the Israelites being told that unfaithfulness will lead to terrible
war and starvation, in which "you shall eat the fruit of your womb,
the flesh of your sons and daughters, whom the LORD your God has
given you" (verse 53).

The New Testament also shows the streets declaring the sinfulness
of man. Paul told the Romans some men "gave up natural relations
with women and were consumed with passion for one another, men
committing shameless acts with men and receiving in themselves the
due penalty for their error" (Rom. 1:27). Christianity is not a *nice*
religion. Just as priests used hyssop to spray the blood of sacrifices on
the people in Moses' time, so Christ had to shed his blood, not just
preach, to free us from sin.

Biblical journalism is the opposite of amoral journalism, the kind
that emphasizes all the sound and fury in the world and presents
people's lives as tales told by idiots, signifying nothing. But biblical
journalism also differs from journalistic moralism, which emphasizes
the good and uplifting parts of life so people can feel better about
themselves, without pointing them to Christ. Sugary journalistic moralism presents happy, smiling church people, removed from the sinful
world and moving from one triumph to the next—but in a world
filled with destruction, divorce, disease, and death, such reporting is
not credible.

Our goal is to honor Paul's injunction: "Whatever is true, whatever is honorable, whatever is just, whatever is pure, whatever is lovely,
whatever is commendable, if there is any excellence, if there is anything worthy of praise, think about these things" (Phil. 4:8). We want
to think of lovely things whenever we can. We also recognize Paul
could not possibly have meant that we are never to think of what is
dishonorable, unjust, and worthy of condemnation, or else he could
not have carried out his evangelistic work in a corrupt, pagan society.

World has to cover man's terribleness, and some of the specific
details might even be too hard for us to handle. Look at this prophetic
passage from Deuteronomy 28:56–57:

The most tender and refined woman among you, who would not venture to set the sole of her foot on the ground because she is so delicate and tender, will begrudge to the husband she embraces, to her son and to her daughter, her afterbirth that comes out from between her feet and her children whom she bears, because lacking everything she will eat them secretly.

By the time of Ahab and his son Jehoram, some of the curses for disobedience were already being realized. One woman told the king of her neighborly arrangement (2 Kings 6:28–29):

This woman said to me, "Give your son, that we may eat him today, and we will eat my son tomorrow." So we boiled my son and ate him. And on the next day I said to her, "Give your son, that we may eat him." But she has hidden her son.

Ezekiel was disgusted at what Israel had become. He wrote of how Judah "lusted after her lovers there, whose members were like those of donkeys, and whose issue was like that of horses. Thus you longed for the lewdness of your youth, when the Egyptians handled your bosom and pressed your young breasts" (Ezek. 23:20–21). *World*'s publication of such language would bring angry letters to the editor, but Jeremiah explained God's methods simply in Jeremiah 19:3: "Thus says the LORD of hosts, the God of Israel: Behold, I am bringing such disaster upon this place that the ears of everyone who hears of it will tingle." How can ears tingle if descriptions are mellow?

Should it be said that those passages are inappropriate for us, we need to be reminded of God's promise: "All Scripture is breathed out by God and profitable for teaching, for reproof, for correction, and for training in righteousness, that the man of God may be complete, equipped for every good work" (2 Tim. 3:16–17). We cannot do better than the inspired authors of the Bible. They show us that even the grotesque, in Bible-based context, is useful for our education and sanctification.

Paul himself wrote about evil in the world because it was important for the Christian community to address sin appropriately. Just as Paul was called at times to write about evil, so are journalists. We are called to witness and describe the bad as well as the good. When and how to run photos of war and disaster, with dead bodies or streaming blood, is sometimes a hard call. We have sometimes shown from a great distance—charred bodies in Fallujah, people jumping from the World Trade Center on 9/11—what we would not show close up.

The one understanding that can cause us to pull back occasionally is our recognition that children look at *World*. One reader wrote me, "I am a 14-year-old homeschool girl who enjoys your magazine very much. However, I have one criticism: Sometimes I think you do not take into consideration that young people may be reading *World*." She saw the importance of sometimes having disturbing details, but suggested, "It would be good if at the beginning of such an article, you could warn readers of such violent content. Sincerely, E. S."

We now go by the E. S. standard: don't eliminate material, but give a warning. Taking into account news value, visual accuracy, and likely reader reaction, editors have to make hard calls on photos—run or don't run, and if run, size and placement. At the same time, we don't want to shelter adults or unduly shelter children.

In portraying wild men and what they sometimes do, *World* follows the path laid out more than 180 years ago by John McDowall, the minister mentioned in chapter 2 who edited from 1830 to 1834 a hard-hitting New York monthly appropriately titled *McDowall's Journal*. McDowall in one article asked "the general questions: "*Shall Vice and Sin be concealed, or exposed?* In deciding this question, I inquire, What does the Bible TEACH? and What does the Bible PRACTICE?" He replied that the Bible teaches us:

> Cry aloud and spare not; lift up thy voice like a trumpet, and SHOW MY PEOPLE THEIR TRANSGRESSIONS, AND THE HOUSE OF JACOB THEIR SINS (Isaiah 58:1). *Show my people their transgressions.*—He must tell them how very bad they really were. . . . He must deal faithfully and plainly with them. . . . God sees sin in his people, in the house of Jacob, and is displeased with it. They are often unapt and unwilling to see their own sins, and

need to have them showed them, and to be told, *Thus and thus thou
hast done.*

More:

He must be vehement and in good earnest herein, must cry *aloud,
and not spare*; not spare them, nor touch them with his reproofs,
as if he were afraid of hurting them, but search the wound to the
bottom, lay it bare to the bone; not spare himself or his own pains,
but cry as loud as he can; though he spend his strength, and waste
his spirits, though he get their ill will by it, and get himself into an
ill name; yet he must not spare.

McDowall then turned to Ezekiel 33, which points out "the duty
of watchmen to blow the trumpet and warn the people of approaching danger." Journalists are watchmen who should make "public
examples" of transgressors:

Endeavor to expose their wickedness, and make the perpetrators
ashamed of them. . . . If it should be said that the preceptive duties
that have been cited to expose vice and sin have special or sole reference to the sins of the *church*, and not to those of the world, then
I reply both the church and the world are under the same moral
government of God—both are amenable to the same laws—both
will stand at the same final Tribunal—and both will be either condemned or acquitted by the same general principles.

McDowall, who had recently graduated from Yale, practiced
what he preached, trampling the muddy streets of Manhattan to
combat prostitution and abortion. He wrote, "Paul, particularly in
the first chapter of the Romans, and the other apostles did expose
and denounce the sins and vices of the *gentiles* as well as those of the
church." Christian journalists should pay as much attention to "the
abominations of the *world*, as to those of the *church*. And as there
is nothing in the Scriptures of an opposite spirit and import to the
general scope of the passages quoted, we are forced to the conclusion

that the BIBLE PRECEPT is, to DETECT, EXPOSE, and PUNISH VICE and SIN."

McDowall then showed how God himself did what journalists should do:

> When Adam and Eve had eaten of the forbidden fruit and thus transgressed the commands of God, *they hid themselves, as vice and sin are wont to do.* Then what did God do? He went into the garden and sought for them saying, "Adam where art thou?" And *detected, exposed*, and punished them. When Cain committed fratricide, the Lord suffered him not to escape, but detected him, saying unto Cain, "Where is Abel thy brother?" "What hast thou done?" And thus did the Lord expose and severely punish Cain.

McDowall gave other examples, including "the case of Achan, whose theft so seriously troubled the armies of Israel. Showing very clearly God's utter abhorrence of concealed vice and sin, and his determination to have it detected, exposed, and punished." God also acted in the book of Esther, when "Haman sought to destroy all the Jews that were throughout the whole kingdom of Ahasuerus. . . . When the plot had advanced so far that the destruction of the people of Mordecai seemed inevitable, then the Lord saw fit to detect and expose the machinations of Haman."

McDowall argued:

> At this time when so many honest Christians are anxiously inquiring and seeking for light, and truth, and correct principles, and for the proper mode of speaking and conversing upon the subject of licentiousness, it is peculiarly interesting and important to know how God spake upon this subject: for true Christians will never hesitate to follow an example set by their Father in heaven. . . . It would be well for us not to become "wise above what is written. Shall we be wiser than God? Shall any teach God knowledge?" (Job 21:22).

He concluded with a passionate plea for journalists to be not only conscientious believers, but also good citizens:

The code of criminal law prescribed by every civilized and Christian government, requires the most diligent and energetic efforts to *detect, expose, and punish vice.* . . . It is only upon the detection and punishment of vice, that the peace and safety of society depend. . . . Abolish the whole system of means and measures, or powers and function, organized for the *detection, exposure, and punishment of vice*—And then shall you see commence the Reign of Terror and the Misrule of Anarchy. Then shall the assassin plunge the dirk and the dagger at noon-day, and blood shall deluge the land.

We should keep in mind, of course, the big difference between God and ourselves. He is omniscient. We are fallen and limited sinners. He reads hearts and minds perfectly. We are sometimes fools and often fooled. Chapters 15 and 16 will discuss ways to investigate Christians and non-Christians, but it's important in embarking on any quest to know what to do if we get lost. Journalists should always take seriously any reporting errors and ethical complaints. We should not use clichéd expressions like "We stand by our story." We should try not to be defensive. Our goal should always be to put readers first and ask whether we have let them down. That means finding out if we erred and, if so, which of our procedures needs improvement so the error does not happen again.

At *World*, we make some readers angry when we investigate Christian groups or take strong positions on controversial issues. That goes with the territory, but we do not and will not shrug off factual errors. A factual error becomes an ethical lapse if we use legal protections as a way not to have to deal with mistakes. For example, the statute of limitations for libel is one year in most states, and two or three years in another, but if we learn we've been inaccurate at a time later than that, we still must apologize and fix what's on our website.

KEY TERMS

Christian hedonism
amoral journalism

journalistic moralism
biblical journalism

STUDY QUESTIONS

1. What are the dangers of misusing sensationalism?
2. On what basis did John McDowall conclude that "the BIBLE PRECEPT is, to DETECT, EXPOSE, and PUNISH VICE and SIN"?
3. McDowall called for journalists to exert "energetic efforts to *detect, expose, and punish vice*"—but when should journalists back off?
4. How much graphic detail is appropriate in stories describing great evil?
5. How should Christian journalists decide whether to prioritize particular areas of vice and sin?
6. Before publishing images of death or gore, how should journalists weigh the effect on victims, the bereaved, and audiences generally?

FOR FURTHER READING

Marvin Olasky, *Prodigal Press* (Crossway, 1988).
John Piper, *Desiring God* (Multnomah, 2011).

8

Sojourning in Non-Christian Lands

IN THE LONG RUN, many Christians aspire to create Christian-run websites, publications, social media channels, and broadcasts. Nevertheless, many Christians work and will work in secular media under the authority of non-Christians. In such positions, we should aspire to glorify God by being good employees who follow the high principles embodied in many codes of conduct, and not the low practice that often violates those principles. As far as possible without sinning, we should aspire to be good employees who improve practice.

In the United States, many newspapers say they offer balanced coverage of differing opinions. In practice, many have tilted to the secular left, and a Christian reporter on such a newspaper can improve it by providing balance. For example, instead of writing a pro-abortion story that excludes pro-life views, a reporter can improve practice by giving equal treatment to pro-life and pro-abortion sides. In China, when officials ask reporters to ignore wrongful actions, the journalists can refer to the 1982 Constitution that guarantees basic freedoms.

Given the worldview differences between believers and nonbelievers, and the differences between biblical objectivity and standard subjectivity, media goals and procedures will inevitably clash. Christians and media analysts continue to watch President Xi's statements closely.

But a more basic question also needs discussion: to what extent are the lessons God gives us regarding life in the Promised Land normative for Christians living as minorities in lands ruled by non-Christians?

My suggestion is to follow the Bible literally, which means trusting the Bible's own clear indications that parts of it are historical description but not prescription, parts are poetry, and parts include rules for life in the Holy Land, but not necessarily for society in the unholy lands in which we now live. The Bible teaches that the goal in ancient Israel was to subtract, not add. The goal outside of ancient Israel was and is to add, not subtract.

The early books of the Old Testament emphasize subtracting a family and then a nation (and its land) from the idol worship that surrounded first Abraham and then Israel. The emphasis was on purity, not evangelism, so God sent Ishmael and Esau into the wilderness, told Joshua to destroy the Canaanites, and instructed Ezra to insist that the Israelites put away foreign wives. To make the Holy Land holy, God commanded a zero tolerance policy: no abominations among you.

The Holy Land was man's greatest opportunity to set up a new kind of Eden. It wasn't the Eden at the beginning of Genesis, because sin still burdened man, the earth yielded its produce reluctantly, and earthly life still ended in death. But it was a semi-Eden—a land flowing with milk and honey—and it had God's semi-presence as he facilitated prophecy and gave specific advice via the casting of lots and the mysterious Urim and Thummim.

Furthermore, God chose a particular nation to live in his semi-Eden, provided commandments so they would know what to do day by day, inspired a history so they would know where they came from, and promised them (in Deuteronomy 28 and elsewhere) that if they obeyed, all would go well. Mao demanded a Great Leap Forward. U.S. President Lyndon Johnson in the 1960s, hoping to create "The Great Society," emphasized the use of "Model Cities," urban renewal projects that would show how all could live. God established ancient Israel as a model nation, a perfect test case of whether good rules would engender a good people.

The Promised Land was supposed to be a model land. The Old

Testament is highly location-specific. For example, in Leviticus 18:3, God tells the Israelites plainly, "You shall not do as they do in the land of Canaan, to which I am bringing you." He then provides a long list of what the Canaanites do and what his people should not do. He summarizes, "You shall keep my statutes and my rules and do none of these abominations, either the native or the stranger who sojourns among you . . . lest the land vomit you out when you make it unclean" (18:26, 28).

Chapter 20 lists penalties for disobedience in the land, including:

> If a man commits adultery with the wife of his neighbor, both the adulterer and the adulteress shall surely be put to death. . . . If a man lies with a male as with a woman, both of them have committed an abomination; they shall surely be put to death. (20:10, 13)

God established many specific practices for that land. For example, Israelites could not sell familial property permanently, and they had to establish cities of refuge.

This emphasis on not only pure people but also a pure country is frequent in Deuteronomic passages about life in Israel: "When you come into the land that the LORD your God is giving you, you shall not learn to follow the abominable practices of those nations" (Deut. 18:9). The emphasis is on "when you come into the land." The land must be cleansed from defilement. It must be preserved as holy.

The prophets were indignant when the Israelites trashed their semi-Eden. God had Jeremiah proclaim, "Thus says the LORD . . . 'I brought you into a plentiful land to enjoy its fruits and its good things. But when you came in, you defiled my land and made my heritage an abomination" (Jer. 2:5, 7). Jeremiah denounced the betrayal: "The LORD once called you 'a green olive tree, beautiful with good fruit.' But with the roar of a great tempest he will set fire to it, and its branches will be consumed" (11:16).

The charter of the ancient Israelites was to protect the purity of the land that God had given them. Evangelism was not a priority. When some Israelites married foreign women, leaders did not celebrate an opportunity to evangelize the newcomers and increase the numbers of Israel. Instead, they looked upon intermarriage with horror. The Israelite charter was to purify the Holy Land by killing or driving out the nations that inhabited it and surrounding their land with a theological and cultural fence to keep others out. The primary directive was defense. The primary goal was the maintenance of holiness.

Most Christians understand that Old Testament history teaches us not to become prideful and think we can create earthly utopias or even sustain the ones handed to us. But other questions also arise from Israel's experience: If ancient Israel's laws, given by God, did not bring about righteousness in this most hospitable of environments, how likely are holiness laws to succeed in less favorable environments? Should those who want to be strong and courageous strive to make whatever country they inhabit the semi-Eden that ancient Israel was to be?

Several Old Testament writers considered the situation of God's people living outside God's model country. Significantly, Jeremiah— the same Jeremiah whose godly fury led to our word *jeremiad*—had a very different tone when he spoke to Israelites living not only outside the semi-Eden, but in the anti-Eden, Babylonia. He wrote to Israelites living in the capital of that very ungodly country:

> Thus says the LORD of hosts, the God of Israel, to all the exiles whom I have sent into exile from Jerusalem to Babylon: "Build houses and live in them; plant gardens and eat their produce. . . . Seek the welfare of the city where I have sent you into exile, and pray to the LORD on its behalf, for in its welfare you will find your welfare." (Jer. 29:4–5, 7)

Other parts of the Old Testament also indicate that Israelites outside the borders of Israel could have a different political agenda than those inside. God banned from ancient Israel "anyone who practices divination or tells fortunes or interprets omens, or a sorcerer or a charmer or a medium or a necromancer or one who inquires of the dead, for whoever does these things is an abomination to the Lord" (Deut. 18:10–12). And yet the book of Daniel shows how

Daniel had to hang out with enchanters, sorcerers, and the other wise men of Babylon. Daniel thought and acted independently, but he nowhere indicated a plan or desire to wipe out those ungodly people. A stranger in a strange land, he had to coexist with them.

The books of Ezra, Nehemiah, and Esther show how the Jews of Persia, part of an empire comprising 127 provinces and a vast number of ethnic groups and languages, also lived under laws not their own. The evil that God had said Israel must ban was often just around the corner in Persia, but Israelites often showed themselves to be the most patriotic of subjects. Cupbearer Nehemiah was the last line of defense against attempts to poison the king. Mordecai in the book of Esther broke up an assassination plot. When Esther and her uncle Mordecai later had an opportunity to have the king promulgate legislation, they only requested that the Jews of Persia have the right to fight back militarily against their persecutors.

It might be said that these societies had no tradition of free speech and public demonstration, and so the relevance of the Bible commanding a hard line in ancient Israel and a tolerant posture elsewhere, is limited. But in New Testament times, when greater liberty did exist for Roman citizens in some parts of the empire, the apostle Paul and others emphasized proclaiming the gospel at every opportunity, without calling for the imposition of biblical law.

Judges 6 shows that Gideon destroyed an altar of Baal in Israel. About one thousand years later, the Maccabees destroyed Greek altars erected in Israel. Paul, though, did not damage the numerous altars he saw during his walk through Athens. Instead, as Acts 17:17–31 relates, he reasoned "in the marketplace every day with those who happened to be there" and also spoke before the city's philosophical elite. Paul never hesitated to demand his rights as a Roman citizen, but he also never tried to eliminate pagan altars and idols from the city streets. Proper action in one place was not proper in another.

The bottom line: location, location, location. We even see this in the work of Jesus. He drove the Jewish moneychangers out of the temple, the holiest place in the world, but did not drive Romans out of other places. Israel had already become a most unholy land by A.D. 70, when Roman soldiers destroyed the temple. After that, one land was not holier than others. Some spaces, though, were: churches were to aspire to be model cities.

Many Jews in New Testament times still emphasized the subtraction of anything impure, but others got the message. They realized that God's model country delivered a pessimistic message about what we can do on our own. The great tragedy of ancient Israel was that God's people sinned in a land that of all lands should have been the least conducive to sin. The great lesson is that sin comes from within, not from our surroundings. God was teaching that sin crouches at our door even in the best of environments, whether the original Eden or Israel's semi-Eden. He was teaching man's desperate need for Christ: accept no substitutes!

As early Christians came to understand the meaning of Israel's history, they were ready to understand the New Testament emphasis on adding. The Jewish answer to the question "Who is my neighbor?" was at the most "your fellow Jew," and more often just the Jews who lived close by. Jesus added to that understanding by eating with tax collectors and others seen as sinners, by stating that anyone in need is our neighbor, and by adding women, Samaritans, and even enemy soldiers to the list of God's people.

Jesus' embrace of others braced the early Christians. Instructed to take the gospel to all nations and not concentrate on defending one, Christians were free to evangelize and admit to church membership anyone who confessed faith in Christ, regardless of pedigree, past sins, race, or ethnicity. Would some get in who should not, and as a result would the visible church display visible sin? Absolutely, but a Christian understanding of the ubiquity of sin makes even the best screen only as effective as bed nets against malarial mosquitoes in Africa. They will find a way to get in.

The early Christian church dropped the defensive posture that had characterized Israel and went on offense. Without a land to preserve, but with a gospel to proclaim, the primary directive was evangelism rather than maintenance of purity. New people rapidly joined the church at the risk of dilution, but leaders impelled by the Great Commission of proclaiming the gospel in all nations took risks that Jewish leaders seeking to maintain purity were never willing to accept.

Neither the United States nor China is the new Israel. That means the Bible's Daniel, living in Babylon, is a role model for us. For at least sixty-six years, from 605 to 539 B.C., he lived and worked under Babylonian authority, always trying to serve a strange public while remaining true to God. He faced down two death threats and saw his friends survive a third.

Daniel declined to eat the rich food available to him in Babylonian dining halls, and instead lived on vegetables. It's possible that Daniel abstained from meat for dietary reasons (although he apparently ate it later) or because it would have been sacrificed to idols (but vegetables were as well). Reformation-era commentator Heinrich Bullinger (1504–75) offered a better explanation, that "the king should not entice him by this sweet poison." John Mayer (1583–1664) similarly noted the temptations of "dainty and delicate keeping" and said Daniel's example shows "it is no part of felicity in respect of worldly things to have the wherewithal to eat and drink daily of the best." Current scholar Iain Duguid points out in his commentary on Daniel that if Satan can "instill in us a sense of dependence upon the material comforts that make up our way of life . . . then he can far more effectively draw us away from the Lord."

Daniel and his colleagues studied Babylonian culture. "In every matter of wisdom and understanding about which the king inquired of them, he found them ten times better than all the magicians and enchanters" (Dan. 1:20). When King Nebuchadnezzar dreamed of statues, God revealed to Daniel the information the king needed. Daniel then couched his news analysis in terms that resonated with the king. Babylonians worshipped mountains, so Daniel's description of a boulder that struck the statue and "became a great mountain" struck home.

The Israelites publicly tolerated differences, but they kept God's commands in their own lives and within their own households. When Nebuchadnezzar set up a ninety-foot-tall image of gold and commanded all his officials to bow down and worship it, Daniel's three friends did not harangue the assembled pagans; chapter 3 shows that they merely refused to bow. That was enough to get them arrested and thrown into a fiery furnace, where they miraculously survived.

But what if a journalist today, facing potential death, fails to be bold and courageous?

Where was Daniel in chapter 3 of his book? Some commentators say that Daniel must have been somewhere else, since he could not have sat quietly as his friends faced fire. Some Reformation theologians went deeper. John Calvin suggested that Daniel was in Babylon but escaped prosecution because the king liked him. English clergyman Andrew Willett suggested that Daniel protested at first, but then was silent.

Those speculations lead to thoughts that could be depressing: During the events of chapter 3, was Daniel, like Peter six centuries later, warming his hands by the enemy's fire? Instead of hearing a rooster crow three times, did he stand to the side as three of his friends faced death? If that's so, it's not depressing, but inspiring, as is Peter's story. Who can turn a skulking coward into a hero? God can. He reached into a prison cell to make Joseph fit to rule. He reached into desert brush to light a fire in Moses. If Daniel was not brave in chapter 3, his courage later is even more impressive.

Chapter 4 portrays a king who started thinking of himself as a god, and courageous Daniel warning him. Daniel's prediction was accurate. When Nebuchadnezzar bragged about "the glory of my majesty," the true King condemned him to seven years of insanity. Chapter 5 tells us that a later king, Belshazzar, summoned Daniel to interpret frightening handwriting on the wall, and that Daniel spoke of the king's imminent doom.

Chapter 6 shows King Darius ordering that for thirty days all prayers had to be addressed to him. When Daniel prayed to God in his own home, as he always did, enemies spied on him and arrested him. Biblical heroes typically do not go looking for trouble. Trouble goes looking for them. Over the centuries, some commentators have asked why Daniel didn't shut the windows and draw the curtains. Why make it easy for his enemies? But Calvin pointed out that had Daniel prayed secretly, those foes "would have counted him timorous and without all courage. . . . It was necessary for him to do as he did that his faith, courage, and constancy to his first principles might appear to all people."

Daniel had to learn patience, and so did his Jewish successors within the Persian empire. The book of Esther tells how Mordecai, officially trusted enough to sit in the king's gate, had to watch helplessly as his beautiful cousin and adopted daughter, virgin Esther, "was gathered" with other young women and "was taken" into the king's harem. The English words, which reflect the Hebrew, are maddeningly passive.

What Daniel gained by intellect, Esther gained by beauty, and Mordecai gained by patience. When he heard of a plot to assassinate the king, he did not take revenge for Esther's captivity by assisting the assassins, as a moviemaker today might have him do. Instead, he saved the king's life. When Esther first received Mordecai's request that she enter the king's inner court, without preauthorization, to plead for the Jews who faced genocide, she turned down what seemed like a suicide mission.

Mordecai, instead of giving up on Esther, emphasized what was at stake and asked the question we all need to answer when asked to go on a mad mission: "Who knows whether you have not come to the kingdom for such a time as this?" Esther then replied, "I will go to the king, though it is against the law, and if I perish, I perish" (Esth. 4:14, 16). She did not act out of a sudden rush of emotion, unaware of the risks. She was a true heroine, counting the cost, but acting nevertheless.

The books named after Daniel and Esther suggest they were not brave from birth. They were sinners like the rest of us, needing to be born again. It seems God loved them and gave them the grace to conquer their fears. That may be God's plan for us too. Journalists should try to have good relations with all people, but when bullies tell us we need to profess views contrary to biblical teaching, it's good and right to refuse.

KEY TERMS

the Promised Land
evangelism
jeremiad

STUDY QUESTIONS

1. How can Christian journalists follow Daniel's example?
2. How should we react when Christians forget that America is not the new Israel?
3. How can a Christian journalist bring a Christian worldview to bear when writing stories for a secular publication?
4. If a reporter, when writing a profile, includes information about the Christian faith of a subject, and a secular editor says "take it out," how should the reporter react?
5. Discuss: "The Bible teaches that the goal in ancient Israel was to subtract, not add. The goal outside of ancient Israel was and is to add, not subtract."
6. Discuss: "Biblical heroes typically do not go looking for trouble. Trouble goes looking for them."

FOR FURTHER READING

Philip Hamburger, *Separation of Church and State* (Harvard University Press, 2002).

Daniel L. Driesbach, *Thomas Jefferson and the Wall of Separation between Church and State* (New York University, 2002).

Christopher Wright, *Hearing the Message of Daniel* (Zondervan, 2017).

Rodney Stortz, *Daniel: The Triumph of God's Kingdom* (Crossway, 2004).

9

Third Brother Journalists

CHAPTER 8 DISCUSSED how Christian journalists should coexist with the laws and mores that rule non-Christian lands. This chapter will look at how we should coexist with others by emulating neither the younger brother nor the elder brother in the parable of the prodigal son.

To review quickly the parable in Luke 15: The younger brother takes his share of the family wealth—one-third, according to Middle Eastern convention. He wastes it all in libertine living until perilous poverty forces him to change. He heads home prepared to grovel, since tradition demands the entire village chastise him. He places his hope in an artfully prepared speech.

The younger brother prepares himself to grovel because he has grossly insulted his father. Sons typically receive their inheritance when their father dies, so the younger son's request to receive his one-third immediately was akin to wishing his father dead. The conventional Middle Eastern patriarch would have slapped his son, but the father in the parable gave the son what he wanted. Now, though, the prodigal has wasted all that money and expects punishment.

When the prodigal returns, the father astonishes the son by running out to meet him. That is uncouth behavior in the Middle East. Patriarchs do not pick up their robes and run to a child. A lot of Muslims and Jews do not like the idea of a compassionate God who runs to embrace sinners—what kind of God is that? But the father in the parable shows his extraordinary compassion.

We often understate the problem of the elder brother. When the father puts on a feast to welcome back the younger son, the older son is resentful. He complains to the father, "These many years I have served you"—not *developed my talents,* not *exercised my creativity,* but served you, like a drudge. Since that was the attitude of the elder brother, it's not surprising that the younger brother didn't want any part of what looked like slavery.

As New York pastor Tim Keller has pointed out in sermons and in *The Prodigal God,* the elder brother has done everything right, but joylessly. Reliable but self-righteous, he did not go out searching for his brother, which would be an act of love as well as an obligation in Middle Eastern culture. He refuses to celebrate the brother's return or even acknowledge their relationship; he complains to the father about "your son," not "my brother." His lack of love leaves him ready to shame his father by boycotting the party. The eldest son at banquets has the duty, but also the honor, of checking to make sure guests are adequately fed and watered.

Strikingly, the father shows his compassion once again by leaving the banquet he is hosting—again, an unusual event in Middle Eastern custom, especially when guests are eating the fatted calf—to plead with his elder son. The parable ends with us left in suspense as to what the elder son will do—because, by tradition, he has a strong case. Should not the just father punish the prodigal, instead of giving him what looks like a reward?

Here's the key: the father forgives; the elder brother does not. The father does not forget, but he purposely puts aside the younger brother's conduct. The elder brother remembers. The father is willing to accept the younger brother in a way that will change future family dynamics. The elder brother—much as he dislikes what he sees as his current servitude—does not want change.

The heart of the problem, though, is not the past or the present, but wistfulness. The elder brother apparently wants revenge because he thinks the younger brother had fun, and he wants that fun too. He works hard, but desires a prodigal life style. The difference between the two brothers is that the younger was obnoxious enough to act out his desires, while the elder repressed his. Then and today, if we are jealous of those who live out a playboy philosophy, we are no better than they. The essential difference is that we are cowards.

Jesus, of course, was speaking to Pharisees who lived by the elder brother's rulebook—upholding Israel's traditions, but redlining grace. Today we still have younger brothers who live merely to fulfill their own desires. Many Christians fight against a libertine culture. Of course, younger brothers need to grow up—but don't those who are orderly but loveless also need to change?

As Keller puts it, the parable teaches "that a man who has violated virtually nothing on the list of moral misbehaviors can be every bit as spiritually lost as the most profligate, immoral person. . . . Elder brothers believe that if they live a good life they should get a good life, that God owes them a smooth road if they try very hard to live up to standards."

Journalism is an arena for competition between younger and elder brothers. In the United States, younger brother magazines along the lines of *Playboy*, *Rolling Stone*, and even *People* sell the libertine life. Supermarket tabloids and television shows make money off of lascivious sensationalism without explicitly approving it. Elder brother journalists, on the other hand, are self-righteous faultfinders—and it's always someone else's fault. Elder brother journalism lacks love, charity, compassion, and any sense that all of us, because of the human condition, are in this mess together. Christian publications that only look at sin among secularists can also be elder brothers.

Third brother journalism is different. One important report in the book of Acts is Stephen's history lecture in chapter 7. He has neither an elder brother's self-righteousness nor a younger brother's scorn for righteousness. He realistically emphasizes the sinfulness of his people and the holiness of God. He understands Christian love and, even when facing a murderous mob, has joy in seeing God's glory.

Christians throughout the centuries have taught the importance of joy, not just in the future, but in the present as well. Chapter 15 of John's Gospel teaches that Christ came so that our joy could be full. Philippians 3 tells us to count everything as loss for the surpassing worth of knowing Christ. First Timothy 6 emphasizes the great gain in godliness with contentment.

The eighteenth-century theologian Jonathan Edwards observed, "God is glorified not only by his glory's being seen, but by its being rejoiced in. When those that see it delight in it, God is more glorified than if they only see it." Pastor John Piper concluded,

> We should *pursue* happiness, and pursue it with all our might. The desire to be happy is a proper motive for every good deed, and if you abandon the pursuit of your own joy you cannot love man or please God.

That's something for Christian journalists to keep in mind when the going gets tough. With Piper and his colleague Sam Storms, we should say,

> Everyone longs for happiness. And we will never tell them to deny or repress that desire. Their problem is not that they want to be satisfied, but that they are far too easily satisfied. . . . We will labor to wean them off the milk of the world onto the rich fare of God's grace and glory.

This teaching is also useful because investigative journalists often tilt toward legalism. We can't measure states of mind and heart, but we can measure external compliance, so the conduct of elder brothers doesn't make for as colorful a story as the antics of libertine prodigals. Journalists can act like beleaguered schoolmarms who tend to praise compliant kids and condemn rambunctious ones.

In higher education, numerous younger brother colleges are party schools that proffer sex and stimulants. Evangelicals might support Christian colleges that try to avoid that by imposing tight rules in elder brother fashion, but those rules may lead to external conformity and self-righteous attitudes, rather than deep belief. Both elder and younger brother colleges divert students from learning more about God.

A third brother journalist has a different view of the nature of work. As Keller points out, God in Genesis 2 brings order out of chaos and then says to man, "Now you create more order." Adam is a gardener, not a park ranger. Work is rearranging the raw material in a particular domain so that it helps everyone to flourish. Music, for example, is taking the raw material of sound and arranging it so it brings meaning. Architects take wood or steel or other basic materials and create ordered space. Writers bring order to letters and words, and so on.

Since we are made in God's image, work should also be play, a way for us to develop and use God-given creativity. We need to make money, as Adam amid thorns needed to wrest his bread from the dirt, but work is not primarily for making money. "It is," to quote Dorothy Sayers, "the gracious expression of creative energy in the service of others." The elder brother apparently never rejoiced as he worked. A younger brother who witnesses joylessness is unlikely to value gardening over loitering.

When Christians write about work, we tend to cheer for elder brothers against younger ones who put play before work and then put off work altogether. But we need to recognize that elder brothers also have problems, as Dorothy Sayers points out in her classic book, *Creed or Chaos?* She describes those who work to make money and view the actual result of their work as a by-product:

> Doctors practice medicine, not primarily to relieve suffering, but to make a living—the cure of the patient is something that happens on the way. Lawyers accept briefs, not because they have a passion for justice, but . . . to obtain money.

In being in, reading about, and writing about organizations, I've seen what happens when work becomes mere moneymaking without creativity. Precise work rules negotiated between New York unions and management have often given employees one specific assignment on the assembly line. For decades the deal was: become a robot at work, so as to have lots of cash for evenings and weekends, when real living occurs. Elder brothers accepted that and worked efficiently but joylessly, but many younger brothers wanted no part of that. Others compromised by smashing out parts during their eight hours and then getting smashed.

How should we report the big debate that has gone on in the United States about same-sex marriage? A third brother journalist knows it's vital to defend marriage, but when we talk about faithfulness in marriage as a duty, or as a standard to uphold, we're defending an elder brother marriage. Yes, traditional marriage fosters superior health and longevity, economic benefit and security, healthier and better-adjusted children, and so forth, but if our marriages are not filled with love, they are only resounding gongs or clanging cymbals.

Since the idea of falling in love is sometimes a conduit toward younger brother irresponsibility, some Christians have pooh-poohed the notion of "love" and even suggested that arranged marriages are better. That won't work. Marriage is more than a contract. Our goal is also to inspire hearts.

When Christians protest against homosexuality, we should not act like elder brothers. Several years back I covered Manhattan's annual Gay Pride parade, and saw that marching homosexuals refrained from kissing each other except when they passed a dozen souls from a church who waved Bibles and yelled at them, "You're going to hell, sodomite," or, "You're an abomination in the sight of God."

One of the protesters told me, "Someone's got to stand for the truth." But elder brothers sometimes forget that truth without love is like sodium without chloride: poison, not salt. The presence of these self-righteous elder brothers allowed the prancing younger brothers to feel self-righteous. Ironically, ranting reminders about sin provided the opportunity to forget about sin.

What difference does it make when a reporter thinks as a third brother and not as an elder or a younger one? Let's look at politics. Elder brothers who are Christian conservatives tend to think that the right laws will help America to be the new Israel. Elder brothers who are secular liberals tend to think that the right laws will help America to be the new Europe. Both sets of elder brothers emphasize preaching at people. But third brothers know we can never have enough laws to banish sin. Law fails. Only Christ truly changes lives.

As Christians, we are more likely to fall into elder brother rants if we start thinking that America should be or once was a new Israel. But with Christ's coming, churches rather than any particular country are the new homeland of those whose goal is to glorify him. The failure of ancient Israel proved man's desperate need for Christ—and there's no need for any more proof. Given such failure, imitating Israel is nothing to be proud of.

If we start idolizing our own country and demonizing others, we are making the same mistake as ancient Israelites made and some of their modern portrayers do. Stephen in Acts 7 angered his listeners as he recounted Israel's history of sin and emphasized that hope is only found in Christ. The United States and China are both wonderful countries with great but also sinful histories, so when we review that history from a third brother perspective, we should follow Stephen's example of stressing God's blessings, but pointing to how Christ saves sinners.

Younger brothers tend to underuse the Bible. Elder brothers tend to overuse it. The dangers of underuse are obvious. Younger brothers rationalize killing via abortion, committing adultery, stealing, bearing false witness, and coveting. Elder brothers treat the Bible like a book of rules about what we should and should not do. But the Bible isn't mainly about rules and what we should do. It's about what God has done. Both younger and elder brothers need to take to heart the Bible's basic teaching.

God created the world and it was very good—but it wasn't perfect. The very good apparently wasn't good enough for human beings who sought what they thought was perfection. A renegade angel, Satan, tempted the humans to rebel. Adam and Eve fell for Satan's lies and the world changed. It's not very good any more. Evil exists in our hearts and decay mars the creation. Death has come into the world.

Most of the Bible is about what God did after evil came into the world. He was not content to let the world decay and rot. Even as he pronounced the consequences of sin, he also promised that one day a special human being would outwit and defeat Satan, and that the earth would one day be restored.

The rest of the Bible is the story of how this works out. God forms a people and protects them against enemies. They sometimes fight wars, but they survive. They keep messing up, but he doesn't abandon them. He shows this people his character. He teaches them about evil and the need for sacrifice. He shows them their inability to keep the law. They keep messing up, committing spiritual adultery, but God never abandons them. They are often unlovable, but he always loves them.

When Christian journalists become solemn, like some full-of-themselves pundits, we are not truly following Jesus, who regularly in the Gospels flashes his sense of humor. Instead, we're acting like disciples of the eighteenth-century German philosopher Immanuel Kant, who saw the moral value of any action as inversely proportional to the benefit we derive from it. Kant argued that we should do what's good simply because it's good, and any benefits we derive lessen the goodness of our action. Good actions are "disinterested." Duty is meritorious. Enjoyment is selfish. The logic of this leads to a hard conclusion: the best actions are those that make us miserable. The elder brother in the parable of the prodigal son is a Kantian hero.

The Bible, though, does not teach us to be stoics. The Bible weaves a story of love and rescue, promise and deliverance. It shows how a Redeemer brings the blind, the lame, and the lost to safety. It tells of a love so terrific that God willingly sacrificed his own Son to make redemption possible for these people. Sin still exists in the world and in the hearts of man. Until Christ comes again, creation still groans. But we see glimmers of the promised redemption. We see examples of self-sacrificial love, tastes of undeserved kindness, and glimpses of holiness.

The greatest stories that journalists can tell grow out of such glimmers and glimpses.

KEY TERMS

> younger brother
> elder brother
> third brother

STUDY QUESTIONS

1. Discuss the application of the parable of the prodigal son to journalists.
2. To what extent could defining protagonists and antagonists in a story (as discussed in chapter 4) tilt it toward an "elder brother" perspective?
3. How does a writer avoid crossing the line into legalistic moralizing?
4. A third brother journalist takes joy in his work and is "a gardener, not a park ranger." Since joy is contagious, this should result in a huge competitive advantage for Christian media outlets over secular ones whose journalists are "bored with life, which they see as purposeless." Has it worked out that way?

FOR FURTHER READING

Tim Keller, *The Prodigal God* (Penguin, 2011).
William Farley, *Gospel-Powered Humility* (P&R Publishing, 2012).

10

Interacting with Atheists

CHRISTIAN JOURNALISTS IN the United States have an easier time interacting with government officials than do Christian journalists in China. One reason for that is the American history of press freedom and limited government. Another reason is that officials are less likely to be doctrinaire atheists. In China, though, officials have often learned in schools that religion poisons everything, and what seems benign to Christians is an evil that must be fought.

For years, the most popular proponent of atheism in the United States and England was a British journalist who became an American citizen, Christopher Hitchens (1949–2011). I debated him once at the University of Texas and twice moderated debates between him and Christian apologists at The Kings College in New York City. Hitchens was a far better debater than me, but he did need fuel from a flask of alcohol he sipped from during the Texas debate. After a midday New York City debate, when we were about to break bread, he said he desperately desired a fifth of whiskey, so I violated the dry college policy in the spirit of hospitality. At the table, he drank a sizable lunch.

All of this suggests that Hitchens sadly needed the opiate of the masses—not religion, but alcohol—but the examples I offered in my debate with him may be useful when dealing with other hardened atheists. Since the title and subtitle of his best-selling atheist primer was *God Is Not Great: How Religion Spoils Everything*, I started by asking him to defend his generalization: "Everything! That sounds improbable. Are all 1.3 billion Muslims murderers? Are one billion Hindus all nutty? Would you concede that Christianity might have produced 50 percent evil and 50 percent good?"

I then followed the style of Abraham's pleading in Genesis: "How about 40 percent? 30 percent? 20 percent? Will not Christopher relent from his anger if we can find 10 percent that is good?" He said statistics would never show that atheists "commit more crimes of greed or violence than the faithful," so I told him about my visit to a prison near Houston, where inmates who go through a prison evangelism program have much lower recidivism rates than others.

Hitchens said religious believers all fight with each other, so I told him about the annual pro-life march in Washington, where more than 100,000 Christians walk side by side with groups from Jews for Life, Buddhists for Life, and so on. Concerning the events of September 11, 2001, Hitchens said, "The nineteen suicide murderers of New York and Washington and Pennsylvania were beyond any doubt the most sincere believers on those planes." I told him about Todd Beamer, a strong Christian believer who led the fight against the terrorists on one of the hijacked planes and made sure it didn't crash into the U.S. Capitol.

Turning to exegesis, Hitchens argued that "none of the gruesome, disordered events described in Exodus ever took place. . . . All the Mosaic myths can be safely and easily discarded." Such sweeping pronouncements have been common since the nineteenth century, but again and again biblical accounts considered mythical back then have gained new archeological support. For example, scholars at one point said the Hittites described in the Bible did not exist, nor did rulers such as Belshazzar of Babylon or Sargon of Assyria. Archeologists now have records of all those civilizations and reigns.

Turning to cultural analysis, Hitchens said, "One knew, of course, that the whole racket of American evangelism was just that: a heartless con." I asked him to consider Christians I had reported on who were spending their lives in a racket that yields them almost no income. The same could be said about many Chinese Christians.

I told him about Mount Zion Church near Washington, where Hitchens lived, that included at least thirty families who had adopted children, often ones with disabilities. For example, the Cooneys had adopted nine children. Their nineteen-year-old was autistic, with mild mental retardation and severe bipolar disorder. Their sixteen-year-old with daunting medical needs grew up in Ghana, where people set her on fire ten years before. Their fourteen-year-old weighed only two pounds when he was born with cerebral palsy. Their eleven-year-old was the sixth child of a drug-addicted prostitute. They adopted these children and others because of their Christian beliefs. How could religion poison everything?

Christians from Mount Zion also founded and funded the Children of Zion orphanage in Namibia. I had visited there and met fifty children, most of whom had lost at least one parent to AIDS. Several—including one boy who had been living in a tire—came out of slavery. Two deaf boys had lived on the streets. Eleven of the orphans carried the HIV virus. That orphanage would not exist except for Christian belief. How could religion poison everything?

I was able to tell Hitchens about Freddie Garcia in his San Antonio home. He had been a drug addict. He had hated white people who were not Hispanic like himself. Then he became a Christian and started a ministry, Victory Outreach, which has helped thousands of drug abusers. He counsels those from many races and ethnic groups, whom everyone else has abandoned. Dozens of ex-addicts have told me that Christianity fought the poison that almost killed them. How could religion poison everything?

Because I had reported on different ministries, I could tell Hitchens about a Christian gymnast who trained others in Indianapolis, a paraplegic weightlifter who changed lives in Philadelphia, and a pastor in Minneapolis who worked with Hmong and Somali refugees. Christian reporters in China should become familiar with the works of mercy performed by Chinese Christians and the positives of Christian history.

Hitchens needed to hear about Charles Brace, a nineteenth-century minister who walked the streets of New York City to gain a personal understanding of problems, and then built forty lodging houses there that provided shelter to tens of thousands of abandoned children. He placed 91,000 of them in adoptive homes. He needed to hear about Helen Mercy Woods, who from 1881 to 1903 ran a shelter in Chicago for pregnant and unmarried women. Month after month she gave personal attention to each newcomer and rejoiced as their babies were born. She helped some women to get married, others to place their children for adoption, others to get jobs.

Officials or antagonistic journalists often take aim at biblical teachings they consider unreasonable, such as Christ's birth to a virgin or his resurrection. Christians in responding can provide context: are any of these acts incredible when we think of the origin of life? A chance of one out of a trillion is considered a virtual impossibility, but when DNA codiscoverer Francis Crick calculated the possibility of a simple protein sequence of two hundred amino acids (much simpler than a DNA molecule) originating spontaneously, his figure was one out of ten with 260 zeroes after it.

Biologist Frank Salisbury, who died the day after Christmas in 2015, described the odds this way: Imagine one hundred million trillion planets, each with an ocean with lots of DNA fragments that reproduce one million times per second, with a mutation occurring each time. In four billion years, it would still take trillions of universes to produce a single gene. So the really odd story is that we are here at all. If God created the entire world, resurrection or other miracles are easy tasks.

Another often-used attack is to claim that the Gospels were written long after the fact and were propaganda booklets. Here are two reasons to the contrary: First, if the Gospels are fictional, their authors were idiots for giving women vital roles in the founding of a religion. Naming women as the first witnesses to the empty tomb would add to suspicion as to whether Christ truly rose from the dead. Overall, it's worth comparing the positive New Testament view of women with the negative one that dominated ancient Greece and Rome.

A second reason is that precision in specific detail shows the first three Gospels were composed soon after the death and resurrection of Christ. Here's a rough parallel: Archeologists have pulled up from the ocean bottom the USS *Monitor*, a ship used during the U.S. Civil War that's famous because it was one of the first ships to be clad in iron. Experts were surprised to find undocumented braces on the gun turret and mustard bottles where the crew ate. If we found in some musty library a document asserting that the crew had added some braces and braced their taste buds by pouring mustard on otherwise inedible biscuits, we would be much more likely to give that manuscript an origin stamp of 1870 rather than 1970. Similarly, some specific details in the Gospels would only have been known to someone alive in the middle of the first century A.D.

We could go on with other defenses of the Bible's veracity, but many other books specialize in that. Instead, let's do a thought experiment. Imagine that in the twentieth century, in the biggest country by land area and also in the biggest country by population, leaders who gained power persecuted Christians and decreed that all schools should teach atheism. If man is naturally good and "religion poisons everything," wouldn't life have gotten better and warfare have ended in those countries?

We don't have to do a thought experiment. The Soviet Union and China did establish atheism, and the results were horrific. Hitchens said, "It is horrifying to remember how many people were tortured or killed" over arguments about God. It's true that the Inquisition over the centuries killed thousands, but Josef Stalin and his Soviet associates killed not thousands, but millions. How many in China died during the Great Leap Forward and the Cultural Revolution?

It used to be that when atheists talked about the evil of church dictatorships, no one could show the problem was broader than religion, because we did not have a track record of secular dictatorships. Now we do. Hitchens spoke of atheists respecting free inquiry and open-mindedness and not excommunicating each other. Maybe some did—but the twentieth century was a century of atheists resolving their disputes not by excommunication, but by murdering each other.

In the twenty-first century, radical Islam has left a deadly trail. Many other religions also emphasize bargaining: "I'll do this for you, Allah, or Vishnu, and you'll do something or me." Bargaining religions can sometimes cause big trouble, but Christianity is about grace. We can't buy God off. We can't trade with him. God is our

Father, so we don't have to win his love by mortifying our flesh or giving some money to religious authorities. We cannot lose his love by asking hard questions. Believers who understand this find it enormously liberating.

Religion poisons everything? No, our fallen, sinful human nature poisons everything. The question is: how can we change? Many pundits talk about changing the world, but when the *Times* of London a century ago asked a splendid journalist, G. K. Chesterton, to write an essay on "What's Wrong with the World?" he responded with two words: "I am."

I suspect Chesterton's life shows that Christianity does not poison everything. I know my life does. I entered Yale University in 1968 as an atheist and a socialist. Many professors and students believed the United States was in decline and needed radical change. Some placed their hope in genetic engineering. Yale professor José Delgado had faith in ESB (electrical stimulation of the brain). In *The Religious Situation: 1968*, Huston Smith wrote that the intellectually best students were checking out "meditation, then Yoga, then Zen . . . then I Ching . . . witchcraft, and magic. . . . And underlying everything of course, the psychedelic drugs."

Instead of embracing drugs or Buddhism, I headed toward Communism. I considered myself realistic about the costs. Of course the revolution would meet with opposition from the bourgeoisie. Of course a terrible struggle would inevitably result. Of course the progressive forces, to be triumphant, would have to be united. Of course the most efficient way to unite those forces would be to centralize all authority in the hands of those who most clearly understood the revolutionary imperative: the leadership of the Communist Party.

I had faith that this would not be a dictatorship for personal gain, but only a transitional stage required to eliminate capitalists and capitalism from the body politic. During the transition, terrible things would be done, but shrinking from them would simply create more misery by prolonging the birth pains of the new era. Thus, more killing means less killing, more dictatorship means less dictatorship, war is peace, and totalitarianism is freedom—all in the long run.

By the time I graduated from college in 1971, I had participated in demonstrations in Washington, political organizing in Philadelphia, and a five-day hunger strike in New Haven. Did I really believe this? The following year I wrote grandiosely,

> Around the world revolutionary societies are developing; what is holding them back is the power of the American empire. The most we can do right now is to neutralize that power to enable revolutionary societies to spring up without hindrance.

I also wrote,

> People are always being killed by governments, one way or another. The point is, how many, and which ones, and why. . . . Some radicals take a soft-headed approach to revolution. They can't understand that Communist Party work is bad work which must be done, sin whose time has come. Communism may be sin, in its revolutionary power enthusiasm, but it is sin going somewhere.

Today I wonder where that idea of "sin" came from, because that was not something learned at Yale. Ironically, Lenin wrote, "If you are not inclined to crawl in the mud on your belly, you are not a revolutionary but a chatterbox." Snakes have crawled on their bellies ever since the days of Adam and Eve, and now it was my turn. In June, 1972, I joined the Communist Party USA.

Later that year I passed out CP newspapers in San Francisco, met CP chairman Gus Hall, took a Soviet freighter across the Pacific Ocean, and traveled across the Soviet Union. The next year I worked as a Communist on a major newspaper, *The Boston Globe*, started work on a PhD at the University of Michigan, attended meetings of the Young Workers Liberation League, and arranged for a visit to Michigan and a speech by Georgi Arbatov, the Kremlin's expert on American politics.

The common denominator of our activities was hatred. We read *Left-Wing Communism*, in which Lenin called hatred "the basis of every socialist and Communist movement and of its success." We read in the *World Marxist Review* that "Lenin hated the enemies of the working class, for struggle was impossible without hatred." Hate, hate, hate, and pay dues of 25 cents per month for students and the unemployed—where hatred costs so little. Hatred is an equal opportunity virus, but proud hatred was a Communist characteristic.

Near the end of 1973, I wasn't dissatisfied with Communism. On November 1, I stuck another monthly dues Lenin stamp onto my CP card. That afternoon I sat in a chair in my room reading Lenin's famous essay, "Socialism and Religion," in which he wrote: "We must combat religion—this is the ABC of all materialism, and consequently Marxism." Lenin's hatred for the "figment of man's imagination" called God was not new to me, but some surprising thoughts began battering my brain: What if Lenin was wrong? What if God does exist?

I pondered this hour after hour, suddenly thinking I had done something very wrong by hugging Marx and Lenin. When I sat down in that chair at 3 P.M., I was an atheist and a Communist. When I got up at 11 P.M., I was not. I was not doing drugs. I was not sleeping. I remember hour after hour looking at the clock, amazed that I was still in that chair. I had no new data. I had, through a process I did not understand, a new way of processing data.

At 11 P.M., I got up and spent the next two hours wandering around the cold and dark University of Michigan campus, crying out to—Someone. During the next three weeks, I stopped doing my coursework and read works by Alexandr Solzhenitsyn, Andrei Sakharov, and other Russians, along with Whittaker Chambers's *Witness* and essays of ex-Communists in *The God That Failed*. Partway through this process, I still didn't know what I was, but I knew I was not a Communist.

From 1974 through 1976, slowly, I started to have faith in Christ, and at the end of 1976 I professed that publicly. That's another story, but the relevant matter here, since Hitchens claimed that religion inevitably poisons everything, is what Christianity did to my life. When I was a Communist, I broke nine of the ten commandments— all except "Do not murder" (if we restrict that to the physical act). I attacked God in many ways, dishonored my parents, mistreated women with whom I had sexual relations and then ignored, stole, bore false witness, coveted—and had murderous thoughts.

Since becoming a Christian, I've been a faithful husband for forty-three years. My wife and I have four fine sons. Before becoming a Christian, I favored abortion. If I hadn't come to believe in God, some or all of those sons would not exist. Christianity doesn't poison everything. In my own case, and for millions of other people, it's the antidote to poison.

This personal experience, as well as what I've read, seen, and studied, has made me resist the tendency of the Hitchenses of the world to condemn God. When we read Shakespeare and do not understand the words or the motivation of a character, do we immediately say, "This is garbage. Shakespeare is an idiot"? No, because Shakespeare has a lot of credibility. How much more credibility does the God of the whole universe have?

KEY TERMS

bargaining religion
materialism

STUDY QUESTIONS

1. What are three of the arguments an atheist may use against religion? How might you respond?
2. What do you see as the main differences between Christianity and all other world religions or systems?

FOR FURTHER READING

Tim Keller, *The Reason for God* (Penguin, 2008).
Alvin J. Schmidt, *How Christianity Changed the World* (Zondervan, 2001, 2004).
Rodney Stark, *The Victory of Reason: How Christianity Led to Freedom, Capitalism, and Western Success* (Random House, 2005).
Arthur C. Brooks, *Who Really Cares: The Surprising Truth about Compassionate Conservatism* (Basic, 2006).

Vincent Carroll and David Shiflett, *Christianity on Trial: Arguments against Anti-Religious Bigotry* (Encounter Books, 2002).

Norman Geisler and Frank Turek, *I Don't Have Enough Faith to Be an Atheist* (Crossway, 2004).

Michael Reeves, *Delighting in the Trinity: An Introduction to the Christian Faith* (IVP, 2012).

Marvin Olasky, *Unmerited Mercy* (World & Life, 2010).

PART 2

PRACTICAL APPLICATIONS

11

How to Interview

NOW, WITH THE basics laid out, let's see how to put some of our journalistic goals into practice. Both American and Chinese leaders sometimes treat reporters as stenographers whose job it is to take down their words without question. Chinese reporters sometimes have no choice but to take dictation from dictators. American journalists have more freedom, but fall into unforced errors because some have not thought through how to conduct good interviews.

Richard Ben Cramer, a masterful political reporter, once pinpointed a common journalistic error:

> I've been interviewed a lot during book tours. I see how newspaper people, in particular, do it. They'll ask you a question. And as you start to talk they bend their heads to their notebooks and try to get down every word. They barely look at you again for forty-five minutes. Now that's entirely the wrong way to get any sense of anybody!

What are other wrong ways? Some newspaper reporters conduct interviews to check off a name on a list, to get a story-"balancing" quotation. (Associated Press editor Kathleen Carroll in 2016 razzed reporters: "Do you email someone asking for 'a quote' to stick into a story you've already put together? That's not interviewing. That's decorating.")

Others play journalistic ventriloquism, in which the reporter quotes sources who utter opinions identical to his own or his editor's. Former *New York Times* reporter Michael Cieply in 2016 reminisced about a colleague who told a source, "My editor needs someone to say such-and-such, could you say that?"

It's easy to go wrong by asking yes/no questions, asking multiple warhead questions so interviewees can dodge the main ones, or making statements rather than asking questions. Some interviewers like to ask broad questions: How is this affecting you? What do you enjoy doing? What would you like to see happen? Such questions tend to evoke overly general answers, so it's better to ask for superlatives: What is your most pressing issue? What was your greatest disappointment?

I've made up the names of two diseases that may strike reporters: quotosis (stringing together quotations) and puffitis (doing public relations for an interviewee). The way to stay healthy while interviewing is to realize the goal of an interview is not primarily to elicit words or give the interviewee a megaphone. The main goal is to get stories, not to put together a string of quotations with linking sentences.

Wise reporters, therefore, ask questions likely to elicit unusual answers, or questions about things the interviewee might prefer not to discuss. They do not use quotations just for the sake of showing they've talked with someone. They probe for information and anecdotes. They verify all information and check the honesty of interviewees by asking questions to which they already know answers.

Interviews are sometimes fishing expeditions, but it is usually better to turn them into searches for specific information and insights. Journalists develop particular lines of questioning, depending on the intent of the article, and should ask general questions only to allow interviewees to open up entirely new areas of which they may be unaware. Sometimes interviews can lead us in a direction opposite to what we anticipated—but we still need to anticipate.

Interview questions to use for eliciting specific detail include: What happened? What's an example of that? What is it like? What did he say? What was the turning point? How would you characterize that? Other good questions to push an interviewee toward specificity:

What do you mean by that? Where do you get your information? How do you know you're right? What happens if you're wrong?

Specific detail rarely pops up without pushing. For example, when interviewing a young mother who has made the transition from salaried professional to full-time mom, settling for a vague statement about tighter budgets is dull. It is much better to probe for the concrete and elicit a statement like this:

> I buy store brands, I compare prices. When we buy a car, we won't buy the Volvo, which would be our vehicle of choice if we were both still working. Instead, we'll go with a less expensive four-door domestic. . . . I buy generic dishwasher detergent. I've found that generic corn-chips are okay, too.

We should always look for stories within the story. In *The New New Journalism*, Alex Kotlowitz recalls asking one interviewee,

> "Tell me about the moment you got the phone call about Eric's death." When he answered that question he started to relive the experience. . . . I walked him through every minute: What he did, what he said, what he thought, what he was wearing. I want him to go into so much detail that I could close my eyes and see the events as if I had been there with him. Now if I had simply said, "Tell me about Eric's death," he would have said something vague like, "Well, it was a terrible thing." Kotlowitz adds, "I ask my subject to tell me a story. . . . It's after people tell me their tales that I begin to poke and prod. The more specific they get, the more reflective and truthful they become."

When interviewees generalize—for example, "The church-growth movement is counterproductive"—we should push them to talk about what they have seen or studied. Good reporters demand descriptive information: What exactly did you see? What did he look like? Ask for names, dates, times, colors, locations, ages, numbers. We want specific detail that helps readers to see.

After an interview has elicited stories, it's time to get more of a sense of what the interviewee believes—and confrontational questions can sometimes help. The list of pointed questions put together by Jeff Myers, who leads Summit Ministries, includes:

> Why do you believe that you are right? So what? Why is this significant? How do I know you are telling me the truth? Why should I believe you? How did you come to this conclusion? What's an alternate explanation? Could you give me two sources who disagree with you? Why do they disagree?

With reluctant interviewees, questioners may have to follow the information-eliciting techniques learned by parents: avoid questions that can be answered yes or no; encourage the recalcitrants to go further by asking, "And then? What happened next?" When stuck, we can ask five W questions: "Who taught you that? What did you read that was influential? When? Where? Why?"

Good reporters talk little, listen much, and listen for what isn't said. With well-known interviewees who have repeatedly answered standard questions, it's important to cut through boredom by starting with unusual questions, watching their body language, and making eye contact. It's fine to repeat questions if the content of the answer is significant, but the interviewee responds in a meandering way. Experienced journalists who are taking notes and need a little more time to record a response may ask a question that will yield an unimportant response so they can write down the exact wording on what was important.

Conversational pauses are fine, except during live interviews. When an interviewee is not answering questions, it's fine to stare: eye contact helps to elicit a response. Expectant silence is also helpful. Radio and television have led us to believe that every second of airtime must be filled with talk, but good interviewing (like good professor-student interaction) requires patience.

Experienced journalists take charge of an interview and retain flexibility while pushing hard for specific material. We have to be prepared to change a theme, if initial assumptions appear incorrect, and to be careful not to put words in an interviewee's mouth. At the same time, we have to guide the interview enough, so interviewees will not neglect the story's theme.

Whether we are interviewing a friend or a foe, we learn to follow the standard used for arms-control agreements: trust, but verify. We remember the interviewee, no matter how famous or infamous, is neither God nor a cockroach. If we have reason to suspect the interviewee's honesty, we ask some questions to which we already know the answers, and see if he is telling the truth. If he tells us something different from what we have heard, we challenge him.

Some interviewees are not particularly personable, but we should avoid getting too friendly with those who are, or being influenced by the interviewee's apparent friendliness. Some interviewees push reporters to talk about themselves, but journalists should not have egos big enough to warrant spending valuable time in that way. If that happens, it is better to turn the questions back on interviewees. Some journalists advise interviewers to pretend to be on the interviewee's side, but when an adversarial story comes out, that experience adds to the bad reputation of reporters and makes sources skittish about accepting invitations to be interviewed in the future.

Journalists should never volunteer to go off the record. Off-the-record conversations may be necessary when a source's safety or job is in jeopardy, but as journalists we work for readers, not for interviewees. We should tell the reason for going off the record with particular sources, and avoid statements like "The source preferred to be off the record." When a source insists on off-the-record status, and an interview seems worth continuing, we should find out whether he means his information cannot be used at all, whether it can be used only for background, whether it can be attributed to an unnamed source in Department X, whether it can be fully used but not quoted, etc.

Unattributed quotations that disparage a person are worthless, unless the reporter has many on-the-record quotations saying the same thing. Attribution should be kept simple. For a short quotation, we should place the attribution at the end, on the grounds that what the speaker said is usually more important than who said it. If the opposite is true, attribution belongs at the beginning. A long quotation should include an attribution in the middle, both to break it up and to let the reader know who is talking.

Reporters still debate whether an interview should be recorded, because taping interviews is both a blessing and a curse. Taping produces among some interviewees the wary-wording syndrome and among others dreaded oratorical tendencies. Recording facilitates concentration on the subject instead of a notebook, provides an accurate record of just how a person speaks, and makes interviewees less likely to throw around accusations of misquotation—which is important in our litigious age.

Most reporters do not send or read back portions of stories to sources. We check facts with sources, but try to avoid reading back quotes unless a valuable source absolutely and insistently refuses to be interviewed without that agreement. Sources often want to reduce the intensity of their statements, resulting in a duller story if we agree to modify them or an irritated interviewee if we refuse to do so.

Here are two questions with which to end an interview: What questions should I have asked that I didn't? Who else should I interview, and why? When concluding an interview, say a follow-up question may be needed, and request a personal email address or cell phone number for that purpose. The subject will usually offer those. Experienced reporters also come away from interviews with printed material, when possible. Like pack rats, we collect speeches, articles, and books.

Although the following should go without saying, journalists should remember basic manners. Some reporters have given the occupation such a reputation for rudeness that we can win respect by not staying overly long, by saying thank you, and by not using a person's first name unless invited to do so. After the interview, experienced journalists record additional impressions immediately and then go to work trying to write a strong article by combining interview material with narrative.

Interviewing works best in person, where we can see sweat and other body language, but often we have to write a story from afar, with words over the phone being all we have. That can leave us with insufficient descriptive material and narrative. Talking heads are usually less interesting than moving feet. The way out is to interview trustworthy people who can become proxy eyes, and elicit from them the type of specific detail we could see if we were there. That's making the respondent an ally in writing the story—it's risky, but necessary at times.

Here is how *World* used an interview with David Hooten, a missionary in Rwanda, who described how he and his wife had made it through a couple of roadblocks, but saw trouble ahead:

> I slowed down, but there was no blockade. No logs or tree stumps or rocks like they normally use to stop you—except just the people, the mob was there. I forced my way with the vehicle through them. I did not want to stop in the middle of them, because I had a pretty good idea what was happening. I tried and was able to get through them. I slowed down on the other side to see if I could get a sense as to what they were doing.

The story continued:

> That pause could have cost the missionary and his wife their lives, had they not been alert and able to keep going: "Sure enough, they came charging after us. One guy got ahold of the side of my door. I had my window down. He hung onto it, trying to get me to stop. The rest of the crowd came at us with machetes and clubs and different implements." Hooten rammed the vehicle into gear and tore away from the crowd.

Especially in phone interviews, we're asking interviewees to help us, and sometimes we can be explicit: "Help me create a picture for the reader." Good reporters don't just settle for, "I walked up the hill." Ask: What was the grass like? Weeds? Flowers? Was it hot? Did you sweat? Were you excited? Tense? What did it sound like? If we do not have time to visit or are not allowed into a maximum-security prison, we should push for a description from a trustworthy guard.

Sometimes the best we can get is a summary report, but that can be helpful. One report told how villagers waving Chinese flags "have taken to the streets in the past few days to protest the detention of a local leader allegedly forced to confess to corruption. Surrounded by a heavy police presence, residents marched around the village holding a banner covered in their signatures."

Interviewing by phone is hard, but it has some advantages. We can look regularly at our lists of questions. (We should also have a list for in-person interviews, but it is important to maintain eye contact with the interviewee, not with our notebook.) Whether interviewing by phone or in person, we start with easier questions and move away from the list as the conversation dictates. Some journalists prefer asking tough questions over the phone. Journalist Susan Orlean said, "I once had to ask someone about incest in his family. It was the hardest question I've ever had to ask, so I waited until we were on the phone."

Phone interviewing allows the reporter to write out important questions in advance and refer to the list. Reporters should also have a list of questions for in-person interviews, but much of that should be in our heads, so we're not looking at questions rather than making eye contact. It's fine to refer to a notebook at the end of an interview to make sure the interview has covered the essentials. Either way, reporters should avoid questions that can be answered with a simple yes or no, and should ask short questions.

Magazine writer Richard Preston points out:

> While the conventional wisdom is that it is always better to do an interview face-to-face, I've often found that people are actually more forthcoming over the phone because they are not distracted by looking at you to see how you are reacting to what they say. Over the phone they are speaking in the comfort of their home or office.

The etiquette of telephone interviewing often involves calling the interviewee to set up a time for questioning. When making such a request, experienced reporters do not say, "I'd like an interview." It's better to say, "I'd like to ask you about x, y, and z," and to specify how much time is needed. When reporters are able to proceed directly to the interview, the best way to start is to explain quickly what the story is about and how the subject can help.

Sometimes a reporter does have to write about an earthquake from afar. The key then is to get graphic description from someone who was there. No, make that more than one person, for just as we need two eyes for depth perception, so we need the testimony of two or more reliable witnesses before settling for detail garnered from afar.

KEY TERMS

stenographers
journalistic ventriloquism
quotosis
puffitis

STUDY QUESTIONS

1. When requesting and doing an interview, how does using specific detail encourage a possibly reluctant interviewee to respond?
2. Why should journalists ask some confrontational questions?
3. If an interviewee asks to go off the record, what are some appropriate responses?
4. How does moving down the ladder of abstraction work in interviewing?

12

How to Research and Write Profiles

EXPERIENCED EDITORS STRESS the importance of human interest in stories. That's both practical, judging from studies of what interests readers the most, and biblical. God made human beings after his own image, so nothing—not forceful waterfalls, not elegant deer, not extraordinary artifacts—is more complicated and more beautiful.

Profiling is interviewing on steroids. The goal of interviewing is to discern the essence of an often complicated problem. The goal in profiling is to discern the essence of an individual, what makes him tick. That's harder, because while problems are often complicated, individuals are often complex. Given enough time, we can understand complications, but we can know people for a lifetime and still find them mysterious.

The first step in writing a profile is to do background research. Reporters run down newspaper and magazine stories about subjects and get basic biographical information, including residence, age, marital status, the number and ages of children, educational and work background, and so on.

The second step is talking with the subject's friends and enemies, including colleagues, competitors, neighbors, and relatives. Reporters press them for revealing stories and anecdotes. Most will start high on the ladder of abstraction, using glowing or glowering adjectives, so it's important to push them lower. One way to do that is with "superlative" questions: What was the happiest you've seen him? The angriest? The most excited? The most afraid? If a particular approach yields an anecdotal pearl, more diving is fine: What was the second happiest time?

The third step is spending time with the subject. Remote-control profiles based on news clips or telephone interviews are almost always inferior to those that give a sense of the whole person. Profiling with discernment requires not only perceptiveness but the kind of close, in-person observation that leads to three-dimensional portraits, with the subjects almost seeming to walk off the page. If a phone interview is all a reporter gets, superlative questions still produce the best results.

Good profiles require not only interview time but also hanging-around time that allows seeing as well as hearing. Writers describe their subjects physically, but since photos generally accompany profiles, a focus on facial features is less important than a description of how a person moves or sits (stolidly or shifting). The ideal way to learn that is to shadow subjects for a day as they go about their ordinary business, and watch how others respond to them.

Especially for profiles, it's important to describe the interviewee's home or office, mannerisms, and style of dress. What is not in an office can be as important as what is:

> Don Wildmon does not have embroidered Bible verses hanging around his office. His small office, which has the faint aroma of cigar smoke, has absolutely nothing hanging on the walls. His desk serves as a cluttered file cabinet, yet he knows where everything is.

Good reporters give subjects a context and surroundings, and try to convey a sense of the person by relating perceptions of him with description of the environment. For example,

> Ron Lewis's church is not easy to find—unless you know your way around Hardin County, Kentucky, like he does. White Mills Baptist Church sits on a hill away from Highway 84, tucked between the White Mills Christian Church and a campground. Though the

church's exterior looks like it might have appeared a century earlier, the steps are covered with new indoor-outdoor carpet. Central air conditioning is evident inside the glassed foyer. Like Lewis, there's subtle sophistication here—a savvy about technology that works. An advanced electronic soundboard blinks just inside the rear doors.

After tying together setting and person, the next step in profiling is to look closely at the person, including elements that may not be evident in photos that will make it into a magazine: are shoes scuffed or polished, fingernails manicured or chewed? It's important to watch gestures and mannerisms: Does he speak quickly or slowly? Does he move his hands as he talks? Does he pause before answering questions? Reporters note not only what people say, but what they eat, drink, or smoke, and whether they smile just with the mouth or also with the eyes.

Since profiles are great ways to express ideas and make points, some committed reporters have the tendency to make them a set of sound bites. That is a mistake. The goal of a profile is to bring a person to life through descriptive detail and narrative, along with contextualized use of quotation. Good reporters watch body language and facial expressions when they ask hard questions. One ex-pastor, who had "grown" from his evangelical background and could easily dance around abstract theological questions, poured out buckets of sweat when I asked the straightforward, classic question, "What do you think of Christ?"

Good reporters always try to get beneath the surface. That is particularly true for writing biblically directed profiles that can get into deeper questions about beliefs and faith in Christ, or lack thereof. It's sometimes necessary to ask several times about a person's attitudes toward God if the subject tries to dodge what's most important. The acronym PROOF—Purpose, Road, Obstacles, Overcoming, Future—is helpful: Ask a subject about his *purpose* in life, and ask how he started down the *road* to fulfilling that purpose, encountered *obstacles*, and *overcame* them. Finish by asking what he expects *future* obstacles to be.

If possible, the sit-down part of time with the subject should be an hour, allowing time for such questions as: Who or what has had the most impact on your life? What is the most important thing you have learned during the past year? What was your most frustrating experience? What would you change about yourself if you could? What do people say about you behind your back? If you could invite any person or persons for dinner, whom would you invite? What do you like most about your job? What do you dislike the most? What are your best and worst habits?

Other questions might be: What do you expect to be doing ten years from now? If you could make that decision over again, what would you decide? Was there a turning point in your life? Are you satisfied with your present job or way of life? People who take pride in their craft are generally willing to explain how they accomplish a particularly difficult task, so it's good to ask some how-to questions. We should also ask about parents and children: What did your parents teach you? What do you hope to teach your children?

When we gain insight into difficult experiences—tragedies, births of children, military experience—and beliefs about God, man, and death, we can then try to connect the dots and show how a person's worldview affects actions on the job as well as habits. We want to show how a hero or a beast became what he is. For example, an examination of how a rogue American doctor, Jack Kevorkian, pioneered in promoting euthanasia, noted that "more than 30 years ago Kevorkian found his style cramped in an oil painting night class with little old ladies whose artistic tastes ran from clowns to kittens." The story showed his reaction:

> "[I painted] a skull, with the top of the skull leaning back a little, the jaw twisted to one side, like it's kind of laughing out of the side of its face . . . Then, there were some bones coming underneath, and a broken femur. . . . Tacked up on the wall behind, where you can barely see it, I have this pasty yellow-green skin, peeled off the head and hanging there. . . . I called it 'Very Still Life.'" They loved it.
>
> Paintings followed: "Fever," "Nausea," and "Coma."

We want to provide readers with a sense of the person as a member of a family, not a disembodied voice or a lone ranger—unless he is one. It's good to ask questions in a down-to-earth style: What do you really hope to do? What do you have to do to fulfill that hope? What problems have you faced; how did you handle them? What is your next step? In general, start with specific questions—not "Do you enjoy being a basketball star?" but "How does this particular play work?"

Here is a basic checklist of what reporters generally should know by the time they complete profiling research:

- Physical Characteristics:
  - Description of home or workplace, outside and inside.
  - Subject's overall appearance, clothing style, hair style.
  - Subject's mannerisms.
- Basic Background:
  - Birthdate, birthplace.
  - Schooling.
  - Military service?
- Religious Experience:
  - If a Christian, when he became one, how has he developed since then, how he puts faith into practice, plus denominational and church affiliation.
  - If not a Christian, what he believes, why he believes it; does he think that what he believes is objectively real, or is it something that makes him feel good?
- Family:
  - Spouse—when married, spouse's activities.
  - Children—ages, names, activities.
  - Parents—what he learned from them, what he did not.
- Personal:
  - Hobbies, recreations, pets.
  - Favorite books, movies, hymns.
  - Volunteer work, other community service.
  - Memberships in organizations.

Whatever the structure, we should not fall into a series of sound bites. Couching quotations in brief descriptive material helps:

> Henry Hyde is relaxed as he rocks softly in his office chair, but his voice has an edge as he talks about colleagues who roll over under media pressure: "People want to do what's right, but . . . the adoration of the secular press is heady."

Weaving is superior to listing. Relating physically descriptive material to current cares led to this comparison:

> Hyde is concerned about future leadership for the pro-life cause. He was once square-jawed and lean, but years on the rubber-chicken and chocolate-mousse circuit have softened the lines. He senses a similar aging taking place in the pro-life movement. The future of abortion, he argues, is tied to development of a new generation of pro-life leaders.

Hyde may not have liked that physical description, but it doesn't matter. We're not doing public relations for him. Similarly, when we profile someone who does not believe in God, but takes biblical positions, we try to get at the why. American columnist Nat Hentoff became a pro-life activist in the 1980s when he realized abortion was leading to infanticide, but he remained an atheist. In response to my questions, he said, "I've always wished I could make the 'leap of faith' and believe, but I can't." Not leaving it at that, I asked if he had ever read any evangelical theology, and he snapped, "I'm an atheist. I'm really not interested." We're not doing our job as reporters or Christians if we stop before the snap.

When profiling Christians, we should not focus so much on their conversion story that we ignore what has happened to the person since then. How has the subject walked the talk? All have sinned and fall short of the glory of God, and those who are redeemed remain sinners. The question to ask is whether that sin is decreasing as the years go by and whether the enjoyment of God's grace is increasing.

In my profile of Hentoff, I resisted the temptation to explain why he was illogical; readers could come to that conclusion by themselves. Profiles should not attack the people being profiled, nor should they do public relations for them. That means reporters should check facts with them, but not let them read stories in advance or revise them—because they often want to look better or reduce the intensity of what they said. The goal of the profile is to be truthful and educate readers, not to make the subject necessarily feel warm and cozy.

Master reporters work hard to see in action someone they are profiling. As Michael Lewis put it,

> Characters are always so much more interesting when they are moving through space than they are when they are at rest (especially when they are behind a desk in their office). Even when what they're doing is irrelevant to what I'm writing about, I just want to participate in something with them.

By participating, we hope to see stories unfold. We also need stories from our subjects and those who know them. If someone says he is generous, we should push for an anecdote that shows generosity. If a person says, "I was worried, and I was praying," we push for specifics: "What were you praying? Were you praying out loud? What did you say?" We push interviewees to use metaphors or similes by asking, "What was it like"? If we get a bland answer, we should be more specific: "What did the punch feel like?"

Overall, journalists should avoid formal interviews whenever possible and seize the opportunity to see more of a subject's life. Jonathan Harr tries "to do interviews in the character's own environment, whether that's an office, home, laboratory, courtroom—anywhere he spends time. I notice what books are on the shelves, what paintings are on the walls, how they keep their house, what kind of car they drive."

Susan Olasky's profile of a U.S. family that adopted many children introduced them as "not an ordinary family, but a Rainbow Family," because incredibly patient Terri and Jim Cooney adopted kids of various races, ethnicities, and disabilities. Instead of just listing them, the reporter showed one of the most troubled in action: "Joshua comes up the stairs with his pants around his ankles, and

Terri exclaims, 'Yay! You left your pants on!' then confides, 'Usually he strips.'"

Next came comedy:

> Joshua comes up the stairs wearing matching purple T-shirt and underpants, but the underpants are on his head. "Well, it was nice of you to match!" Terri says. . . . Joshua reappears with his shirt on his head and his pants down. "Sweetie, I love you, and it's a good thing," Terri says to him, and whispers to me: "Lithium causes very loose bowels."

The profile poured out more background about the children, not textbook style, but in the context of a flowing narrative:

> Two-year-old Stephen comes in wearing yellow star-shaped sunglasses, and Terri exclaims, "Look at you! You are downtown!" We learn that Stephen was born nearly three months early and weighed only two pounds. Doctors said he would probably never walk, and it appears they were right: He runs everywhere, and has broken the blades off two ceiling fans by hanging from them. Then, a real-life example: "As we watch, Stephen steps up on the hinge of the storm door and, reaching up with a book, flips the hook latch open. He is immensely pleased with himself."

Finally, with readers given a vivid sense of the who-what-when-where-how of the Cooney home, discussion of the why comes naturally. "Our story challenges everybody's reasons for not adopting," Terri says. "Age, income, space . . . we had all of those problems. But if everyone in the body of Christ would adopt just one! Thousands of kids out there need homes, but they're older, black, or special-needs. If we could just embrace one, we could take care of the kids. Why save them from abortion if you're not going to save them for the kingdom?"

The Cooneys did not try to put on a show—the show happens every day. Sometimes the subjects of profiles put on a false front, and may even try to buy good press through an offer of material help.

Reporters should not worry about hamburgers—few journalists can be bought that easily—but offers of fine lodging or dining should be turned down. On the other hand, invitations to a subject's home are usually worth accepting. We learn much more about people by eating in their homes than by eating in a restaurant. Staying overnight is also useful in that we get to see people in the morning, preferably before they've had coffee. Journalist Susan Orlean describes being in her subjects' homes as the opportunity to run a lint brush over their lives, to "pick up a thousand little threads of who they are."

The bottom line is to know yourself. Know what sways you. Be aware your job is not to make friends, but to tell the truth, so if you do feel obliged to write something nice about a person because you've stayed in his house, stay instead at a moderately priced hotel. Always remember a Christian reporter's job is not to glorify the person being profiled. Our goal is to glorify God and educate readers by telling the truth.

KEY TERMS

profiling
PROOF

STUDY QUESTIONS

1. When and how should you ask a person you're profiling about his religious beliefs?
2. What are the pluses and minuses of staying in the home of the person being profiled?
3. How do reporters avoid writing public relations stories?

13

Organizational Strategies

U.S. NEWSPAPERS IN the twentieth century had a simple formula for reporting stories: an inverted pyramid, with the wider part at the top showing graphically that the most important material should be in the first paragraph, followed by less important material, and an eventual trickling out at story's end. A reporter's goal was to answer six questions, 5 W's and an H—who, what, when, where, why, and how—as close as possible to the beginning of the article.

That structure is still appropriate when reporting hard news. For example, here's the lead of a December 2016 *World* website article: "A prominent Chinese Christian human rights lawyer and two publishers of human rights news websites [*who*] in China [*where*] disappeared [*what*] in the past two weeks [*when*], renewing fears of a crackdown on human rights defenders [*why* this is significant]." The article then gave details of *how* Jiang Tianyong, Liu Feiyue, and Huang Qi disappeared. Here is another example:

> For months many people had suspicions about the finances of an American-funded evangelical group, Gospel for Asia, and a draft of one *World* article noted concern that the ministry had hoarded money rather than using it for church-planting, missionary work, or charitable help to the poor. But the big news was that GFA had admitted that the charges were true, so it was important to say so:

"We have done wrong," said David Carroll, GFA's chief operating officer.

That was the who and what of the story, and it quickly went on to give the when, where, why, and how. The 5W1H format is still useful as a logical exercise in thinking about news, and as a way to structure stories that requires little artfulness. But as newspaper editors have realized most Americans today hear top news online or on television or radio, more news stories have been featurized. U.S. news magazines and feature stories within newspapers now tend to use more flexible structures that go by a variety of names. I've called five of the most popular ones chronological, linear, circular, parallel, and multigrain.

Let's run through the five, starting with the *chronological* story, a natural choice because children hearing bedtime stories want to know what happens next. "And then . . . and then . . ." is a story-telling mode that has suspense built in. For example, a *World* story about growing up in a poor, gang-dominated neighborhood of Los Angeles started with twelve-year-old David Trujillo joining a gang, then seeing his friend murdered, then attending his friend's funeral, then becoming more tolerant of violence, then being ready to stab or shoot others who disrespected him, then coming to believe in Christ, and then becoming a pastor.

A *linear* story is the equivalent in space of a chronological story in time. The linear story gives readers a closer look at a subject by moving them from outside to inside, or room by room through a house, or house by house down a street. For example, the profile of cultural radical Nat Hentoff began with a description of him working within a building plastered on the outside with posters advertising nihilistic bands like Lunachicks, Suicidal Tendencies, Haunted Toilet, and Hide the Baby. A huge trash pile along one side of the building smelled of urine and sparkled with empty liquor bottles.

That specific detail showed the type of culture Hentoff and his newspaper, New York's *Village Voice*, promoted in its articles. The story then moved readers inside, up a dark staircase brightened only by a taped-up flyer offering comfort to "Lesbian Survivors of Abusive

Relationships." That staircase brought readers to the editorial offices, then into the office of Hentoff, who believed in absolute existentialist freedom, except on abortion. He fought the newspaper's policy on that issue, deviating from the American cultural left, and so became a pariah. As Hentoff showed me around the offices, no one spoke to or smiled at him.

This linear story was the equivalent of beginning with a wide-angle lens and then moving in. A linear story can also start with a telephoto lens that provides a close-up and then move out, contextualizing the individual.

A third kind of story, *circular*, starts like a linear story, but eventually swings around and ends up in the same location or situation where it began. For example, one *World* story began with a focus on a brass cross, the focal point of the chapel in a Texas prison. That cross, inmates explained, was to be removed, to the dismay of Eugene, a 35-year-old convict: "Ain't that something?" he asked. "It's about the only thing in here doing any good."

The story then provided information and perspectives before coming back to another statement from Eugene, who had spent many hours thinking about what can change a criminal's heart:

> People talk a lot about education. Let me tell you, there's a whole lot of educated people in prison. Education doesn't do it. Buildings don't do it. You've got to change a man's heart. Then you'll see some rehabilitation.

The article eventually ended where it began, with Eugene pointing to the cross and saying: "If I had not been sent here, I'd be in the ground by now. Here is where God talked to me. . . . They took God out of schools. Hope they don't do that here."

Another *circular* story in *World* came from our China bureau. It began:

> Inside a sleek steel building in an artist community on the outskirts of Beijing, editors, producers, and videographers gather for a brainstorming meeting in their heavy snow jackets and boots. The

temperature is in the teens outside. Dirty snow and slush cover the parking lot, but the landlord has turned off central heating to save money, meaning the staff of 7g.tv, a Chinese Christian video production company, must plan the week's upcoming short videos in the cold.

After surveying the Chinese media, the story came back to its first scene:

> Back at the chilly 7g.tv office, the new generation focuses on seeking inspiring testimonies, filming talk shows on motherhood against a green screen in the studio, and brainstorming music video ideas with unsigned Christian artists.

This is all valuable work, but a Chinese Christian writer notes that few Christian publications dare to cover political topics: "The biggest issue facing house churches is government interference and the lack of religious freedom."

A fourth story structure useful for comparing rhetoric and reality is the *parallel* story, which uses a cutting-back-and-forth approach familiar from movies. For example, a *World* story set in Washington, D.C., first described American legislators showing their "compassion" by spending other people's money. Then came a contrasting sentence:

> Several miles away from the Capitol, residents talk of four children found locked up by their mother in two filthy, roach-infested rooms. None was able to speak more than simple sentences.

Then back to the legislators:

> On Capitol Hill, where lawmakers say the word and create a federal bureaucracy out of nothing, the child welfare program has a simple solution—more money. Whenever a child is killed emotionally or even physically by an abusive parent, the story is the same—the system is overloaded and underfunded. While Congress is trying to give more money to child welfarists in order to "preserve families,"

critics charge that the child welfare system is so deeply flawed that bigger bucks will not help.

Then back to the streets:

> Quintessa Murreld of New York City died in foster care last year at the age of three. Her uncle, who was also her foster father, pleaded guilty of manslaughter. Quintessa had been placed in foster care because her mother, a crack addict, neglected her. After six months in that foster home, she was not placed for adoption, but was moved into foster care with her aunt and uncle, who made it clear that they had no intention of adopting the child.

The alternating portraits directed readers' attention to the legislators' distance from reality.

Some parallel stories begin with a catchy lead and then deliberately alternate individual or group achievements and warts. Such a story often concludes with an anecdote that tries to reconcile the contradictions.

Let's call a fifth useful story structure *multigrain*, because it is a healthy melding of various images. After reporting in Cuba, I wrote a story that started this way: "Three Spanish expressions common in Havana summarize what I saw during a recent trip to Cuba." Then came a paragraph for each:

> First, heard regularly: *No es facil* (It's not easy). Every aspect of life—from gaining basic material sustenance to traveling across town to remaining psychologically relaxed when any neighbor or associate might be an informer—is difficult.
>
> Second, heard as an explanation of why a failing government resents attempts to fill the gaps, *Ni comen ni dejan comer* (They don't eat, neither do they let others eat). Churches are ready and willing to do better than the government in helping the poor and particularly the elderly, but it is officially and ideologically the responsibility of the state to provide all social services. Officials turn down church requests to build homes for the elderly and even

citizen attempts to organize the collection of garbage rotting in the streets. Everything compassionate people do is an indictment of government failure—and Cuba's Communist Party is desperately trying to avoid facing the truth.

Third, abundantly seen on billboards, the favorite Castroite slogan: *Un mundo mejor es posible* (A better world is possible). Marxist sloganeering tends to have three stages: belief, cynicism, and flipping the slogan on its head. Some Cubans may still believe the regime can produce a better world; many appear to be cynical; but the future is with Christians who have faith a better world is possible and are willing to take reasonable risks in striving toward that goal.

These five—chronological, linear, circular, parallel, and multi-grain—are the big five among story structures, but others, such as *opening question*, can also work. Journalists sometimes start off with a big question—say, "What is an immigrant?"—and proceed to answer it. Or journalists may ask "Who are the immigrants?" and then paint portraits of a person or persons.

Journalists may choose a particular structure because it goes well with the theme they plan to emphasize. Circular structures often contribute to a sense that many people are talking about problems, but few are finding solutions. Alternating (parallel) structures work well when we are contrasting biblical and ungodly approaches. Linear stories give readers the sense they are looking deeper into an issue, situation, or personality.

When it's hard to figure out which structure to use, we need to ask ourselves questions: What interested me about this story? What is it really about? What do I want to teach the reader? The key to the successful organizing of a major story is a firm grasp of the theme. It's helpful to summarize a main theme in a sentence that has a noun and a verb—in other words, subject plus action. Then we can see if we have sharpened an angle enough to be able to write a tight article rather than a dithering report.

As we organize, we may realize the story we thought was about "X" is actually about "Y," with "X" as a subtheme. Some journalists outline elaborately before they write, but others find getting into the flow of writing will help them understand more about the nature of their story. Outlines should be spines, not corpses, and brief enough that journalists can do quick spinal taps while thinking about the material.

As reporters prowl through notes and think through organizing the sections of a story, it's important to consider narration, description, and quotation. Interspersing those three can keep telling to a minimum. The tendency of many inexperienced journalists or those only trained in newswriting is to take down lots of quotations and write stories that are successions of soundbites linked by expository sentences. That's a boring type of reporting, one that might please the person quoted, but will excite few others. It's much better to provide description, then pause to introduce major characters, and then show those characters in action.

Pacing is vital. Feature writer Lynn Vincent speaks of alternating medicine and sugar: after readers read through statistics or difficult exposition, reward them with anecdotes, colorful detail, or humor. Other writers speak of scattering gold coins throughout a story, so readers who find several will keep on reading for more. Successful publications are often travel guides, taking readers to areas or situations foreign to them and introducing them to people they are unlikely to meet.

For example, a story about big-city addiction began:

Walking down Brooklyn's Fourth Avenue, Leroy Shepherd isn't talking about the New York mayor's race coming next month. Instead, he's explaining how to spot a crack cocaine addict: They walk along the sidewalks, and you'll see them looking into the gutters for old crack vials, in hopes of finding one with a little crack left at the bottom. Sometimes they find enough; maybe that day your car won't get broken into.

Good journalists are always on the lookout for anecdotes that can illuminate issues. For example, one story about Mexican political changes pointed out what was new this way:

Mexicans for years have told a little inside joke. They grin and say that citizens of the United States have nothing on them when they brag that they can know the results of a presidential election within a few hours after the polls close. "In Mexico," residents boast, "we know who the next president is before the polls close." For 65 years that has been so. The nominee of the Institutional Revolutionary Party (known by its Spanish acronym PRI) has been assured the presidency. . . . Something is different this time.

Good editors would rather coach early in the process than fix organizational errors later on. Both methods improve stories, but coaching improves journalists as well. A reporter should not be offended if an editor reads the draft and then comes back with questions like these: What's your theme? What are the most interesting things you saw? What's your evidence for this? What did it look like? What does the reader need to know? How can you clarify this?

The editor's key role at this point is *structural editing*, based on an analysis of how the story moves from start to finish. Editors may demand reorganization. The editor's job is to explain why, and the reporter's task is to be of good cheer through what is at times painful. Reporters may feel everything they have written is important, but a story in which everything is equal most often has the excitement of a posed class or team photograph. A good editor is antiegalitarian, emphasizing certain elements and downgrading the importance of others.

Good journalists learn to emphasize material by placing the most important words at the beginning or end of the sentence, the most important sentences at the beginning or the end of paragraphs, and the most important paragraphs at the beginning or the end of stories. It's also possible to emphasize words within a sentence from least to most important by varying sentence length, by repeating key words or phrases, and by parallel structure.

Introducing character and action at the right pace is art, not science, like all writing. A good storyteller does not list the plot details at the beginning of his story, and good journalists do not recite facts without drama. They introduce characters who are forced to confront problems in realistic ways, and do so at a pace that places readers on a slope with a gradual ascent.

KEY TERMS

> inverted pyramid
> 5W1H
> chronological
> linear
> circular
> parallel
> multigrain
> pacing
> structural editing

STUDY QUESTIONS

1. What are advantages and disadvantages of inverted pyramid structures and feature structures?
2. How might chronological and linear stories suggest a view of reality different than that which circular and parallel stories convey?

FOR FURTHER READING

Jack Hart, *Storycraft* (University of Chicago Press, 2011).
William Blundell, *The Art and Craft of Feature Writing* (Plume, 1988).

14

The Parts of a Story

MANY GOVERNMENT AND corporate heads want stories to start out with their words and be filled with propaganda. Captive journalists have no choice but to obey such commands. When freedom rings, though, reporters who have finished their research often start by deciding on a lead. Sometimes that decision is easy, but sometimes it's a struggle, and reporters need to remember that in journalism the perfect is often the enemy of the good. We need to look for good beginnings, not the ideal lead.

Often it is better to rough out an article and then come back to wrestling with the lead. That's why the previous chapter on organization came before this discussion of leads. Many writers either get hung up on the lead or construct a pretty one that does not connect well with the bulk of the article.

Feature leads, like other parts of stories, vary in length according to the size of the overall article, but their purpose remains the same. They are to give the reader a sense of what the article is about, establish a mood, and entice the reader to march on. Feature leads are *not* supposed to summarize the news. Old-style inverted pyramid newspaper leads and feature leads are opposites. The former makes it possible for readers to skip most of a story, while the latter pushes them to read on.

Leads come in many different flavors. Anecdotal, descriptive, situational, and multi-vignette leads are in the toolbox of experienced reporters. The *anecdotal lead* is often the best because it gives readers characters with whom to identify and actions to grasp. In directed reporting, an anecdotal lead is a specific mini-story that begins teaching the reader about the nature of the overall problem.

Here is an example from *World* in 2016:

> Wearing a loose gray button-up shirt with a priest's collar, 84-year-old former Cardinal Joseph Zen Ze-kiun walked down the walkway outside the Salesian Mission House in Hong Kong, where he studied as a student in 1948. With white hair, wire-framed glasses, and slightly stooped shoulders, Zen has a gentle smile reminiscent of a grandfather's. Yet when the topic turns to the Vatican's warming relations with Beijing, Zen passionately raises his voice, at times banging his hand on the table, at times shaking his head while exhaling "Ai-ya-ya-ya."

Good anecdotal leads arouse immediate interest, humanize what could be dry, or personalize what could be merely sensational. The anecdotal lead should be colorful but directed, accurately representing the article and pointing the reader to the rest of the story. An anecdote that is colorful, but does not push readers toward deeper understanding, may be used further down, but should not be the lead. Anecdotes should be factual, not a composite or a product of the imagination.

Second on the superior list is the *descriptive lead*. It presents a scene without including characters or action. For example, here's the lead of a story on how China is developing economic ties with Nigeria:

> Away from the swerving traffic and honking cars of the busy Ojota highway in Lagos, Nigeria, lies a quiet, untarred street where pedestrians walk in an unhurried pace and a middle-aged woman stirs a steaming pot on a circle of firewood, the smoke rising above her. Down the street, the typical Lagos scene suddenly ends as a red, castlelike wall looms with the words "China market" written in Chinese characters over its arched entrance.

A descriptive lead works particularly well when the writer wants to create a mood of sadness or happiness, as in this example:

On a hot summer's day in Beijing's outskirts, 2-year-old Jack carefully studies the plastic water gun in his hand. A New Day Foster Home volunteer squirts him in the leg and he squeals, then gleefully dips his own water gun into a bucket of water. Alfred, at 18 months, sits nearby on a Mickey Mouse waterproof play mat: His bowed legs prevent him from standing, yet his eyes carefully follow the flight of a stray bubble blown by another volunteer.

Third on the superior list is the *situation lead*, which presents a problem that needs resolution. For example:

It's just after 11 P.M., and Houston police officer Al Leonard has his gun drawn as the elderly black man approaches the patrol car. The 9mm pistol is out of sight, pointing through the car door. Leonard rolls down his window and casually greets the man: "What can I do for you?" The man shakes his head in disgust. "Some kids," he says . . . . "Broke my windshield. Musta been 10 or 12 of them." Leonard nods. "When did it happen?" "Few minutes ago."

The lead leaves readers in suspense. What will Al Leonard do? The lead pushes us to read on. It is a purposefully incomplete anecdote. A situation lead should end with a sense of imminent trouble.

Fourth on the superior list is the *multi-vignette lead*. The use of several real examples communicates a realistic sense that many people face a similar problem. For example:

Although she wanted more children, Janet White felt that a tubal ligation—severing the fallopian tubes—was "the thing to do." Never questioning the "pressure from society for small families," she felt she had pushed the limit with three. But since then, her desire for more children has intensified—after her ability to have them was gone.

Then, other vignettes:

John Barja underwent sterilization surgery because doctors warned that pregnancy might endanger his wife's health. It nagged at him

for 11 years. . . . Jennifer Barfield took the bus to a doctor's office
and had the option of more children surgically removed from her
life. It became a decision she and her second husband later regretted.

These stories led into the article about childbearing and adoption
options.

Quantitatively and qualitatively, lead writers have great variety
to choose from. The length of a lead often is tied to the length of the
article—short for short, long for long. A good rule of thumb is that
the lead should not be more than 10 percent of the story. The crucial
point to keep in mind is that the lead should draw attention to the
theme of the story, not to itself.

Lead construction is not either-or. Reporters can combine forms,
as long as the lead does not dither, but comes to a point. For example,
this lead is both descriptive and anecdotal:

Inside a small Bedouin goods shop in Jerusalem's Old City, the
smell of strong Arab coffee cuts through the foreign aromas that
have combined into a confusing but unforgettable blend. Outside
the shop, a commotion . . . reaches a peak.

The reporter then describes Arab men carrying off a shirtless youth as
blood from knife wounds flows freely.

What comes directly after the lead goes by many names—point
statement, theme-paragraph, thesis, justifier—but the pungent journalistic name is nut graf. The nut graf is the essence, the underlying
idea of a story. Generally following an anecdotal or descriptive lead,
the nut graf gives the basic news value and describes the significance
of the story under way. The nut graf is show-and-tell expository writing. After a lead that shows, the nut graf tells. The nut graf is vital
because it explains the problem the story addresses and shows it affects
many people.

Construction of a nut graf begins with the most crucial question
a journalist can ask himself: what is my story about? Reporters normally have more reporting than they can use, so the answer to that
nut graf question helps them decide which details are important. Lack

of a nut graf confuses readers and opens the door to dithering. Lack of one also wastes a good author's tool. Once the nut graf is in place, reporters can measure sentences, and paragraphs throughout the body can be measured against it: those that do not help to make the point or provide reflection on it can be discarded.

For example, here's the nut graf following the lead from New Day and its plastic water guns:

> It's all typical toddler's play, yet these children may never have had the chance to enjoy that summer day without the work of New Day Foster Home. . . . Government orphanages, especially those in more rural areas, rarely have access to doctors who can treat severe conditions. Through New Day, though, children with diseases like hydrocephalus (water in the brain) and congenital heart disease receive the medical care, therapy, and love they need.

Here's the nut graf of a story about one persecuted person:

> Gao became China's No. 2 target (after Nobel Peace Prize winner Liu Xiaobo) for his work as a lawyer defending house churches, the banned religious sect Falun Gong, and property owners harassed by government officials. His public opposition to the "inhumane, unjust, and evil" CCP led to his detentions, first in black prisons at undisclosed locations, and then at Shaya Prison in Xinjiang. Gao says prison guards took great pains to ensure he could not hear or see anything at the official prison, afraid he would expose more abuses.

The nut graf should be one paragraph, sometimes one sentence. For example, one sentence summarized a feature about the organization and ideology of abortion in America: "This abortionist shortage represents the soft underbelly of the multi-million dollar industry that has grown up around the concept of choice and personal sovereignty."

Ideally, leads flow smoothly into nut grafs. Lead: "In early July, authorities approached a Wenzhou church network with an ultimatum posed to thousands of other churches: 'Take down the crosses on top of your churches, or else.'" Nut graf: "'It wasn't the first time authorities had approached the church,' explained Timothy, a preacher and network leader. . . . Authorities asked his network of two dozen churches to take down some of the taller, more noticeable crosses from atop churches along main roads."

Ideally, a descriptive lead carries readers all the way to the nut graf. One *World* story began:

> In Africa, mosquitoes go blood hunting after dusk. They often drift in through open windows or doors, but any crack or crevice will do. Inside, they sniff out their prey: a mother scrubbing pots after dinner, a child's ankles as she finishes her homework.

The next paragraph deepened the tone of inevitability:

> Bedtime is the best time for feeding. Through the quiet darkness comes a mosquito's reedy whine when it zips past your ear. But in Africa mosquitos mean more than itchy bites; just one can bring death through malaria. And trillions breed anywhere there is fresh standing water, even puddles. Sleepers sometimes use insecticide-treated bed nets as a defense—the nets often hang over floor mats, not beds—but the mesh turns stifling in the heat. Badly-hung nets have gaps, and any tear renders them useless. Trying to stop every mosquito is a dead man's game: They will find a way in.

Then, the nut graf: "The only winning way to fight Africa's malarial mosquitoes is the law of the jungle: kill them before they kill you." This is a story of how those who would save human lives lost their most effective weapon, and how some policy wonks are moving beyond their academic journals and seclusion in order to say, loud and often, give us back the weapon.

With evocative leads and clear nut grafs, journalists are then ready to run the race by developing the body of a story. Many stories that start well become mushy in the middle, with no sequence of ideas and sensations, no pattern of cause and effect, no narrative, no pearls—just puddles. The body of the story should help readers understand what the reporter has learned while researching an article.

The journalist does that by telling pointed stories, translating jargon into everyday terms, and giving a face to a fact by explaining macro matters in human terms. Let the small represent the large.

It's vital to keep thinking of readers, and to help them by relating the unknown to the known (for example, faraway place X is like nearby place Y). We should not overuse confusing statistics or technical information. A little goes a long way. Keeping readers in mind is especially important when dealing with big numbers. Instead of merely mentioning that New York spent $2 billion in ten years on 25,000 homeless people, a reporter should do the division problem for the skimming reader and note the per person per year expenditure was $80,000.

Logical transitions contribute to the cause of moving readers from one chunk of information to the next. Strong writers do not bury crucial information in the middle of a paragraph. Key points of emphasis are the beginnings and ends of sentences, paragraphs, and stories. The best stuff should be in the most emphatic locations.

Reader-friendly English prose places the subject before the verb and uses the active voice rather than the passive. Reporters should normally use the past tense when writing about things that have occurred. Some novice writers think that the present tense is better because it supposedly makes the action more immediate, but it also can make a well-reported story sound like a breathless romance novel.

Writers who are trained in writing for newspapers or writing for children sometimes fear long sentences, on the theory that they slow down readers. Actually, a well-organized longer sentence takes no longer to read than a series of short sentences, because periods are like stop signs. The real issue is complexity of material. The more complicated the idea, the shorter the sentences and paragraphs should be, in order to slow down the reader. But a narrative sentence can be long if it is good.

The most important thing to remember throughout the body of the article is the inclusion of specific detail. Beginning writers often fall in love with their material and try to compress anecdotes and description so they can force everything in. Sometimes even experienced reporters with a lot to say cut out descriptive and narrative material so they can include all their points. But good stories require showing, not telling, and showing takes space. Selection, not compression, is the key. When in doubt, the reporter should turn to the nut graf and remember the goal of telling stories in support of a central point.

One way to summarize material quickly is to quote public-policy jargon, but it's better to place it under a biblical lens. For example:

> He defines behavioral poverty as a "cluster of social pathologies including dependency and eroding work ethic, lack of educational aspiration and achievement, inability to control one's children, increased single parenthood and illegitimacy, criminal activity, and drug and alcohol abuse." In a word, sin.

Endings give readers a sense of closure and a sense that the writer knows what he is doing. We need to ask ourselves what we want the reader to remember. Last is often most in memory. The lead and the ending should make the same point. (Sometimes, they can be more effective if switched.) Four popular kinds of endings are the metaphorical, the next step, the nail-it-shut, and the circular. All four kinds ideally appeal to the emotions as well as to the intellect.

A *metaphorical* ending works well to evoke a response, either by making a biblical reference or by placing the problem reported on in some other cultural context. For example, a story on a highly publicized tug-of-war concerning an adopted child ended, "No one is proposing that the child be cut in half physically. Most people are hoping that Jessica will not be sliced and diced emotionally."

The *next-step* ending tells readers what happened after the time span of the article. Here is the end of a story about a woman who did abortions in China, but escaped having one herself. "As for Chi An and her family, they live in the southwestern United States. Now that Mahwae is in kindergarten, Chi An is studying for her nursing credentials. She hopes one day to work in a maternity ward, helping to deliver babies, not destroy them."

Sometimes the next-step is literally a note about the next step:

> In spite of seemingly insurmountable challenges, former *Reform* editor Chu remains hopeful about the future as he watches a new batch of Christian leaders rise in China . . . such as Pastor Wang Yi

in Chengdu. "Every generation has its responsibilities," Chu said: "The older generation has taken their stand; now the new generation is not only persevering in the Christian faith, but bringing Christianity into society and influencing it."

The *nail-it-shut* quotation has a key individual strongly elucidating the story's central theme. Here's one:

Hong Kong Chief Executive Leung Chun-ying said he would write to Beijing concerning Lam's case and review a notification system for when residents are detained by mainland authorities in mainland China. Albert Ho, a pro-democracy lawmaker, told CNN he was disappointed by Leung's meager response: "his is utterly disappointing. What Hong Kong people need is not a letter."

Here's a longer one from a police officer that creates an evocative setting:

At his funeral, they were saying what a tragedy it was—that Gary was a Christian and had even been a missionary. I didn't know anything about that part of his life. I knew he was a good officer, a good person. But I told God right then that people I ride with aren't going to hear [for the first time] at my funeral that I was a Christian. I knew I had to do better at letting people know what I am. Because like I said, without God I couldn't make it.

We have already discussed circular structure in stories; *circular* endings bring back a central character for a final look. For example, a story that began with a focus on one Chinese Christian, Yu Jie, ended with these two paragraphs:

Yu Jie said his Christian faith has sustained him through government pressure as well as his exile from China. He's seen many activist friends compromise their values as officials offer them cushy jobs and prestige as long as they vow to stop criticizing the government. He's watched as friends "in the struggle" turn to tactics employed by the Communist Party—refusing to listen to dissenting opinions and squelching opposing ideas. . . .

For Yu, the Bible reminds him that all men—including intellectuals and human rights activists—are sinful and in need of a Savior. His faith also bolsters him as he continues writing, spending time with his family, and worshipping at a Chinese church in the suburbs of Virginia, far from the clamor of Beijing: "Most Chinese people feel homesick about China, but I know that on this earth I am a sojourner. So in Beijing I was a sojourner, and in America I am also a sojourner."

KEY TERMS

newspaper lead
feature lead
anecdotal lead
descriptive lead
situation lead
multi-vignette lead
nut graf
active voice
passive voice
metaphorical ending
next-step ending
nail-it-shut ending
circular ending

STUDY QUESTIONS

1. What is the main purpose of a feature lead?
2. When writing, what is the best way to stick to the point of the story?

FOR FURTHER READING

Francis Flaherty, *The Elements of a Story* (HarperCollins, 2009).

15

Investigating Christian Groups

ONE OF A Christian journalist's most important functions is to help church leaders who have gone astray understand that the harm they do to others in secret will become visible, not only in a future judgment, but in this world as well. The presence of investigative journalism, done well, can forestall some problems, correct others, and help wrongdoers repent and return to Christian fellowship.

Investigative work often begins with someone within a congregation or denomination contacting a reporter or editor and providing evidence of a problem. Journalists should always be sympathetic but skeptical. Some church members may exaggerate difficulties or envy leaders. Some eyewitnesses are unreliable. Sometimes details that seem too bad to be true are not.

When a story seems valid to us at *World*, we start asking: What good can we accomplish by pursuing it? Will a story help to protect the innocent and be a voice for those who would otherwise be voiceless? Can we help the "uns": the unborn, the unschooled, the unemployed through no fault of their own, the unfashionable because they stand for Christ?

Then come other questions: Are we examining a well-known/influential institution or individual or one who is significant only to a small group of people? Is the subject a public figure or someone readers support financially? Is the objectionable behavior we've heard about recent or old? Is the problem an exception or part of a pattern, and is it a matter of organizational policy or culture or a personal rogue sin? Are we confident that our sources are not perpetual malcontents who have exaggerated a problem?

Our state of mind in asking and answering such questions is important. Christians need to distinguish between being on the Lord's side, sticking as closely as we can to his revealed Word, and being on the side of any person or group of people, no matter how distinguished. Psalm 118's warning to put no confidence in princes is good advice for everyone and especially for journalists, whom princes readily try to influence.

The tendency to confuse journalism with public relations is a common failing among Christian magazines and newspapers. God-respecting and self-respecting editors should not run pieces puffing particular organizations, especially those that offer incentives to do so. One of the most telling signs of the generally low level of Christian journalism in America is the expectation of many publicists that Christian magazines and newspapers will do their bidding. Some Christian groups express irritation at *World* for publishing anything negative about them, even critical paragraphs within generally positive reports.

Overall, Christian publications that wish to practice biblically directed journalism should stand firm against propaganda in five ways. We should not pretend that all is well with Christian organizations that are having problems. We should be willing to investigate and expose the wrongdoings of political allies. We should be willing to praise opponents who act rightly in particular circumstances. We should not cover up embarrassments that befall even strong organizations. We should not place great church leaders above criticism.

That last one is often the hardest. We know from the Bible that all have sinned and fall short of the glory of God, but when *World* criticized some leading American pastors and evangelists for being silent about the evil of abortion, some readers were shocked. And yet, Christian journalists should always be willing to speak up sadly if the facts warrant. That's one other reason to remember the great cloud of Christian journalistic witnesses. Were some of our predecessors tortured and killed so that we can live lives of fear under much less intimidating circumstances?

Once our hearts are set on doing what's right in an investigation, we need to think hard about procedural questions: Will our sources of information go on the record? Publications should not make their pages available for anonymous accusations. When journalists use unnamed sources because their testimony is essential and credible, it's important to tell readers why we're not naming them. We should never see a statement like, "The source preferred to be off the record." Many sources do prefer that, but legitimate reasons are when identification of the source could leave him (or close family members) unemployed, imprisoned, or dead.

At *World*, when we do agree to go off the record with sources, we need to define what that means. Should the information be used for background only, or used but not attributed at all, or attributed merely to "a source in the xyz department"? Unattributed quotations that disparage a person are worthless unless we have lots of on-the-record quotations saying similar things.

We point out to reporters that the word is "sources," not "source." The Bible repeatedly tells us of the importance of establishing fact through the testimony of two, three, or more witnesses (Num. 35:30; Deut. 17:6; 19:15; Matt. 18:16; 2 Cor. 13:1; 1 Tim. 5:19). And, since witnesses are fallible, we usually need to see documentation, and we always need to give the accused a chance to respond.

Another question is whether a Christian organization has put biblical processes for accountability into effect. We are more likely to get involved when we see biblical process intentionally subverted or ignored, so our investigation is not derailing a biblical process but derailing a railroading. We also ask whether a Christian leader makes wide use of print and electronic media to win the support of the Christian public well beyond his own local church. If so, we believe that same Christian public has a right to know what's going on in that leader's life.

Even if all the answers to these questions suggest a green light, journalists sometimes have to pass up some stories because a time-consuming investigation may demand more resources than the news organization has. We also need to recuse any editors or reporters from any story in which they have connections to key players. Investigations are not times for settling scores or covering up misdeeds of friends or relatives.

What all this adds up to: Are we glorifying God by potentially overturning an idol? If the organization is a Christian one, and if a secular publication is likely to expose the practice, can we minimize the damage by contextualizing it and showing the world Christians do not cover up problems?

Ethical questions emerge as investigations continue. We sometimes have to deal with issues of leaked documents and deception, which we accept in times of war—for example, making Adolf Hitler think the D-Day invasion in 1944 would be at a different place. We can extend that thinking to those who are clearly at war with biblical truth, such as abortionists, but it's easy to fall down a slippery slope, so we need to be careful. Journalists should have reputations for telling the truth, and if we deceive others in pursuit of a story by creating our own sting operations and doing hidden-camera investigations, we may win a battle but lose a war.

Once reporters have sent in drafts of investigative stories, the work continues. On many investigative stories, editors go line-by-line with the reporter: How do you know this? How are you sure about that? At least three persons should look carefully at every story before it is published. Editors sometimes ask reporters for additional checks, such as underlining anything that says or suggests a person has committed a crime. This underlining is the reporter's attestation that he has double-checked those facts.

When an article makes accusatory statements about a person or an organization, the accused party needs to be given the opportunity to respond in the article. When a publication criticizes a person by name in a way that could harm his reputation, and his view was not presented within the article or a column, it's right to offer guaranteed response space in a letters-to-the-editor section of the magazine or its equivalent.

Our state of mind is important here. We should humbly realize the ninth commandment—"You shall not bear false witness"—indicts us all. If it merely said, "Do not lie," then sometimes we could defend ourselves, because lying implies a conscious state. But we can be bearing false witness even when we think we are sincere, if our presuppositions and attitudes propel us away from honest accounts. Operating from our own understanding, none of us can hope to stand before God and be told, "Well done, good and faithful reporter."

When the apostle Paul thought and wrote about sexual immorality within the church in Corinth, legalism in Galatia, hypocrisy in Jerusalem, and many other false, dishonorable, unjust, and impure practices, was he breaking his own rule about emphasizing the pure, lovely, commendable, and excellent? No. When a family drives to the beach on Saturday past garbage heaps, parents and children should concentrate on what is lovely, so as not to drown in the sewage of the world. Still, the world would be a better place if a newspaper columnist on Monday describes that garbage dump and insists it be cleaned up. Part of Paul's task was to look at and write about rotten stuff at times. Journalists also have that unpleasant calling.

As we have wondered at times whether we should take the easy way out and drop a story on clergy sexual abuse or other evils, Paul's words to the Ephesians have heartened us: "Take no part in the unfruitful works of darkness, but instead expose them" (Eph. 5:11). It's shameful to have to do this, but actions exposed by the light become visible, and that's how evildoers are pushed to change their lives. As commentator Matthew Henry wrote three centuries ago, evil acts "should be made to appear in their proper colors to the sinners themselves, by the light of doctrine or of God's word in your mouths, as faithful reprovers."

John Calvin's point on Ephesians 5:11–12 is also good. Would evildoers

> lay aside all shame, and give loose reins to their passions, if darkness did not give them courage, if they did not entertain the hope that what is hidden will pass unpunished? But do you, by reproving them, bring forward the light, that they may be ashamed of their own baseness. Such shame, arising from an acknowledgment of baseness, is the first step to repentance.

That should be the Christian journalist's message to anyone who thinks he can act evilly and cover it up: don't. If the thought of God watching doesn't stop you, be aware others may see. By bringing this question out into the open, we hope Christians will work toward establishing sexual-abuse policies in their own churches, and church leaders will educate members about the problem and how to prevent it.

World has had to confront problems within the church much more often than we would like. When our reporting contributed to the demise of one Christian organization that had gone astray, it seemed right to quote scriptural sadness about bad news: "How the mighty have fallen! Tell it not in Gath, publish it not in the streets of Ashkelon, lest the daughters of the Philistines rejoice" (2 Sam. 1:19–20).

Here's how that column continued:

> Some Seattle residents who despise Christianity are rejoicing now at the demise of the organization known as Mars Hill. But they don't realize that a church is not a building and not an organization. It's a group of saints who once were sinners and still do sinful things. We sin by using ministries for personal glory, or by lording it over others, or by idolizing others, but J. I. Packer's three-word summary of the gospel is succinct and true: "God saves sinners."
>
> Those who rejoice don't realize that because the church is made up of people, it doesn't die when an organization dies. Some who suffered abuse will give up, but many Christians sing in church that we should "put no confidence in princes." The Mars Hill saga is more proof that we should put our confidence in God alone. Or, as Earl Atnip, the uneducated but wise deacon who heard my first, weak confession of faith in 1976 told me, "People will always disappoint you. Christ never does."

Within the limits of resources, Christian journalists should not leave it to the secular press to expose wrongdoing within the church. We should investigate problems within the redemptive hope that God turns weakness into strength. *World* is a Christian publication but not a movement organ, so we have publicly criticized Christian leaders and organizations when they did not respond to the private criticism that always follows abuses of authority. But *World* has published in the streets of Ashkelon while knowing that Christ came into the world to forgive all who put their faith in him. Sometimes uncovering sin helps both perpetrators and readers know we desperately need Christ's covering.

Exposure of corrupt individuals might not seem to coexist with a famous passage from Matthew 18:

> If your brother sins against you, go and tell him his fault, between you and him alone. If he listens to you, you have gained your brother. But if he does not listen, take one or two others along with you, that every charge may be established by the evidence of two or three witnesses. If he refuses to listen to them, tell it to the church. And if he refuses to listen even to the church, let him be to you as a Gentile and a tax collector.

Christian journalists should keep three aspects of that passage in mind. First, the injunction refers to "your brother." Non-Christians should also be confronted with the facts against them and given an opportunity to comment, but this particular procedure is for use among Christians. Second, the passage refers to private offenses ("sins against you"), rather than instances of community-affecting corruption, such as stealing from the temple treasury. Third, the passage deals with the initial way in which a person is helped to confront sin. Normally, by the time a reporter learns of a public-affecting, sinful activity deserving exposure, the steps listed in Matthew 18 already will have occurred—at least in part.

The overwhelming majority of exposure situations that reporters face do not involve Christian brothers in private situations concerning issues with which they have never before been confronted. Typically, the offender already will have been challenged by an associate or associates, and will have decided to continue on his downward path. The reporter should attempt to find out if that initial confrontation has occurred—and if not, why not. The logic of Matthew 18 suggests great care must be taken in reporting public as well as private offenses, but it does not argue for nondisclosure.

But what about those situations in which a Christian brother who was engaged in personal rather than public offenses has acknowledged his sin following confrontation and shows signs of repentance and reconciliation? This is where it is helpful to remember the title of the first American newspaper, *Publick Occurrences Both Forreign and Domestick*. A news publication should emphasize public occurrences, not private affairs, unless those affairs have public ramifications. A minister's adultery, for example, can have an effect on a congregation different from that produced by the waywardness of a regular church member. For people in public positions who are supposed to model virtue and elicit trust, every offense has public ramifications.

Investigation is often difficult because many people in sensitive situations and aware of potential repercussions do not want to talk on the record. Reporters in stressful situations should be forcefully honest with sources about the hardships as well as the benefits to be gained by telling the truth. It is better to delay a story than to violate a trust.

The good news about investigation is that often, sooner or later, someone who has been part of a cover-up decides to talk. Sometimes God has been at work on the person. Sometimes he is simply sick of the deception. When a source during an investigation does talk, verification is vital. Those with strange tales should be asked to repeat them several times, to different people, as reporters listen and see if the details change. Documentation is important. We ask sources to get verification of their stories on paper from files to which they have access.

Reporters ask sources to describe specific places at which incidents occurred—and the weather at specific times. Journalists follow the money: "They rob widows," the Bible laments, and organizations in recent times have done the same, misusing funds designed for orphans as well. *World* reported that in Brazil a project director of one children's fund gave his fiancée $31,000 in bonuses, and in Oklahoma funds meant for Cherokee Indian children became capital for a video rental business.

Sometimes investigations do not require undercover searches, deep-throat interviews, or any other behind-the-scenes work. Sometimes the information is out in the open, but requires someone to scoop out bits of data and analyze their significance. For example, one *World* story took a complaint frequently heard at American pro-life meetings—that many ministers shied away from taking a stand on abortion—and concluded, in a cover story headlined "Silence of the Shepherds," that large numbers of evangelical pastors have "offered their flocks little or no leadership" on abortion. Few pastors preached on the subject, and only one-third ever encouraged walking in a march for life or showed a pro-life film.

To summarize: It's good, for three reasons, to expose Christian ministries that have fallen into corruption. First, exposure might help the ministry to reform before it's too late. Second, 1 Corinthians 10:12 instructs us to take heed, lest we likewise fall in our own lives, ministries, or churches. By drawing out lessons, we can help other Christians avoid similar falls. Third is the benefit to a watching world: we want to show that anti-Christian propagandists are wrong, that Christians do take sin seriously and are willing to expose it. Our God is a God of truth, and he does not need our public relations help.

When the secular left gloated about ministry tragedies, and its propagandists declare Christians are hypocrites and liars, it's particularly important to show some Christians stand for truth.

KEY TERMS

the "uns"
the great cloud of Christian journalistic witnesses
off-the-record sources
testimony of two or more witnesses

STUDY QUESTIONS

1. In what ways can biblically directed journalism stand firm against propaganda?

2. What are good reasons to expose Christian ministries that have acted unethically?

FOR FURTHER READING

Clifford Christians, Kim Rotzoll, and Mark Fackler, *Media Ethics* (Longman, 1983).

16

Investigating Government Officials

IT'S ONE THING to criticize pastors who may get mad at us but do not have the power to imprison us. That takes some courage, but it's far more costly to stand in front of a tank or to upset those with the power to jail, torture, or even kill us. In this regard, American journalists have it easier than our Chinese counterparts. The United States has a tradition of journalistic freedom, as we have seen.

And yet, the tendency of many American journalists to play it safe and go with the crowd is a depressing reality. As noted in chapter 4, a soft despotism within the U.S. molds stories. Even if journalists acknowledge they are conforming because of soft pressure, many like to stay that way because it keeps their career paths smooth.

Such journalists may be sarcastic about their peers who are employed by corporations or government offices and charged with making those who pay their salaries look good. Facing soft despotism, though, reporters tend to do the same toward those in power. Journalists with the courage to be critical are rare, even under soft despotism, so I do not want, from my American vantage point, to tell Chinese Christians what to do in their dangerous situation. But I do have five suggestions for those who are willing to be exceptionally bold and courageous.

First, journalists should compare official claims with reality. That seems obvious, but some journalists are lazily content to write stories off press releases and interviews with leaders. I've seen this firsthand since my first professional reporting job in 1970, and I suspect it happens even more frequently when the government threatens independent journalists.

Earlier I mentioned my experience reporting from Havana a decade ago, at a time when Cuban propagandists and American socialism-favoring reporters were praising Fidel Castro for bringing about "healthcare for all." They even said Cuba has primary care physicians who get "to know their patients and even make house calls." Havana doctors told me that was a joke. They earned so little that some were becoming cab drivers so they could get dollars from tourists and move from peso stores, where little was available, to dollar stores, where they could buy items that were expensive but at least available.

The governmental system was so bad that some churches were distributing medicine to church members, even though state health officials threatened them with "severe sanctions" for doing so. One priest gave the needy vitamins, antibiotics, aspirin, and anti-diarrhea medications brought to him by trustworthy Spanish tourists. He operated illegally and officials knew what he was doing. He said, "The needs of the people are so great that the political cost of shutting us down is too great for the government."

Other Christians had asked for permission to build homes for the elderly and organize the collection of garbage that was rotting in the streets. Officials said no. Some churches were ready and willing to do better than the government in helping the poor and particularly the elderly, but it was officially and ideologically the responsibility of the state to provide all social services. Everything compassionate people did was an indictment of government failure—and Cuba's Communist Party was desperately trying to avoid facing the truth.

Several Cubans, telling me officials acknowledged the inadequacy of government programs but still did not allow private programs, said, "*Ni comer ni dejan comer*" ("They don't eat, neither do they let others eat"). I learned, as I've seen elsewhere as well, that if reporters roam and talk with those who are not officials—such as Christians who have set up compassionate programs in the face of government opposition—we can learn much.

Second, while it is important to get statistics, when possible, to back up or challenge personal observation, human interest is always crucial. Reporters need to understand a story well enough to find a "face"—an individual with whom readers will sympathize—who will bring out the human consequences of a mistaken or evil government policy. Reader interest highly correlates with the human interest of stories. More people like to read about people than issues.

It's vital to protect the people who risk their own necks by providing information. At *World*, we dislike using anonymous sources, since politicians and others often want to influence debate on policy issues without jeopardizing their own security, but we have given anonymity to Chinese opponents of the government's post-abortion policy. We created a pseudonym for one source:

> Zhang felt convicted about the sanctity of life on the night his wife gave birth to their firstborn daughter in 1997. He remembers waiting at the hospital and being awakened in the middle of the night from the sounds of pleading and crying in a neighboring ward. The next day he found out the pregnant women who entered that ward had to abort and bury her unborn babies, and it left a deep impression on him.

The story described how, when Zhang's wife became pregnant again,

> Zhang's in-laws, friends, and even church members told them they should submit to the government and abort the baby. His in-laws even tried to persuade the couple's doctor to tell them the baby might be deformed because Zhang's wife had taken medication while pregnant. But "my wife and I agreed on one thing—that we are Christians and God is very clear that you cannot murder," Zhang said. "We really decided that we will keep this child at any cost and we think that it's a gift from the Lord. If I don't keep it, my faith would be in vain, my faith would be a lie. I cannot do that."

The story described how Zhang's wife gave birth to a beautiful boy. Zhang had some problems with officials, but was able to work them out with payments. He spoke from the pulpit of his 100-member church, saying all human life is from God: "Since then, at least 10 families in his congregation have given birth to a second child."

The last paragraph:

> Zhang doesn't think Chinese Christians should openly challenge the government. They should quietly follow the Bible instead. But that doesn't mean Christians should go along with policies at odds with God's Word. He sees the current situation in China as comparable to that in Exodus 1, where Jewish midwives disobeyed Pharaoh's order to murder all Jewish male children: "Christians need to get rid of fear. We still abide by the government's law, but I would empower them to be filled with the spirit of God; God can make a way within the framework of the administration."

Government officials can, of course, do their own investigations, which may include psychological and physical pressure on journalists to identify their sources. Sometimes reporters hold out and sometimes they give in, and we should celebrate those who resist without judging those who succumb—but we should never make it easy for officials to act wrongly.

Third, a staple in American movies now is the journalist who thinks he knows more than almost anyone else, and maybe God as well—and that's why investigative journalists need humility. We must not think we are better than the officials we are investigating, even if we see them using their positions to gain illicit financial or sexual benefits, as is all too often the case. Nor should we think of ourselves as avenging angels. We record what we see, and it's rightly up to others to decide what the penalty should be. Our task is to be strict constructors of stories and to avoid trying to legislate from our notepads.

Our first reaction to new information should not be "What do I think about it?" but "What happened?" That's in the spirit of Luke, who stressed at the beginning of his gospel that he relied on eyewitnesses, "followed all things closely for some time," and was offering the recipient of his letter, Theophilus, "certainty concerning the things you have been taught." When an official tells us what happened, we should not bow and accept what he says. We should ask probing questions: How do you know what you're saying is true? Where do you get your information?

Wise reporters are humble before God and before their own hearts. Tough-minded journalist Lynn Vincent noted once,

> This job is fun, but it also sometimes hurts. It hurts to pry open the stinking corpse of a heinous act and recount it so that others can see it in all its ugliness. But if it didn't hurt, I would be worried. If I ever stop hurting when others hurt, it will be time to quit.

Fourth, journalists who are afraid of numbers should learn not to fear them. Investigations without any data leave readers wondering whether the human interest stories reporters tell represent big problems or anomalies. For example, the *Las Vegas Sun* before 2010 presented anecdotes about hospital problems, but its computer-assisted analysis of three million hospital records revealed more than 3,600 surgical mistakes, infections, and preventable injuries, and 300 cases of deaths due to medical error. The *Sun* included graphics showing how infections spread and which hospitals were the worst.

Reporters in many cities have built homicide databases showing which areas have had more murders. Useful discussions about policing followed. Other journalists have examined U.S. Department of Education data and found which states offer rich and poor students unequal access to high-level courses. Investigative reporters have used public records of cases treated in hospitals to learn some hospitals were getting more reimbursement from the government than they deserved. Doctors in one hospital chain were saying elderly patients they treated had a protein deficiency syndrome at a rate seventy times higher than the average for all hospitals.

Data journalism, sometimes called computer-assisted reporting (CAR) or precision journalism, has spread around the world. In Germany, *Zeit Online* ran stories on the evacuation of everyone within thirty kilometers of the Fukushima, Japan, nuclear plants when radioactive material escaped from it—and then showed how many Germans lived within thirty kilometers of their nuclear plants. In the United Kingdom, a "Reading the Riots" investigation showed how looters in 2011 used social media, and a "Where Does My Money Go?" project showed the taxes people paid in different parts of the country and the services they received. In Argentina, reporters researched what had happened to 30,000 people who "disappeared" following a 1976 military coup. Several hundred convictions of people who had engaged in "crimes against humanity" resulted.

Finally, worldview makes a huge difference. In the 1930s, why did many Western writers and intellectuals journey to the Soviet Union and report only what government officials wanted them to report? For example, Maurice Hindus, a foreign correspondent who wrote *Red Bread* in 1931, visited a Soviet Gulag slave camp in 1931 and wrote that "the dictatorship . . . actually overflowed with kindness." Writer Lionel Feuchtwanger traveled for three months in the Soviet Union in 1936 and 1937. He saw how Josef Stalin put his former comrades on trial and then executed them. Nevertheless, Feuchtwanger rhapsodized about "the individual's feeling of complete security, his comfortable certainty that the state is really there for him, and not he for the state."

Only a handful of journalists told the truth. One, Britain's Malcolm Muggeridge, described in his autobiography, *Chronicles of Wasted Time*, the thinking and actions of most of his peers. They "resolved, come what might, to believe anything, however preposterous, to overlook anything, however villainous, to approve anything, however obscurantist and brutally authoritarian, in order to be able to preserve intact the confident expectations that one of the most thorough-going, ruthless and bloody tyrannies ever to exist on earth could be relied on to champion human freedom, the brotherhood of man, and all the other good liberal causes to which they had dedicated their lives."

Western leftist journalists who visited China during the mid-1970s produced similar propaganda. Professor Edward Luttwak of Johns Hopkins University described in "Seeing China Plain" that the reporters typically missed an important detail:

Perhaps the most transparent of all the simulations of social equality one sees in China is the mock-equality of dress. Almost everybody wears the standard boiler-suit, the Mao uniform. But some are made of rough cotton and others of delicate gabardine, and still others of good-quality wool. Senior party men would wear their equality in carefully tailored worsted wool, and their Mao suits had much more in common with Pierre Cardin than with the blue cotton outfits of ordinary people. And yet in the post-1972 reports of China it is the theme of visible equality that is most insistently advanced.

Those experienced reporters were either sell-outs or lazy. They did not push for specific detail. Half a century ago, when Whittaker Chambers was trying to show he had been the courier for Alger Hiss's disclosure of diplomatic secrets to the Soviet Union—more about this in chapter 28—he mentioned Hiss had been excited about seeing a prothonotary warbler during a bird-watching expedition. Hiss had denied knowing Chambers, but his deception began to unravel when he was questioned about his hobbies and mentioned how he had been entranced by the sight of that particular kind of bird.

Whether an investigation requires undercover work or reading not only the covers but the insides of many reports, the hard-and-fast rule is: Be very careful, and verify everything numerous times. Reporters should avoid inflammatory words. "Sensational Fact, Understated Prose" remains our motto regarding investigations.

KEY TERMS

soft despotism
face
CAR

STUDY QUESTIONS

1. How can editors and writers prepare themselves to push back against the pressures of despotism?

2. Are readers influenced more by sympathetic faces or hard numbers?

FOR FURTHER READING

Gene Goodwin, *Groping for Ethics in Journalism* (Iowa State University Press, 1983).
James Emery White, *Serious Times* (InterVarsity, 2004).

17

Good Writing in English

THIS CHAPTER IS for those with a good knowledge of English and the desire to become good journalistic writers in that language. Others should skip it. I do not know if the advice that follows is useful for writing in Chinese. In English, journalists should strive to use nouns and strong verbs rather than adjectives and adverbs. Our goal should be to use specific detail, stay low on the ladder of abstraction, keep it simple without oversimplifying, and use big words and fancy sentences only rarely.

Sadly, some students at around age ten become bad writers because American teachers give them points for "dressing up" their writing by using sentences beginning with *after, while,* or *because,* clauses beginning with *who* or *which,* and lots of adjectives and adverbs. One popular textbook gives this example of a sentence improved by dressing up: "The fox *casually* mentioned how pleased he would be to hear the crow sing." (The prized addition, "casually," makes the sentence worse, because it's redundant: a mention *is* casual.)

One fifth-grader I know received a low grade because his paragraph about a school trip lacked dress-ups. Here it is:

> On Tuesday we visited NASA in Houston. My group built a rocket and went on a scavenger hunt. The next morning we rode the tram, had fun on the playscape, ate lunch, and watched a movie

about the space station. On Thursday we hurried to the Museum of Health and Sciences and saw amazing and disgusting things, like the insides of a brain and a heart. Then we ate lunch and wandered around the gross museum.

That paragraph could be improved, but it cogently provided specific detail. The teacher, though, told the fifth grade boy to use dress-ups. Here's his rewritten paragraph:

After traveling to NASA in Houston on Tuesday, my group excitedly built a stupendous rocket. While there we spent time scavenging. When the next morning dawned we merrily traveled on the tram and played happily on the playscape. Since it was lunchtime we ate delicious food and viewed a lively film. The next day we enjoyably galloped through the Museum of Health and Sciences, which displayed the insides of a brain and a heart, and then relished our food.

That paragraph received a high grade—but the writing seems like that of a precious British duchess rather than an American boy. Here's better advice from several generations of writers who dressed down those who dress up. British poet F. L. Lucas: "Make clear connections between sentences. Be simple. Omit needless words. Write less; rewrite more." Novelist John Gardner: "The abstract is seldom as effective as the concrete. 'She was distressed' is not as good as, even, 'She looked away.'"

Mediocre writers become good writers by becoming conscious of their dress-ups and discarding them. Writing guru William Zinsser advises,

Look for the clutter in your writing and prune it ruthlessly. Be grateful for everything you can throw away. Re-examine each sentence that you put on paper. Is every word doing new work? Can any thought be expressed with more economy? Is anything pompous or pretentious or faddish? Are you hanging on to something useless just because you think it's beautiful? Simplify. Simplify.

Similarly, the fine critic Sheridan Baker advised, "Never use a long word when you can find a short one. . . . Suspect yourself of wordiness whenever you see an *of*, a *which* or a *that*. Inspect all areas surrounding any form of *to be*." Baker said we should examine every sentence to see if we could shorten it. Another critic, Jacques Barzun, wrote, "Look for all fancy wordings and get rid of them."

This does not mean we eliminate every multisyllabic word. By economizing much of the time, we have money to spend at the right time. By not eating sugary food every day, we are free to eat an elegant desert occasionally. Writing with strong nouns and verbs lets us follow Mark Twain's advice: "When you catch adjectives, kill most of them—then the rest will be valuable. They weaken when they are close together; they give strength when they are wide apart."

Since we hope to present readers with evocative images, provocative thoughts, and tension without pretension, we should follow advice from George Orwell:

> Never use a metaphor, simile or other figure of speech which you are used to seeing in print. Never use a long word where a short word will do. If it is possible to cut a word out, always cut it out. Never use the passive where you can use the active.

Good journalists emphasize quality rather than quantity. It is better to have one strong bit of specific detail than twelve nothings. (Miguel de Cervantes's worst nightmare: "Let every man . . . not set down at random, higgledy-piggledy, whatever comes into his noodle.") Good journalists write about what they see, not just what they feel like pondering. E. B. White advised, "Don't write about Man, write about a man."

All this advice adds up to nine writing suggestions (not ten, to avoid any confusion with commandments):

1. The world suffers from overwriting more than underwriting. Make every word count by avoiding throat-clearing (introductory paragraphs) and those dress-ups (lots of adjectives and adverbs). When two words mean the same thing, generally

use the shorter one. As Mark Twain and others have said, "kill your darlings," expressions that seem precious to you. They are almost always examples of overwriting.

2. Write in the active voice: no passivity, please. (For example, change "The cemetery was stormed by them" to "They stormed the cemetery.") Use of the active voice is a matter of ethics as well as style, since the passive voice often signals an avoidance of responsibility, as in the classic, "Mistakes were made." Straightforward honesty suggests putting statements in positive, emphatic form. Instead of "He did not choose well," write "He chose poorly."

3. Remember that no one has to read what we write. Every word has to sell the next word, every sentence the next sentence, every paragraph the next paragraph. Keep it moving. Varying sentence length helps pacing. The more complex the information, the simpler the sentence should be.

4. Persevere. Sometimes when we're stuck, we need to sit at our computer and grind it out. If we're really stuck and suspect we have "writer's block," it's probably because we have insufficient specific detail. It's time to do more research and remember to show, not tell. That's particularly good advice for Christians. God tells us to taste and eat, to see whether his teaching is good in practice, and that is the same invitation we should make to readers. At *World*, our goal is to provide the aromatic food of sensational facts and understated prose, and then allow readers to taste and eat.

   Help from others makes for better journalists. We improve as writers when we find true friends who analyze our work fiercely and initially depress us, dressing us down if we use dress-ups, actively criticizing us when we use passives.

5. Avoid particular phrases that are short on energy or evidence. For example, don't start sentences with *there is* or *there are*, except in rare circumstances. Use *evidently* or *apparently* or a similar expression when we don't know for sure what people are feeling or thinking. A *World* cover story noted that although the crowd was singing a hymn, "this is hardly church, and no one is

feeling worshipful." While that statement may be true, we can't be sure that "no one" in the crowd was feeling worshipful.

Avoid dangling participles, a common disease in bad writing. For example, "Standing on the hotel room balcony, the sun immediately made Carol feel warm." This construction implies the sun stood on the balcony. The sentence should read, "Standing on the hotel room balcony, Carol immediately felt the warmth of the sun." Here is another example: "Completing the graduate theater studies program, David's acting career began." This sentence sounds as if the acting career actually completed the graduate program. The sentence should read, "Completing the graduate theater studies program, David began his acting career."

Avoid words many writers frequently abuse. For example, go on a *which* hunt by replacing *which* with *that* when the clause isn't set off with a comma. Don't refer to a person as a "that," as in "the lawyer that won the case." (Humans deserve the pronoun *who*.) Do not use *finalize*, a pompous word associated primarily with bureaucracy; words like *complete* or *finish* are much better. Remember that *unique* means "one of a kind," so it does not take a modifier. Something cannot be "more unique" or "one of the most unique." Do not say a real person was "legendary." A legend is a tradition or story handed down from earlier times that we now do not accept as factual. Reality is not legendary.

6. Don't make the common grammatical error of using *their* instead of *its* in relation to groups. For example, don't have a band announcing "their breakup." Even though a band, like a company or some other organization, is made up of more than one person, it's still an "it." Avoid sentence structures that imply an attribute was present only in the past. For example, "I interviewed her last week. She was smart." (Her intelligence didn't disappear when the interview was over.)

Learn the peculiarities of English. For example, distinguish between *between*, which is used for two things, with *among*, which is used for three or more.

Know how to use *fewer* and *less*. The first refers to a number of individual people or things ("because of automation, fewer workers are needed"), while *less* refers to a quantity or amount of one thing ("less rain has fallen this season than predicted"). Put another way, we use *fewer* if the word it modifies is plural, and *less* if the word it modifies is singular.

(As I go through some of those frequent mistakes, I feel like apologizing for English, a language that developed a millennium ago by the melding of words and verbal constructions from Romance languages like French and the Germanic languages of northern Europe. That mix gives English nuances and makes it harder to learn—but English speakers also find learning Chinese hard.)

7. Understand how language conveys biblical or antibiblical understandings of the similarities and differences between men and women. One recent language change in the U.S. has been an improvement. For a long time, the language used in relation to certain jobs suggested they were for men only, but we now recognize women can fight fires and crime, so *firefighter* and *police officer* are better than *fireman* or *policeman*. More generally, we use terms such as *workforce* or *workers* rather than *manpower*. At *World* we're fine with using *people* or *humanity* rather than *mankind*, but we don't ban *mankind* from our pages, and we do not use the awkward *humankind*.

Another American trend, though, is unbiblical. God created humans male and female, and transsexuals in confusion and depression kick against that—but changes in hormones and even changes in sex organs do not change a man into a woman or a woman into a man. Instead of writing "Last spring, Jayce transitioned legally from female to male," we might write, "Last spring, Jayce completed the legal process that changed his gender designation to male rather than female."

8. Learn a publication's editing shorthand. Here's a partial list at *World*:
   - AWK: awkward.
   - UGH: super-awkward.

- TEK: this everybody knows.
- MORE: needs explanation or additional detail.
- MEGO: mine eyes glaze over (boring).
- PAMO: Needs protagonist, antagonist, mission, obstacles.
- SCENE: Needs something the reader can visualize.
- BW: Broken window (grammar, spelling, or punctuation error).
- MBD: Man bites dog (unusual event worth reporting).
- DBM: Dog bites man (dull, everyday event).
- SD: Specific detail needed.
- LA: Ladder of abstraction (too high up it, needs SD).
- PR: Public relations, to be avoided in journalism.
- SFUP: When we have sensational facts, we should use understated prose.

9. Some young writers bristle when edited, but the usual reaction—eventually—is like this one from someone who went on to be a book writer: "I wanted to thank you. You challenged my writing style so much. You'd say, 'It's good, but it needs work.' You made me realize that anything we write can always be better. You also taught me about brevity, so I'll stop now." As one writing professor said when teaching a seminar of twelve students, "Some of your fellow students will be nicer than they should be, but I won't, because I'm the only one in this room who's paid to tell you the truth."

Advanced students who are thinking about becoming professional writers need to add temperament to talent. Novelist Isaac Asimov, commenting on a classic editor's statement—"We don't reject writers; we reject pieces of paper with typing on them"—added,

> Don't stay mad and decide you are the victim of incompetence and stupidity. If you do, you'll learn nothing and you'll never become a writer. . . . Don't make the opposite mistake and decide the story is worthless. Editors differ and so do tastes and so do magazines' needs. Try the story somewhere else.

Mark Twain suggested this way of discerning a calling:

> Write without pay until somebody offers pay. If nobody offers within three years the candidate may look upon his circumstances with the most implicit confidence as the sign that sawing wood is what he was intended for.

The way *not* to learn is to assume that friends who say "you're great" have good judgment. Young writers need true friends who are willing to make them cry. They need teachers and editors willing to tell the truth, even if it hurts. All are hard to find in this age of inflating grades and emphasizing self-esteem, rather than offering tough honesty.

For a good, brief compilation of basic stylistic pointers on writing in English, the classic little book by Will Strunk and E. B. White titled *The Elements of Style* is unbeatable.

KEY TERMS

dress-ups
active voice
passive voice

Five important *World* editing terms:
AWK
LA
PAMO
SD
TEK

STUDY QUESTIONS

1. What are right and wrong ways to respond to criticism?
2. Who are the best friends of writers who want to improve?
3. How should freelancers respond when an editor turns down a story idea or story?

FOR FURTHER READING

William Strunk Jr. and E. B. White, *The Elements of Style*, 4th ed. (Longman, 2000).

Gerald Graff, *Clueless in Academe* (Yale University Press, 2003).

18

Using Words Accurately

CHRISTIAN WRITERS NEED to be attentive to the manipulation of words to make political points. For example, before the 1960s, American journalists routinely used the word *baby* when referring to the creature in the womb. Then changes in ideology pushed reporters to search for a new term. They grabbed *fetus* from the world of medicine. It was a way to blur the reality of abortion—but good journalists don't run from hard truths.

At *World*, we don't use the term *abortion clinic* because *clinic* implies a facility devoted to health—not death. We use *abortion business* or *abortion center*. We call the person who performs an abortion an abortionist, not an abortion doctor or physician. Physicians who uphold the Hippocratic oath are supposed to preserve life, not destroy it. We don't see pro-life laws as restrictions on abortion. They increase protection for pre-born life.

World's policy book offers other usage guidelines not related to abortion. Here are a few: For historical dates, we still use B.C. and A.D. rather than the more trendy C.E. and B.C.E. (Before Common Era). We know Christ is the fulcrum of history.

We don't use the term *Dark Ages* because it suggests the Roman Empire was a fountain of light, and its fall brought darkness. Not true. Rome was an evil empire that improved with Christianization. We avoid saying *fortunately*. That's a theological term from ancient religion. Fortuna was the Roman goddess of luck and fortune. We prefer the biblical term *providentially*.

We don't use *homophobia* to describe the belief that homosexuality is wrong. It means "fear of homosexuals," not disagreement with them. We sometimes use the word *Christophobia*, not as a reference to the idea that Christianity is wrong, but to left-wing fear of any Christian influence in American society.

We avoid the term *progressive*, except when it's part of an organization's proper name. The term suggests that one faction supports progress, while the rest of us are against it. We refer to *biblical theology* in describing belief that the Bible is God's word, not *conservative theology*, because what conservatives believe varies widely.

We don't like the term *faith-based*. Everyone has a faith of some kind, so the term does not supply useful information. We try to say *religious group* or use some other descriptive term. We also minimize use of the word *unbeliever*. We will use *agnostic, atheist, pantheist*, or whatever, but *unbeliever* just isn't accurate, because everyone believes in something. As Bob Dylan sang, you gonna have to serve somebody.

We capitalize *Church* when referring to the universal body of Christ, and lowercase it elsewhere. Jesus died for the Church, and churches have been proclaiming the gospel ever since.

We try to use the word *compassion* accurately. It's a willingness to suffer with a person in need. It's not suffering for the sake of suffering, but active personal involvement, rather than just feeling sorry for someone. It is especially not to be used in reference to the passing of a piece of legislation that purportedly indicates concern for the poor. *Empathy* denotes a close understanding of the feelings of another, vicariously putting oneself in another's place. *Sympathy* is feeling emotionally close to a person, but not necessarily doing anything to help.

And here are some more terms:

devil. Uppercase when referring to Satan, because he is a real being with significant power. Lowercase when used generically about evil and trouble: "The devil is in the details." Lowercase "demons": they're tools, not lords.

evangelical. A person who emphasizes biblical inerrancy, salvation by faith in the atoning death of Christ, and the importance of personal conversion. Best used as a theological, rather than a political, term.

fetus. Use *unborn child, preborn child,* or *child* instead, unless quoting someone (in that case, quote exactly).

fundamentalist. Normally refers to a defined set of Christians (those who adhere to *The Fundamentals,* a series of twelve books published a century ago). Liberal journalists have applied it to unsavory folks of other religions as a way to knock Christian fundamentalists. We refer to Hindu burners of Christians or Muslim knifers of Christians as "extremists," not "fundamentalists."

gender/sex. Sex divides male and female (persons, animals, plants) and also refers to the character of being male or female. Originally, *gender* was strictly a grammatical term, but it became a way of referring to maleness or femaleness without using the word *sex,* and now it is a politically correct term best to avoid when possible.

gospel. Capitalized when referring to one or more of the four Gospels in the Bible.

he and *she. He* is the default in the English language, but it is usually fine to recast sentences to the plural (except in translating the Bible) so that *they* can substitute for it.

jargon. Christian writers should seek to communicate with non-Christians, not just with members of the evangelical tribe, so avoid jargon like "get into the Word," "laid upon my heart," and "share a verse."

Judeo-Christian. Avoid, since the two faiths are different. On some social and cultural issues, it's fine to say "the Christian and Jewish traditions."

LGBT or *LGBTQ.* Use for succinct references to "lesbian, gay, bisexual, transgender, questioning or queer" people.

LGBT community. Today's journalists overuse *community* generally, and particularly in this instance. Sentences are usually easy to recast. Instead of "X was once an influential, zealous leader of the LGBT community," we should write, "X was once an influential, zealous LGBT leader." Instead of "many members of the LGBT community," we should write, "many who identify as LGBT." Instead of "lawsuits and political attacks from the LGBT community," we should write "lawsuits and political attacks from LGBT activists."

nonsexist language. People, humanity, and *human beings* can be substituted for *man* and *mankind,* although *mankind* is acceptable at *World.* Do not use *humankind.* Instead of using *average man,* use *average person.* Instead of *man a project,* use *staff a project.* Instead of *manpower,* use *workforce, personnel,* or *workers.*

Use *he* and *she* when writing specifically about one person, but when talking about both men and women, use plural constructions, such as "the nurses . . . they." When that is awkward or changes the meaning, the use of *he* and *his* is acceptable when referring generically to a human being. Sometimes a general noun or adjective can be substituted.

Quotations (especially quotations from the Bible) should not be changed, and verses should not be altered to support ideological objectives. Do not, for example, change Psalm 1:1, "Blessed is the man who does not walk," to "Blessed are those who do not walk." That changes the meaning from individual heroism to a collective intransigence.

Many sentences in our own, uninspired speech, do not lose their potency by going from singular to plural. Instead of "A professor needs to think about what his words convey," it's fine to say, "Professors need to think about what their words convey."

Do not mix singular and plural forms, as in "He asked any student who knew the answer to raise their hand." Instead, write, "He asked students who knew the answer to raise their hands."

Do not alternate *he* and *she,* or *him* and *her.* Do not use the passive voice or the stuffy "one" as an escape hatch.

Be careful of stereotyping. Avoid *woman doctor, lady lawyer, male nurse* or other similar constructions. *Doctor, lawyer,* and *nurse* are sufficient. Instead of *foreman,* use *supervisor;* instead of *policeman,* use *police officer;* instead of *stewardess,* use *flight attendant;* instead of *mailman,* use *postal worker* or *letter carrier.*

Use constructions like "Research scientists often neglect their families," rather than "Research scientists often neglect their wives and children." Avoid nonparallel structures, such as "ten men and sixteen females." Unless you literally mean "men and girls," use "men and women" instead.

Describe men and women in parallel terms. *Housewife* indicates sex, marital status, and occupation, excluding men; *homemaker* indicates occupation and includes men. Instead of using constructions like "ambitious men and aggressive women," use "ambitious men and women" or "ambitious people."

pro-abortion. Use except when an individual clearly expresses horror at abortion but believes philosophically that individual liberty trumps preservation of life, in which case *World* might describe him as pro-choice.

pro-life. Accurate to use in relation to those who oppose murder, i.e., the deliberate killing of innocent human beings.

religious terminology. Avoid clubby, insular expressions like "The Lord laid it on my heart," "Look to the Lord in prayer," and "prayer warrior."

restrictions on abortion, or *pro-life victory*. May be true, but the real result is "increased protection for unborn children," and we should say so.

saint. None of us is wholly sanctified in this life, and Protestants don't think of people as being in two distinct classes, so use *Augustine* rather than *Saint Augustine* and *the apostle Paul* rather than *Saint Paul*. (Christians are lower-case saints.)

they and *them*. Always plural. Do not use *they* as a synonym for *he*. If you want to use *they*, change sentences from singular to plural (unless they occur in the Bible or you are changing their meaning).

The Associated Press now says *they* can refer to one person if the person doesn't want to be referred to as *he* or *she*. But subjective preferences don't change objective reality. Use *they* only for more than one person, unless the one person you're writing about has multiple personalities. In transgender or (extremely rare) cases of ambiguous sexuality, use proper names if necessary, not pronouns.

unbeliever. Use *agnostic, atheist, pantheist*, or whatever. Everyone believes in something.

Word and *word*. Capitalized in reference to the Bible and the speech acts of God, lowercase elsewhere.

worldview. Useful term, since everyone has one, but not everyone has a religion.

KEY TERMS

compassion
worldview

STUDY QUESTIONS

1. Discuss the problems with some conventional journalistic words: abortion clinic, homophobia, faith-based, gender, community, progressive.
2. What are some problems with removing "sexist" language in Bible translations?

FOR FURTHER READING

Associated Press. *The Associated Press Stylebook* (2013, 2018).
Diane Ravitch, *The Language Police* (Knopf, 2003).

19

The Character and Personality of Good Journalists

IN AMERICA WE have tests that measure intelligence quotient, IQ. At *World* we discuss at times spiritual quotient, SQ. A chain of fast-foot eateries called Dairy Queen—DQ for short—is popular across the United States, so we also talk about the importance of a high DQ: determination quotient. DQ differentiates those who are successful in investigative journalism from those who merely play at it.

DQ means getting to the site of an interview ten minutes ahead of time, and then redeeming the minutes by observing. DQ, when a meeting is being covered, generally means staying afterward and eliciting reactions. DQ means constant collecting. Experienced reporters typically have more observations written in their notebooks than a story will have room for. (Writers who do not have adequate material and try to make up for that lack by adding rhetoric end up with heat, but little light.)

A *World* reporter's IQ and SQ are important, but so is his DQ. One popular novelist, Tom Clancy, isn't a great stylist, but like the apostle Paul he presses toward his goal, so his advice is worth remembering: "Writing is most of all an exercise in determination."

Every successful writer has a high DQ. Note this advice from two craftsman-authors: Michael Crichton said, "Books aren't written. They are rewritten." James Michener claimed, "I'm not a very good writer, but an excellent rewriter." One of America's top stylists, E. B. White, noted, "A writer who waits for ideal conditions under which to work will die without putting a word to paper."

Telling True Stories and *The New New Journalism*, two books filled with interviews of journalists, repeatedly show the importance of DQ. Journalist Richard Ben Cramer says he once read Tom Wolfe, a top American writer, and thought, "God touched you and made you a genius, and that's the end of it." Then he saw Wolfe toiling at a desk, writing. "I looked in his eyes and saw the haunted, hunted animal look."

Another outstanding American nonfiction writer, Michael Lewis, says, "The most common pleasant thing people say to me about my writing is that it looks 'effortless.'" Then he confesses, "It is the opposite of effortless. . . . I probably do 20 drafts of each chapter. I write something over and over. It's like *Groundhog Day*. My writing process is sweaty and inelegant."

Lewis also notes, in response to a question about whether he needs to write in one particular place,

> I've written in awful enough situations that I know the quality of the prose doesn't depend on the circumstances in which it is composed. I don't believe the muse visits you. I believe that you visit the muse. If you wait for that "perfect moment" you're not going to be very productive.

We've found over the years that the best reporters have curiosity, a gripping desire to see and learn new things. They have a willingness to work hard, fast, and (if necessary) long hours. They connect the dots of different events and go beneath the surface. They have enough charm to get other people to talk and help. They have integrity, the grace to withstand enticements. And they have thick skin, since good reporters inevitably make some people mad.

A peculiarly American way to view this is through the lens of baseball, the most popular sport in America during the twentieth century, one that still grips many imaginations. Baseball scouts talk about five-tool players: those who can run, field, throw, hit, and hit with power. Five-tool Christian reporters are those who can DRAW—discern, report, analyze, write—and tell stories. We can chart it this way:

1. Discern: approach a story within a biblically objective framework.
2. Report: move from abstractions to observation of reality.
3. Analyze: connect the dots, seeing the sum of all the specific details.
4. Write: smoothly and accurately convey information and perspective.
5. Tell a story: weave that information into a compelling account.

Here's how journalist Susan Orlean shows her Determination Quotient:

> I hate going out to lunch because that is exactly when I am usually getting up a head of steam. So I usually just grab a sandwich and eat at my desk . . . rather than taking a break because I can't get anything done. I take a break whenever I write something that I feel really good about. It is hard for me to stop for dinner and then go back to work, so I often stop writing around 8 P.M.

Another fine writer, Anne Hull, displays her DQ in a segment of *Telling True Stories* titled "Revising—Over and Over Again." She says,

> Only editors know the awful truth: how bad even the best narrative stories look in the beginning. Successful rewriting requires a fierce sense of competition with yourself, not anyone else. You must be dogged in reaching for your personal best. When you begin a story's first draft, you must ask yourself hard questions.

Hull asks herself this tough one:

Am I getting to the heart of my subject matter? When we begin redrafting—and, unfortunately, sometimes right through to the printed version—we're at the story's fringes. Finding the story's center is crucial; we usually write our way there. It takes many drafts, and there are no shortcuts.

A high DQ often kicks in even before the writing begins. Lawrence Wright takes issue with journalists who say "they don't want to start a story knowing too much for fear that all this information will dull their own impressions." He says such impressions "might be brilliant and insightful . . . but I believe they'd be even more brilliant and insightful if you really worked at understanding your subject by doing a lot of research."

Curiosity is crucial, as is relishing the process of learning and then explaining to others in ways that communicate. Alex Kotlowitz in *The New New Journalism* says,

> I go back and rewrite, scene by scene, detail by detail. It's the part I love the most. It's all I think about. I'll awake in the middle of the night with a perfect sentence. Or during a game of basketball will find a word I'd been looking for. I'm sure, to some, I must seem like an unholy, scatterbrained mess.

High-DQ writers find ways to take a vacation from one project, not by lying on the beach, but by gaining the stimulation of another project. Michael Lewis says,

> At any given moment, I have at least four projects under way. I write short columns. . . . I'm usually working on a book. . . . I'm usually at some stage of one of the long articles I write. . . . I don't know whether it is a character flaw, or just comes with the life of a freelance writer.

No, it comes with a high DQ in writing—or in any other area of life.

Good journalists are always on the lookout for specific detail. Richard Preston writes about asking a chemist,

"What does DNA really look like? How do you handle it?" He took out a vial of human DNA . . . and pulled out a little mucus-like strand with a toothpick for me to look at. I wanted to know everything about DNA: how it tasted, what it smelled like. So I ordered some calf DNA from a lab supply company. It arrived in powder form and I put it on my tongue. It was faintly salty, and a bit sweet. I used that detail in the article, and I think it helped make the whole idea of DNA more concrete for readers.

Preston also explains he once

had to learn what it felt like for a doctor to cut open a cadaver. A doctor I know in Princeton agreed to call me the next time there was an autopsy, and one Saturday morning he called to say that there was an autopsy scheduled in thirty minutes. I rushed over to the hospital and watched the whole thing: the assistant cutting and opening the body, the pathologist using a bread knife to slice organ samples. When the pathologist cut the skull and lifted the brain out, she handed it to me. It was a soft, gelatinous blob. And the smell during the autopsy was profound. The contents of the large intestine stink, and the freshly cut human flesh smelled, I must say, a little like raw pork.

Preston reported the smell of an autopsy, which he could do only by being there. *World*'s goal whenever possible is to provide street-level, rather than suite-level, reports. Even a public policy story should emphasize the effect of a policy throughout the country, rather than the way it is drawn up in Washington. Most of the Bible was earthy, while much of Greek philosophy was abstract. We want to be earthy. Within Greek philosophy, Plato liked writing about universal forms, but Aristotle found the universal in specific detail.

A former *World* staffer, Jonathan Bailie, interviewed *World* editors and reporters and produced a summary of our goals. It began with an emphasis on true stories: all truth is God's truth because God himself is truth. To glorify God rightly requires all his adopted children to worship him in spirit and in truth. Truth is not one value that can be horse-traded for another. Even though truth can cause immediate pain, it should never be mitigated or avoided. In time, truth will heal and restore.

Bailie noted our view that truth is always an end in itself, never a mere means. Even if truth challenges preconceived notions or dogmas, we cannot sacrifice it for the greater good, because truth, by divine appointment, *is* the greater good. Stories motivated by pride, selfishness, indifference, or envy lack the essential nature of truth: putting things right in this world.

Bailie saw our desire to throw off pretension, false faces, fantasy, and self-delusion. We want to know what really is, not what is artificially masqueraded and peddled as reality. We know God made humans in his own image, so we are people watchers, always learning what makes each of us unique and valuable in our own right, warts and all.

Great reporters are always curious, always willing to take something apart to find out what it's made of, and mesmerized by a symphony or a smile that resists reduction to individual elements. We weep with those who weep, but, even in the face of real evil, we know God's great story sweeps through the darkness. We enjoy having a front row seat at the earthly circus, and delight in what the ringmaster shows us.

Christian publications should show we are pilgrims in a very seductive environment. We are in a Psalm 73 position: "My feet had almost stumbled, my steps had nearly slipped. For I was envious of the arrogant when I saw the prosperity of the wicked" (verses 2–3). We worry when an election goes the wrong way: "When I thought how to understand this, it seemed to me a wearisome task" (verse 16). But that psalm's author, Asaph, enlarges his world when he enters God's sanctuary, comes to understand God's magnificence, and resolves to "tell of all your works" (verse 28).

We try to be deed-tellers like Asaph, showing God's sovereignty through our storytelling. Some publications want to put readers in the panic zone, and others provide a comfort zone, but we are unusual in emphasizing the challenge zone. We want to equip our readers to say, "You have given me perspective. You have helped me raise my family.

You have encouraged me to work hard, but not be fearful. You've encouraged me to keep calm and carry on, with eyes on the prize."

KEY TERMS

DQ
qualities of top reporters
DRAW

STUDY QUESTIONS

1. Why is it good for journalists to see themselves as skilled workers rather than artists?
2. How should journalists take Psalm 73 to heart?

FOR FURTHER READING

Hugh Hewitt, *In, but Not Of: A Guide to Christian Ambition and the Desire to Influence the World* (Thomas Nelson, 2003).

20

When Readers Complain

JOURNALISTS HATE MAKING factual mistakes, but some always occur, and our goal should be to admit errors quickly. All staff members who learn about their errors should inform editors as soon as possible. It's far better to turn yourself in than to be found out. Our ultimate aim is God's glory, not the magazine's glory or our own. A press card is not a license to harangue, hate, or lie: those actions would show we put ourselves first and don't trust God's providence.

Letters from people quoted or otherwise directly involved in a story should receive priority on the grounds that journalists had a shot at explaining the situation, and now they can have their turn. Some publications fill their mailbag pages with letters praising their efforts or offering minor additions to stories, but *World* prints attack letters as long as they are factually accurate. Editors should take ethical complaints seriously and avoid defensiveness or the clichéd expression, "We stand by the story."

A publication will make some readers angry by taking strong positions on controversial issues, and that goes with the territory, but it should not shrug off factual errors. A factual error becomes an ethical lapse if a publication uses legal protections as a way not to correct mistakes. For example, the statute of limitations for libel is one year in most states, and two or three years in others, but if we learn we've been inaccurate at a time later than that, we still want to apologize and fix what's on our website.

When replying to readers, it's good to use a gentle-answer policy based on Proverbs 15:1: "A soft answer turns away wrath, but a harsh word stirs up anger." We fight the temptation to respond, "Dear Sir or Madam, an insane person has stolen your stationery (or hacked your email account). I thought you'd like to know." If a reader persists in making demands, a journalist may respond, "Dear Sir or Madam, you may be right"—and leave the reader to ponder what exactly "may" means.

Journalism that affects readers emphasizes specific detail. Abortion and ISIS stories upset readers, because if we're not upset we'll forget we live in a fallen world with lots of sin, and we won't remember how desperately we and the whole world need Christ. Christian journalists want to drive readers to prayer and action against evil. After all, the Bible very graphically at times describes killing, adultery, and even cannibalism, as God shows us man's depravity. On the other hand, we're not God. He infallibly knows when to show evil and when not to. We make mistakes. We don't want small children to see what they don't need to see until they're older.

The publishers of a central Texas Christian magazine called it *The Good News Journal*, but running only the good news suggests we think ourselves superior to God, who filled the Bible with bad news. Instead of pretending problems don't exist, biblical journalists report them and hope God will conquer wretchedness, in part through its exposure.

Photos are often worth a thousand complaints, sometimes because they show too much skin, sometimes because they display scarred skin. *World* has sometimes shown from a great distance—charred bodies in Fallujah, people jumping from the World Trade Center on 9/11—what we would not show close up. It's hard to have a hard-and-fast rule, because we are pulled one way by our goal of biblical objectivity and another way by the recognition that children look at magazines, particularly the pictures. We have sometimes shown small photos of a knife at the throat of a Middle Eastern man seconds from being decapitated, but we have not gone further.

Both publications and individuals can readily have conflicts of interest. American publications depend on advertising, which is better than depending on the leniency of a political dictator, but still has its pressures. At *World*, we do not allow "native advertising," the attempt to fool readers into thinking ads aren't ads, but lots of publications are heading that way. We try not to have editorial copy about a specific product or development in the same issue as advertisements for that product or development, since readers might think the two are linked. When a person tells a *World* reporter an ad will be forthcoming if we produce a favorable story, our reporters are trained to just say no.

Avoiding personal conflicts of interest is also important. Conscientious reporters do not profile their friends or relatives, or write about companies in which they have a financial interest. They try to avoid stories about start-up ministries that might seem like fund-raising efforts. They refrain from contributing to, or working for, political candidates, because they need to be free to criticize. Romantic involvements also demand that reporters recuse themselves from stories.

Aggressive reporting brings potential conflicts. At *World*, we will not lie to get a story, but we are not obliged to disclose everything. If we're covering a Planned Parenthood demonstration, and someone asks, a reporter can say "I'm from *World*"—without saying we're a pro-life publication. When we mix sight-seeing and reporting in a country that looks askance at independent journalists, we can do so on tourist visas. Reporters, though, do not have the right to break into offices, steal documents, hack computer files, or tap telephones.

For both biblical and business reasons, editors should almost always reply to readers' concerns with gentle answers that turn away wrath. A response should thank a reader, point out why a publication did what it did, and (if appropriate) pledge to attempt to improve. In the dozen years since starting with Gmail in 2007, I've sent 60,000 emails, and below are half a dozen typical exchanges. First comes the initial letter in italics, then the response in regular type, and then any further back-and-forth (with the same font pattern).

WHERE'S GOD?

I recently discovered your magazine, and was pleased to find a Christian publication that pursues investigative journalism. As I've browsed your site this evening, a question occurred to me—one I've wrestled with often of late. It is this: Is God himself actually doing anything in the world? If God were actually actively present, if he actually did some things that humans couldn't take credit for, Christianity would seem like something more than just another religion. Is God actually at work?

One factual answer to your question—Is God actually at work?—lies in six occurrences that have amazed me.

First, it is miraculous that during decades of Cold War we did not have a nuclear war. I'm not aware of any time in human history that a massively effective new weapon hasn't been used for such a long time—and we did come close to disaster many times.

Second, particularly after traveling during the past couple of years in the Baltics, Balkans, and Ukraine, I'm enormously impressed by the end of the Soviet empire from 1989 to 1991. None of the leading scholars predicted it. Ronald Reagan did, but that was at least semi-rhetorical. I had read in the Bible how God suddenly overturned powerful empires, but I'm impressed to see it with my own eyes.

Third, the spread of Christianity in China (a bit of which I've seen myself) may be a sign and wonder. If I were to see someone drop a brick on a bird so the bird is flattened, and later see that bird come to life and fly once again, I'd think of that as a miracle, so the resurrection in China seems like a sign and wonder.

Fourth, I've visited more than one hundred poverty-fighting ministries in the U.S. over the years, and the willingness of many individuals to sacrifice themselves to help others is another sign and wonder. They don't derive any evolutionary benefit from doing so, and seeing long-time addicts and others get a life never ceases to astonish me.

Fifth, I almost always read a book only once, but the Bible is different—I learn something every time I go to it, which makes me think it's a very special book, which makes me think that the very special things it describes are true.

The sixth is also personal. I was interviewing Lon Solomon, pastor of a Virginia church, earlier this month, and he described himself during his years around age 20 as a "sociopath." I could describe myself at that age in those terms as well. That he's now a decent person and so am I, more or less, also seems miraculous. Some people might describe that as maturing, but many people become more self-ish as they age. It's surprising that millions of miracles like Solomon and myself are walking around.

Thank you so much for taking the time to give a thoughtful reply to my inquiry. I really appreciate it. A casual perusal of articles about Christianity recently left me rather discouraged. It seemed like a lot of in-fighting takes place, and a lot of human effort, without a lot of divine presence or action. But he is present, and if we're not asking him to move, or giving him opportunity, what's wrong with us?

NEGATIVE MOVIE REVIEWS

I want to begin by saying that I appreciate World *and eagerly devour its contents every time it comes to my mailbox. However, my emotions boiled over as I was reading your recent unfavorable review of "Faith of Our Fathers" and its actors. My heart screamed, "What must a movie include to get a positive review from* World? *Sexual innuendo? Cursing? Graphic violence? Violations of the Third Commandment?"*

It bothers me that so many movies which include elements that pre-vent Philippians 4:8 Christians from going to see them are given great reviews (with a short disclaimer) by World, *while so many clean movies with no objectionable elements receive bad reviews. My heart also aches for the person who has to sit through the filthy movies to review them.*

Thanks for both your kind words and your thought-provoking negatives. Recently, we have given good reviews to the *In the Footsteps of Paul and Peter* documentaries and others. We want to hold movie-makers on our side to high standards, and we're glad to see some are getting better.

Regarding the negative elements, we have two kinds of readers and viewers: those who say any bad stuff mean "turn it off," and those who look for positives amid a very corrupt society. We value both kinds, and both have good arguments in their favor. We try to include warnings early in the reviews, but we cannot drop such reviews while serving many *World* members and trying not to abandon coverage of much of our culture.

You're right our reviewers have a hard task, but so do our reporters when murder and adultery stalk the world. I'll leave you with questions: Could Paul in Philippians have meant that we should never expose ourselves to objectionable elements? If so, how could he walk the streets of Athens where prostitutes and idols beckoned on every corner?

Thank you for responding to my letter to the editor. I have written several letters to the editor (to different periodicals), and you are the first one to ever write me back.

POSITIVE BOOK REVIEWS

In a recent issue of World, *you listed* The Book of Strange New Things *as the best sci-fi book of the year. So, thinking I could enjoy some summer reading I ordered and downloaded it on my Kindle. I was saddened that a Christian news magazine—one that is widely read and admired—would recommend a book containing graphic sexual content and an ample sprinkling of "f" words. Perhaps this reveals my lack of sophistication, but I still maintain, regardless of some spiritual content, that this was an unsuitable suggestion. Would be happy to hear your response.*

We have two kinds of readers—those who like powerful books so much they'll keep going even when there's a sex scene and some bad language, and those who as a matter of principle and taste say those elements ruin the whole book. I tend to be in the first camp, but I respect those in the second and think there are good theological arguments for both positions.

The other four members of our committee and I were impressed that a book with strong spiritual content regarding the excitement of encountering God's Word was coming from a fine writer (but an agnostic) and a distinguished secular publisher. Sadly, lots of lukewarm Christians are blasé about the Bible. Seeing it as the book of strange new things suggests the excitement of lots of people on this planet when they first hear the Good News. We need to be excited about it and to present it as exciting.

I made the mistake of reading the book early on and a few months later, when writing about it, forgetting about the elements you rightly found distasteful. I could say *The Book of Strange New Things* had a much smaller amount of that objectionable content than most other secular novels, but that's an inadequate defense. We always try to warn readers about books or movies we think have merit, but include some demerits, and it's my fault we didn't do so this time.

Thank you for your thoughtful reply with an attitude that exhibits Christian humility. I will only add that I kept reading the novel in spite of the "stuff," but was not challenged or encouraged by any of it. Did I miss something? Yes, the world is falling apart, and yes, the innocence and sincerity of the "aliens" is something we long to see, but now what? I am a faithful reader of World and appreciate reporting from a Christian perspective.

SEMI-POSITIVE PERSONAL APPRAISALS

How could you compliment Ray Lewis? You say his charitable works and his commitment to spend time with his children show repentance. Really? Many nonbelievers do and say the same things. John the Baptist told followers to "bring forth fruit in keeping with repentance." In the area of his serial immorality, I would like to see some of that fruit from repentance in regard to his sins against his lovers and their children before holding another philandering pro athlete up to the world as a Christian role model.

You're right: Lewis's charitable work and time spent with his children don't prove he's a Christian. Furthermore, since one of his children is 11, that shows he continued to have sex outside of marriage after the killings that occurred 13 years ago, at which point he declared himself to be a changed man with a strong relationship to Christ.

So you're right: He should not be held up to the world as a Christian role model. He's clearly not—but he professes faith in Christ, so we shouldn't assume he's not. His positive deeds show he has improved, but he is still a sinner. Of course, so am I, and so is every reader of *World*. God has justified us, but he's still in the process of sanctifying us, a process that won't be finished until heaven.

I want to be in the middle ground regarding Ray Lewis: Not seeing him as a role model, not seeing him as a villain, seeing him as a person who professes faith in Christ and on whom God is working. I probably could have communicated this more clearly, so thanks again for your emails.

Thank you for your personal response to my letter. I want you to know that I highly value the work World *Magazine is doing. It is the only magazine I "religiously" read cover to cover. I have purchased subscriptions for our pastors and others.*

MISTAKEN IMPRESSION

My husband and I have been longtime subscribers, devourers and proponents of World. *We've influenced many people to subscribe to* World, *quoting it in countless conversations and letters, and we have prayed for its success. We're grateful to God for the impact it's had on our lives. I recognized early-on that* World's *theology is Calvinist, and I am an evangelical Christian with free-will leanings. For many years I felt that* World *and I shared a Love that united us fully, and my respect for* World *kept me reading and learning. In this issue, I was stopped cold by the promotion, on page 39, of William Barclay's book* The Secret of Contentment. *I confess that I don't know the content of this book, but I do know that William Barclay did not embrace the humanity of Jesus Christ, which troubles me very much.*

Thanks for reading and supporting *World* over the years. Your being "stopped cold" by the promotion of William Barclay's book surprised me, because P&R Publishing has a reputation of putting out only biblically orthodox books. Might you be confusing the author of the book, William B. Barcley, with the heterodox William Barclay? Barcley with an "e" is a professor at Gordon-Conwell Theological Seminary and the author of some thoughtful commentaries; Barclay with an "a" was a universalist at the University of Glasgow.

My complaint about William Barclay—what can I say: Embarrassment and shame are such miserable feelings! It was idiotic of me to make a rash judgment without even noticing the spelling of the author's name—and you were generous to upend me with a polite question. I offer my sincere apology. I admit my overall feelings toward Calvinism are raw (some painful encounters) and produce a hyper-vigilance in me, which results in erroneous judgments some of the time. I could go on, but suffice it to say that if you had not extended grace by writing to me, I wouldn't have the opportunity to make amends. Please forgive me.

Thank you for your lovely reply. Of course I forgive you, because by your letter and your continued reading of *World* I take it you've forgiven me for my many goofs. The confusion about William Barclay is certainly understandable; I would only have been concerned had you mixed him up with William F. Buckley.

SMALL MISTAKES

I am thankful for World *magazine. I especially enjoy the book reviews, the articles about successful ministries, the Daniel of the Year awards, and the different interviews at Patrick Henry. I am not looking to get a letter published, I just wanted to point out a misuse of a word that is very common, but still irritating. In your December 8, 2018, issue on the Quick Takes page under "The Final Chapter," the author used the phrase "close proximity." Please, no! Proximity means closeness, so the author basically said 'close closeness.' I believe it would have been more correct to say ". . . who had been living in proximity for four years. . ." Thanks for considering this!*

I checked the offending sentence: "According to a spokesman for Russia's Arctic and Antarctic Research Institute, the relationship between the two scientists who had been living in close proximity for four years had soured." You are correct, and not just correct, but absolutely, completely, totally correct, and not only that, but without any mistake.

Thanks for pointing this out. Writing "close proximity" is similar to giving a restaurant the name humorist Calvin Trillin preferred: La Maison de la Casa House.

I am delightedly happy, pleased, and very glad you found my suggestion helpful!

On a more serious note, I would like to thank you again for what you are doing through World *magazine. In a day of compartmentalization (this is me at work, this is a different me at church, and this is a different me on Facebook), it is helpful to have someone looking at current events through the lens of faith, to remind us all that life is to be viewed through what's true about God and his Word. There are many wonderful churches, many wonderful books about faith and theology, many wonderful books about science and faith even, but very few resources offering what your magazine offers. I have been encouraged by your stories about people living out their faith in practical, often difficult circumstances. I have been challenged by some of your articles that examine deeply held, but not necessarily well thought-out opinions. I have been thankful to find out about events I might not otherwise have known about, or been able to hear about from a different point of view than the secular media offers. And I have been very blessed by some of the books that you have recommended. So, thank you, and keep up the good work!*

Thank you. You've summarized elegantly what we hope to accomplish.

KEY TERMS

native advertising

STUDY QUESTIONS

1. How should journalists respond to complaints?
2. What's the problem with running only good news?
3. Why should Christian reviewers be willing to criticize Christian films?

PART 3

PROGRESS
AND REGRESS

21

The Official Story and the
Protestant Reformation

WE LOOKED IN chapter 1 at some of China's long journalistic history, and there's more in the appendix. Since my own background is in Western journalism and particularly that of the United States, I'd like to draw out some lessons from different eras of Western and American journalistic history.

The story of Western journalism shows how Christians can win freedom of the press and also lose it. This history instructs American journalists who stand on the shoulders of their predecessors in European and early American history. It also instructs Christian journalists in China who can see how their counterparts on the other side of the world sometimes persevered in the face of pressure and sometimes faltered. In every situation, faith in Christ makes a huge difference, even when—especially when—rulers try to suppress it.

Americans still expect journalists to have some independence from government and other leading power centers. We are not surprised to glance at the morning newspaper or television news show and see exposure of wrongdoing. We assume the press has a responsibility to print bad news as well as good. Many Chinese Christian journalists hope to have that freedom as well. What all of us should understand is that such freedom is unusual in the history of the world, and attaining and preserving it is not easy.

How did the unnatural act of independent journalism come to be seen as something within reach? As noted in chapter 1, China had the first newspapers—in the eighth century—but centuries before that, in ancient Rome, came *Acta Diurna*, a handwritten news sheet posted in the Roman Forum and copied by scribes for transmission throughout the empire. *Acta* emphasized governmental decrees, but also gained readership by posting gladiatorial results and news of other popular events.

Acta Diurna set the pattern followed in many lands for centuries. It promoted an official story of government power and wisdom, conveying a simple message: "If you obey, we will take care of you." (A more modern way of saying the same might be, "Depend on us to establish the proper environment for your life.") Official, state-allied religion often received protection also. Published news was what authorities wanted people to know.

Julius Caesar used the *Acta* to attack some of his opponents in the Roman senate, but they could not criticize him or his successors. (Had independent journalism existed in Rome, Caesar might have faced only character assassination on the Ides of March, the day Brutus and other senators knifed him.) Other handwritten publications also emerged during ancient and medieval times. They transmitted news that state or state church authorities wanted leading citizens to know. Sometimes ballads and poems that mocked the official news vehicles passed on orally from person to person, but the official version, with support from the state church, endured from generation to generation.

In Western Europe, kings with support from the Catholic Church were said to rule by divine right, and the official story was the only story allowed. Leaders might acknowledge a different story prevailed in heaven—there, God was sovereign and biblical principles were practiced—but only those who went away to monasteries or nunneries might be able to see God's will being done on earth as in heaven.

This dualistic sense of spiritual and temporal realms removed from each other grew not only in journalism but in artwork and other cultural realms as well. The Bible itself was removed from daily life and available only to the elite who knew Latin; Pope Innocent

IV in 1252 forbade translating the Bible into vernacular languages. In 1275, in a tiny and relatively barbaric part of the world known as England, the statute of Westminster I outlawed "tales whereby discord or occasion of discord or slander may grow between the king and his people or the great men of the realm."

Officials also banned from common use any book that could inspire such discord—including the Bible, which stated laws of God under which every man and woman, whether king or commoner, should live. After Oxford professor John Wycliffe translated the Bible into English during the late fourteenth century, a church synod forbade Scripture translation. Officials burned Wycliffe's books in 1410 and 1412. They dug up and burned his bones in 1428.

The technological opportunity for a big change came around 1450, with the development of movable type in the Mainz workshop of goldsmith and printer Johannes Gutenberg. Innovation creates possibility. Worldviews determine whether, and how quickly, people use inventions. Demand from monasteries, kings, and commercial leaders for big Latin Bibles was growing, and at first printed volumes merely met that demand. The Bibles were often to show off, rather than read. Printing created potential for change, but as long as priests discouraged Bible reading, and governments jailed or killed independent printers, journalism dependent on God, but independent from state (or state church) pressures, had little opportunity to flourish.

Early post-Gutenberg developments in England showed the limited effect of the technological revolution by itself. Printing began there in 1476, but printers were careful to avoid publishing works that might irritate king or prelates. Regulations limited the number of printers and apprentices. Royal patents created printing monopolies. Officials prohibited importation, printing, and distribution of threatening books, such as English translations of the Bible.

English policies were like those of other countries in the early 1500s, but then came the providential sound of a hammer on a door, and the beginning of a theological onslaught (aided by journalistic means) that changed Europe. Martin Luther was a German theology professor and Roman Catholic priest who in 1517 opposed Catholic belief that many who died went to purgatory for a long time that could be shortened if the deceased's friends or relatives gave money to the church. According to tradition, he nailed to a church door his "Ninety-five Theses" of protest.

Over the next few years, Luther expanded his critique of Catholicism and emphasized how Christ's finished work, not our works, save us: "The just shall live by faith." Scholars have described the effect of Martin Luther's theses and his subsequent publications, but many have missed an important aspect of the situation: Luther's primary impact was not as a producer of treatises, but as a popular writer of vigorous prose that concerned not only theological issues, but their social and political ramifications. Between 1517 and 1530, Luther's thirty publications probably sold well over 300,000 copies, an astounding total at a time when illiteracy was rampant and printing was still in its infancy.

Luther and other Reformation leaders emphasized the importance of reading the Bible. Christians were to find out for themselves what God was saying. Literacy rates began to skyrocket everywhere the Reformation took root, while remaining low wherever it was fought off. Luther not only praised the translation of the Bible into vernacular languages, but also made a masterful one himself. In preparing his German translation, Luther so understood the need for specific detail to glorify God and attract readers that when he wanted to picture the precious stones and coins mentioned in the Bible, he first examined German court jewels and numismatic collections. Similarly, when Luther needed to describe Old Testament sacrifices, he visited slaughterhouses and gained information from butchers.

Furthermore, Luther understood it was important to present bad news as well as good. Luther's Reformed theological understanding led him to write:

> God's favor is so communicated in the form of wrath that it seems farthest when it is at hand. Man must first cry out that there is no health in him. He must be consumed with horror. . . . In this disturbance salvation begins. When a man believes himself to be utterly lost, light breaks. Peace comes in the word of Christ through faith.

Reformation leaders believed people would seek the good news only after they became fully aware of bad news. Man needs to become aware of his own corruption in order to change through God's grace. A reporter who makes readers aware of sin does them a service.

Freedom of the press remained nonexistent for a while in England. In 1534, a "Proclamation for Seditious Books" ordered that no one should print any English book without a license from the king's councils or those persons appointed by the king as licensers. The "Proclamation of 1538" left the press with only one master: the king. The British Parliament in 1542–43 ordered: "Nothing shall be taught or maintained contrary to the King's instructions." The law forbade

> annotations or preambles in Bibles or New Testaments in English. The Bible shall not be read in English in any church. No women or artificers, prentices, journeymen, servingmen of the degree of yeomen or under, husbandmen, nor laborers, shall read the New Testament in English.

Under Reformed doctrine, journalists for the first time could be more than purveyors of public relations. They had their own independent authority and could appeal to biblical principle when officials tried to shackle them. The Reformers believed the Bible was clear enough on most matters for ordinary individuals to read it themselves and see its truths for themselves. Some government officials, though, believed opponents of the king who did not recant should be burned at the stake.

During the reign of Queen Mary Tudor, "Bloody Mary," from 1553 to 1558, the British government confronted those who based their lives on *sola scriptura* (the Bible only). One of the first Protestants to go to the stake was John Hooper, who was publicly burned at Gloucester on February 9, 1555. Burned as heretics that year were about seventy-five men and women—and many more during the following two years. Soon reports of those burnings spread illegally throughout England. Ballads and other publications—one was called *Sacke full of Newes*—attacked the queen and praised the heroism of the martyrs.

The sixteenth-century journalist who made the greatest impression on several generations of English men and women originally had no desire to report on current events. John Foxe, born in 1516, was an excellent student. He was a fellow at Oxford, but became Reformed and had to give up his stipend if he wanted to go beyond doing public relations for the king. In 1548, Foxe began writing a scholarly history of Christian martyrdom. It turned journalistic in 1553, when Mary became queen. Facing death in 1554, Foxe left England and began earning a poor living as a proofreader with a Swiss printer, but he continued to research past persecutions and learn about current ones.

Foxe published two volumes in Latin during the 1550s, but switched to English for his journalistic output, with the goal of telling the martyrs' stories in a readable manner. He returned to England in 1558 after Mary died and Elizabeth became queen. He then spent five more years interviewing, collecting materials, and writing, before publishing the sensational account that became known as *Foxe's Book of Martyrs*. To make sure everything was accurate, he worked seven years more before putting out in 1570 an expanded, second edition that contained woodcuts portraying burnings and whippings. Later, large-scale editions increased the number of illustrations.

Foxe vividly described how pastor John Hooper, tied to a stake, prayed as I recounted in the introduction. Here's one detail more: Foxe wrote that "when he was black in the mouth, and his tongue swollen, that he could not speak, yet his lips went till they were shrunk to the gums." Finally, one of Hooper's arms fell off, and the other, with "fat, water, and blood" dripping out at the ends of the fingers, stuck to what remained of his chest. Foxe was not afraid to employ biblical sensationalism, and one result was that his book was the third most likely to be found in American colonial homes in the eighteenth century, after the Bible and *Pilgrim's Progress*.

Foxe also described the deaths of two other Protestants, Hugh Latimer and Nicholas Ridley. Ridley, chained over another of those slow-burning fires, was in agony, but Latimer seemed to be dying with amazing ease—Foxe wrote he appeared to be bathing his hands and face in the fire. Latimer's last words to his suffering friend were

"Be of good comfort, Master Ridley, [so that] we shall this day light such a candle, by God's grace, in England, as I trust shall never be put out."

Foxe used colorful, Bible-based imagery. For example, his report on the impending death of John Hooper described how light overcame darkness as officers led Hooper through London to Newgate prison. They

> ordered all candles along the way be put out; perhaps, being burdened with an evil conscience, they thought darkness to be a most fit season for such a business. But notwithstanding this device, the people having some foreknowledge of his coming, many of them came forth of their doors with lights, and saluted him; praising God for his constancy in the true doctrine which he had taught them.

Writers such as Miles Coverdale maintained Foxe's stress on accuracy. Coverdale wrote in 1564, "It doth us good to read and heare, not the lying legendes . . . triflyng toyes & forged fables of corrupted writers: but such true, holy . . . epistles & letters, as do set forth unto us ye blessed behaviour of gods deare servantes." For a time, it appeared that a free press, with careful fact-checking, might arise, but Queen Elizabeth, while allowing direct criticism of her predecessor, Mary, cracked down on anyone who objected to her reign or to the domination of the established Anglican religion. She offered a reward to those who informed against anyone writing or dispersing books opposed to herself or the nobles.

Brave Puritans—the Protestants most determined to follow the Bible—persevered. After *An Admonition to Parliament*, a sixty-page attack on state churches, appeared, its authors spent a year in prison. John Stubbes wrote a pamphlet in 1579 respectfully criticizing Queen Elizabeth. The government punished him by cutting off his right hand. A contemporary account described his amazing response: "John Stubbes, so soone as his right hand was off, put off his hat with the left, and cryed aloud, God save the Queene." Stubbes, under such duress, set the pattern of respecting those in authority over us, while exposing their unbiblical actions.

In 1588 and 1589, John Hodgkins published tracts that humorously satirized and ridiculed the heavy-handed theological treatises put out by defenders of the state-approved church. He repeatedly dismantled his printing press and moved it around on a cart. Hodgkins escaped harm until he was unloading his press one day before curious onlookers. A few small pieces of metal type fell from one of the boxes. A bystander picked up a letter and showed it to an official, who understood the significance of the discovery and summoned constables. Arrested and repeatedly tortured, Hodgkins refused to admit guilt and implicate others.

The bravery of Hodgkins, like that of Martin Luther, John Hooper, John Stubbes, and many others, had an effect. Persecution of the Puritans, instead of stamping them out, led to new conversions. When James I became king of England in 1603 and Puritans presented petitions for religious and press freedom, he threatened to "harry them out of the land, or else do worse." James, arguing he was "above the law by his absolute power," and that "it is presumptuous and high contempt in a subject to dispute what a king can do, or say that a king cannot do this or that," advised subjects to "rest in that which is the king's revealed word in his law." But that is something Puritan writers, committed as they were to following God's law whatever the cost, would not do.

KEY TERMS

Protestant Reformation
sola scriptura
divine right

STUDY QUESTIONS

1. Why is independent journalism an unnatural act?
2. What impact does technology have on journalism?
3. How was Martin Luther a pioneer of theology and journalism?
4. Why was Reformation understanding crucial in changing journalism?

FOR FURTHER READING

I researched most of the history in this and succeeding chapters through original research into primary documents housed at the Library of Congress and the University of Texas at Austin. Full footnotes are in my *Central Ideas in the Development of American Journalism* (Erlbaum, 1990).

Mitchell Stephens, *A History of News* (Viking Penguin, 1988).
Herman Selderhuis, *Martin Luther* (Crossway, 2017).
Andrew Pettigrew, *Brand Luther* (Penguin, 2015).
John Foxe, *Foxe's Book of Martyrs* (many editions).

22

Revolution and Counterrevolution

EARLY IN THE seventeenth century, the Reformation strongholds of Amsterdam and Augsburg were the centers of journalistic publishing. The first European newspapers emerged in those cities in 1607 and 1609, and printed information on a weekly schedule. By 1620, Amsterdam, known for its Reformed emphasis on literacy and liberty, was the refuge for printers emigrating from France, Italy, England, and other countries. In that year, the first newspapers ever printed in English and French came out—in Amsterdam.

In 1621, another Amsterdam publisher started exporting his English-language newspapers to England, and the king's agents now had to track down bundles of newspapers, not just destroy printing presses. The British government, under pressure, tried to co-opt the opposition by allowing licensed publication of a domestic newspaper, *Mercurius Britannicus*, and some political pamphlets during the 1620s. Criticism of governmental foreign policy became a sore point, however, and King James I struck back at his press opponents, issuing edicts decrying "the great liberty of discourse concerning matters of state." He imprisoned printer Thomas Archer, but the doctrines of those who became known as Puritans—for they were willing to risk their lives in attempts to glorify God by purifying churches filled with centuries of rust—won increasing acceptance, particularly in English towns.

When Alexander Leighton, a Puritan critic of King Charles I, published a pamphlet in 1630 titled *An Appeal to Parliament*, Charles and his court were outraged. Leighton insisted that Scripture was above everyone, including kings, so that subjects could remain loyal while evaluating their rulers against biblical standards. Leighton said his goal was to correct existing problems "for the honor of the king, the quiet of the people, and the peace of the church." The British government saw it differently and termed Leighton's work "seditious and scandalous." On November 16, 1630, officials whipped Leighton, cut off one of his ears, slit his nose, and branded one side of his face. One week later they did the same on the other side.

The penalty did not stop other Puritans. Government officials arrested John Bastwick, Henry Burton, and William Prynne in 1637 and charged them with seditious libel for writing pamphlets that criticized royal actions. They sentenced each man to "perpetual imprisonment" without access to writing materials, and planned to cut off their ears. The royal authorities, believing they had the populace on their side, proclaimed a public holiday that would have as its highlight the public mutilations. But when the three men were allowed to make public statements (according to the custom of the day) as the officials waited with knives, the crowd cheered them. Nevertheless, the maimed trio went back to prison, until the political tides turned. In 1640, Parliament, as part of its stand against King Charles, ordered the prisoners released.

The Puritan-dominated Parliament in 1641 abolished the torture-prone Star Chamber. Soon more newspapers appeared. Puritan Samuel Pecke published weekly *A Perfect Diurnall*, and introduced it with these words: "You may henceforth expect from this relator to be informed only of such things as are of credit." As the battle between Parliament and the Royalists turned into a civil war, Pecke—although clearly a Puritan partisan—truthfully reported Royalist military victories and twice covered wrongful conduct by Parliamentary soldiers. He also gave opponents space to express their views. When Parliament executed archbishop Laud for murder, Pecke included a transcript of his scaffold speech.

Similarly, when John Dillingham began his newspaper *The*

Parliament Scout in 1643, he pledged "to tell the truth" and not to "vapor and say such a one was routed" when no battle had occurred. Dillingham wrote about plundering by soldiers, the bravery of some captured Royalists, and the need for better medical treatment of the wounded on both sides. Partisanship and fairness could go together because Puritan editors believed God would judge them for lying, even if their supporters cheered.

By 1644, London, a city with half a million residents, had a dozen weekly newspapers. This was more journalistic variety on a regular basis than had ever before existed. Some Puritan leaders did not like criticism any more than the king's officials did, but most were committed to the idea of biblical rather than personal authority, and of letting individuals read for themselves. One Puritan leader and friend of John Milton, Samuel Hartlib, reflected general hopes when he predicted in 1641 that "the art of Printing will so spread knowledge that the common people, knowing their own rights and liberties, will not be governed by way of oppression."

Parliament in 1643 did pass a law that restricted the sale of pamphlets and news books, but it received little enforcement and much criticism. Puritan pamphleteer William Walwyn noted licensing might restrict some evil publications, but would also "stop the mouths of good men, who must either not write at all, or no more than is suitable to the judgments or interests of the Licensers." Another Puritan, Henry Robinson, proposed theological and political combat should "be fought out upon even ground, on equal terms," and "neither side must expect to have greater liberty of speech, writing, Printing, or whatsoever else, than the other."

John Milton himself penned the most famous response to the new law. Licensing, he wrote, brought back memories of "tyrannous inquisition" and was inconsistent with the "mild, free and human government" that the Puritans said they would provide. Milton's most famous words in his *Areopagetica* were,

> Though all the winds of doctrine were let loose to play upon the earth, so truth be in the field, we do injuriously by licensing and prohibiting to misdoubt her strength. Let her and falsehood

grapple; who ever knew truth put to the worse, in a free and open encounter.

Milton had faith in God's invisible hand over journalism. He asked,

> For who knows not that truth is strong, next to the Almighty? She needs no policies, nor stratagems, nor licensings to make victorious; those are shifts and the defenses that error uses against her power.

The greatest journalistic talent of seventeenth-century England emerged during this mid-1640s period of relative freedom. Marchamont Nedham tried to walk the tightrope of reformation without revolution. Nedham, born in 1620 in a small town near Oxford, studied Greek, Latin, and history as a child, received a bachelor's degree from Oxford University in 1637, and spent the next six years as a schoolteacher, law clerk, and dabbler in medicine.

During those six years, Nedham underwent a theological and political transformation that led him to side with the Puritans. Nedham's writing was sensational and colorful; rather than staying high on the ladder of abstraction, he provided specific detail about the vices of Royalists. Lord Ratcliffe, for example, was "bathing in luxury, and swimming in the fat of the land, and cramming his Hens and Capons with Almonds and Raisins." Lord Porter was "that Exchequer of Flesh, which hath a whole Subsidy in his small guts and his paunch, and hath bestowed the assessments and taxes of the State in sauces."

Nedham saw himself turning darkness into light by exposing corruption. In describing his journalistic accomplishments, Nedham wrote he had "by an excellent and powerful Providence led the people through the labyrinths of the enemy's plots." He had also shown that

> the King could not keep an evil Councelor, but I must need speak of him. The Queen could not bring in Popery, but I must need tell all the world of it. . . . I undisguised the Declarations, and Protestations, and Masqueries of the Court.

Exposure was his goal. He wanted to take off the "veils and disguises which the scribes and pharisees at Oxford had put upon a treasonable and popish Cause." He enjoyed his effectiveness: "I have served a Parliament and Reformation hitherto in unmaking and unhooding incendiaries of all sorts. . . . Everyone can point out the evil counselors now." But in a question-and-answer note at the end of each issue of *Mercurius Britannicus*, Nedham regularly cautioned against arrogance. When asked, "What are we to do or expect now in this time when our forces are so considerable?" Nedham answered, "Not to trust nor look too much upon them, but through them to a Divine power, lest we suffer as we did before."

Nedham criticized the Royalist newspaper editor John Birkenhead for becoming a propagandist:

> Oh! what Prodigious Service hath he done, he could tell of battles and victories, when there was not so much as an alarm or skirmish, he could change . . . Squadrons and Troops into Regiments and Brigades, he could rally routed Armies and put them into a better condition when they were beaten than before.

Nedham saw his calling as one of truth-telling, rather than promoting allegiance to a certain set of leaders. In 1645, Nedham made it clear to his readers that Parliament did not tell him what to write. He also disobeyed a Parliamentary request that he delete a hard-hitting passage, and received only a reprimand.

Sadly, but typically in revolutionary circumstances, some Puritan leaders gained great power and decided they were above criticism. In 1646, when Nedham criticized Parliament, one writer attacked his "sullen and dogged wit" and suggested "his hands and feet be as sacrifices cut off, and hung up, to pay for the treasons of his tongue." Officials spared Nedham's limbs, but jailed him for twelve days and released him only on condition he do no more newspaper editing.

Nedham abided by his "no editing" pledge, but continued to write. At a time when both Anglicans and Puritan Presbyterians opposed independent churches, Nedham made himself unpopular with both sides by writing a pamphlet that warned those who would not tolerate independent churches, "Take heed therefore lest while ye rail against new lights ye work despite to the Spirit of God." Nedham attacked "compulsive power" in religion, but compulsion increased as tensions between Parliament and General Oliver Cromwell's New Model Army grew.

The Army, with hands and guns and support from those members of Parliament who were disposed to use force rather than reason, ended up on top. Cromwell increasingly seemed determined to brook no opposition. As the Puritan revolutionaries took control, they set up a Committee on Examinations to demolish the presses and imprison press owners found to be part of the opposition. In 1648, officials arrested many pamphleteers, and in 1649 they required every printer to agree not to print anything offensive to the government or pay a huge fine.

Some Puritans, criticizing this tightening, urged the granting of liberty to the press, and pointedly told military leaders that if

> you and your army shall be pleased to look back a little upon affairs you will find you have been very much strengthened all along by unlicensed printing. . . . The liberty [of the press] . . . appears so essential unto Freedom, as that without it, it's impossible to preserve any nation from being liable to the worst of bondage.

Puritan theologian John Owen wrote it is better to have 500 errors scattered among individuals than to have one error gain power over all.

Nedham saw Oliver Cromwell's autocratic rule coming and opposed it. Calling him "King Cromwell," Needham knew dictatorship led to more bloodshed. He noted sardonically, "Tis a godly thing states to reform by murder." Reflecting on how good intentions can lead to sad results, Nedham exclaimed, "Good God, what a wild thing is Rebellion." As the Puritan reforming zeal turned to revolutionary lust for power, Nedham week after week in *Mercurius Pragmaticus* showed the degradation of the movement: "See how Wealth / Is made their Heaven! They swell / With Pride! and live by Blood and Stealth, / As if there were no Hell."

Meanwhile, poverty dominated the countryside, and there "the citizens (like silly sheep) / must fast, and be content." Civil war, Nedham feared, was bringing out the worst in men:

> Faith and religion bleeding lie, / And liberty grows faint: / No Gospel, but pure treachery, / And treason make the saint. . . . Away with justice, laws and fear; / When men resolve to rise, / Brave souls must scorn all scruples where / A kingdom is the prize.

He decried the movement "to a Military government" that would lead to "the utter subversion of our Law . . . and the enslaving of the kingdom."

When the revolutionaries expelled most members of Parliament and executed King Charles, Nedham went into hiding, but published an underground edition of *Mercurius Pragmaticus* that said they "with fresh flames of Zeal grow wild / The State's grown fat with orphans tears, / While widows pine and moan; / And tender conscience in seven years, / Is turned to a heart of stone." Nedham attacked those who "Boast when Royal Blood is spilt, / They'll all be Kings themselves." When the revolutionary leaders celebrated victory with a parade and feast on June 7, Nedham wrote "their paunches out were spread, / While thousands starve for want of bread . . . / Tyrants feast with joy."

Officials captured Nedham, sent him to prison for several months, threatened him with execution, and then offered a deal: become a government propagandist, and live. Nedham signed an oath of allegiance to the revolution and wrote a 100-page pamphlet titled *The Equity, Utility, and Necessity, of a Submission to the present Government.* He wrote that anyone who disobeyed the new government, regardless of "allegiances, oaths, and covenants" formerly entered into, was "peevish, and a man obstinate against the reason and custom of the whole world."

English public opinion eventually turned against the regime. One honest Puritan, Denzil Holles, complained "the meanest of men, the basest and vilest of the nation, the lowest of the people, have got the power into their hands." When Oliver Cromwell died in 1658, some of the generals began to grease the slide on which the slain king's son, Charles II, could return—but Nedham, instead of joining the plotters, warned readers hopes of a peaceful, constitutional monarchy were foolish, because Charles II would be vindictive. Now the Royalists were angry with him again, and Nedham fled to Holland.

Charles II executed many of those who had signed the death warrant for his father, and even hanged (by what was left of their necks) the decaying corpses of Cromwell and two other leaders. He allowed Nedham to come back and stay out of prison on the condition he stay out of journalism. Nedham agreed, and for the rest of his life concentrated on the practice of medicine. He was an amateur in it, but—given the limited knowledge of medicine at that time—probably did no more damage than others. Few people noted Nedham's death in 1678, at the age of fifty-eight.

In 1662, the new, Royalist-dominated Parliament passed a bill enacting a new, stringent censorship system. No more, said Parliament, would "evil disposed persons [sell] heretical, schismatical, blasphemous, seditious and treasonable books, pamphlets and papers . . . endangering the peace of these kingdoms, and raising a disaffection to his most excellent Majesty and his government." Officials in 1663 convicted John Twyn of sedition because he printed a book arguing citizens should call to account a king whose decrees violated biblical law. After Twyn refused to provide the name of the book's author, officials cut off his "privy-members" before his eyes. They then beheaded him and cut his body into four pieces. Each was nailed to a different gate of the city as a warning to other printers or writers.

Independent churches also suffered. In 1664, the First Conventicle Act made it illegal for five or more people not of the same household to meet together for worship except in accordance with the government-approved Anglican liturgy. In 1665, the Five Mile Act forbade ministers ejected from their churches to come within five miles of any place where they had ministered, unless they would swear never to attempt "any alteration of government either in Church or State." In 1670, the Second Conventicle Act imposed heavier penalties on preachers or others who defied the law. Seizure and sale of Dissenters' goods was authorized, with one-third of the revenue gained paid to informers.

After three decades of revolution and counterrevolution, independent journalists and worshipers in England were worse off than they had been before the tumult started. Some sought greater freedom in the British colonies hugging the Atlantic coast 3,000 miles to the west, but problems also emerged there. One critic of government in the colony of Maryland in 1666 received thirty-nine lashes across his back. Five years later in the neighboring British colony of Virginia, Governor William Berkeley said he was glad Virginia had neither a college nor printing presses, "for learning has brought disobedience, and heresy, and sects into the world, and printing has divulged them, and libels against the best government."'

Berkeley was typical in his desire to stifle any who dared to criticize officials. Anyone who called the governor a lawbreaker received a heavy fine. When a printing press finally arrived, Virginia officials carefully regulated its use. One printer received a reprimand and fine in 1682 merely for printing the colony's laws without official permission. Every few years—1685, 1690, 1693, 1699, 1702, and 1704—proclamations condemned the "licentiousness of the People in their discourses." In 1689, the Protestant Association, a Maryland group, complained the government had punished "Words and Actions" it disapproved of by "Whipping, Branding, Boreing through the Tongue, Fine, Imprisonment, Banishment, or Death."

Puritans in the northern colony of Massachusetts, though, emphasized publication and education. In 1636, just six years after their arrival in a wilderness where mere survival was not assured, they had set up Harvard College and a printing press. Creation of the college challenged royal authority. In England, the universities at Oxford and Cambridge were arms of the government, which had a monopoly on the granting of college diplomas. Harvard in Massachusetts, though, awarded its first diplomas in 1642, without royal authorization—and it was in Massachusetts that the official story began receiving severe challenges.

KEY TERMS

licensing
English Civil War

STUDY QUESTIONS

1. Why did the early English newspapers so often have Mercurius in their titles?
2. Discuss Milton's famous statement: "Though all the winds of doctrine were let loose to play upon the earth, so truth be in the field, we do injuriously by licensing and prohibiting to misdoubt her strength. Let her and falsehood grapple; who ever knew truth put to the worse, in a free and open encounter." Was he right?

FOR FURTHER READING

John Milton, *Aeropagetica* (many editions).
Frederick Siebert, *Freedom of the Press in England, 1476–1776* (University of Illinois Press, 1965).

23

A Moderate Revolution That Lasts

MASSACHUSETTS OFFICIALS, with their Puritan under-standings, began to encourage the reporting of bad news because they saw such accounts as reminders from God. For example, in 1674 pastor Samuel Danforth described a crime following by a hanging, and noted that

> God's end in inflicting remarkable judgments upon some, is for caution and warning to all others. . . . Behold now the execution of vengeance upon this lewd and wicked youth, whom God hath hanged up before the Sun, and made a sign and example, and instruction and admonishment, to all New England.

Puritan pastors preached twice on Sunday and once at midweek services, generally for at least an hour. They emphasized biblical exegesis, but also preached what we could call "news sermons" on royal births and deaths, military defeats or victories, election results and government decisions, and crimes (preferably with punishments). Printers moved naturally from the publication of Bible commentaries to the publication of theological treatises and sermons, to the publication of news sermons and pamphlets on current events.

Many seventeenth-century New England publications were

event-oriented. Puritan theology not only allowed but emphasized the reporting of bad news, for the coming of well-deserved calamities was a sign that God still reigned. The best-known Massachusetts minister of the late seventeenth century, Increase Mather, also became its leading journalist. Mather argued in 1674 that God was not pleased with the sins of pride and envy that were common in New England, and that "a day of trouble is at hand."

Mather's forecasts of general disaster hit home in 1675 and 1676, when Indians destroyed twelve towns and killed one in every sixteen colonists of fighting age. A published ballad contextualized the news and offered an explanation: "O New-England, I understand / with thee God is offended: / And therefore He doth humble thee, / till thy ways hast mended." For the Puritans, the war was an exceptionally clear example of judgment upon sinful people, and many ministers and/or writers spoke or wrote about it. Mather's *Brief History of the War with the Indians of New-England* was filled with dispatches like this one:

> March 17. This day the Indians fell upon Warwick, and burnt it down to the ground, all but one house. May 11. A company of Indians assaulted the Town of Plymouth, burnt eleven Houses and five Barns therein.

Like other Puritan journalists, Mather was careful to juxtapose evidence of God's anger with dramatic news of God's mercy. When one house was about to be set on fire by hundreds of Indians who surrounded it, it appeared

> Men and Women and Children must have perished, either by unmerciful flames, or more unmerciful hands of wicked Men whose tender Mercies are cruelties, so that all hope that they should be saved was then taken in: but behold in this Joint of Difficulty and Extremity the Lord is seen. For in the very nick of opportunity God sent that worthy Major Willard, who with 48 men set upon the Indians and caused them to turn their backs. . . . However we may be diminished and brought low through Oppression,

Affliction, and Sorrow, yet our God will have compassion on us, and this his People shall not utterly perish.

Mather reported on man's heroism, but emphasized God's grace. He reported that when New Englanders recognized their reliance on that grace and renewed their covenant with God, the war ended. Mather emphasized the importance of accurate reporting—"a brief, plain, and true story"—in understanding the why of the war: God was punishing prideful colonists. He also offered hope: God's "design, in bringing the Calamity upon us, is not to destroy us, but to humble us, and reform us, and to do us good in the latter end."

The next step for American journalism came in 1681, when a general meeting of the Massachusetts ministers urged careful coverage of "Illustrious Providences, including Divine Judgements, Tempests, Floods, Earth-quakes, Thunders as are unusual, Strange Apparitions, or what ever else shall happen that is Prodigious." Here was a definition of news not unlike today's in its emphasis on atypical events—except that the why was different, since for the Puritans all unusual occurrences showed a glimpse of God's usually invisible hand.

Mather also wanted each minister to be a correspondent, with the responsibility to "diligently enquire into, and Record such Illustrious Providences as have happened, or from time to time shall happen, in the places whereunto they do belong." Second, to avoid the supplanting of fact by fiction, he wanted pastors to rely on eyewitnesses and make sure "that the Witnesses of such notable Occurrences be likewise set down in Writing." Third, it would be important to find a main writer-editor who "hath Leisure and ability for the management of such an undertaking." Mather would not report about an event unless a reliable source made a written, signed statement. After noting one extraordinary occurrence, he remarked, "I would not have mentioned this relation, had I not received it from serious, faithful, and judicious hands."

Mather and others thought accuracy was important because they saw events as their report cards signed by God. They wanted to know where they stood, for better or for worse. Mather wrote about political events, but also about storms, earthquakes, and fires. All such events, he wrote, were "ordered by the Providence of God. . . . When a fire is kindled among a people, it is the Lord that hath kindled it." Some ministers opposed paying attention to earthly things, but Increase's son Cotton Mather wrote, "To regard the illustrious displays of that Providence wherewith our Lord Christ governs the world, is a work, than which there is none more needful or useful for a Christian."

When one Christian in 1690 tried to put out a regular newspaper, he encountered trouble. Benjamin Harris had been jailed in London in 1679 for publishing an independent newspaper, *Domestic Intelligence*. After his release, Harris headed to America and, with help from Cotton Mather, published in 1690 the first newspaper in America, *Public Occurrences Both Foreign and Domestic*. Harris said its purpose was that "Memorable Occurrences of Divine Providence may not be neglected or forgotten, as they too often are."

Harris's combination of reporting and teaching showed when he reported "a day of Thanksgiving to God" for a good harvest and noted, concerning a tragedy averted, that God "assisted the Endeavors of the People to put out the Fire." But when Harris emphasized God's sovereignty over politics, controversy followed. He criticized royal officials for allying with Indians, and he reported on adultery in the French royal family: King Louis XIV "is in much trouble (and fear) not only with us but also with his Son, who has revolted against him lately, and has great reason if reports be true, that the Father used to lie with the Sons Wife."

British officials, hoping at that time for peace with France, were refraining from comments that could arouse popular concern about trusting those of low morals. Since sexual restraint was not common in the British royal family, they may have thought such news was non-news. Four days after Harris published, officials suppressed his newspaper and said any further issues would give him new prison nightmares. Harris gave in.

Other newspapers emerged over the next four decades and provided a service in helping readers to know "how to order their prayers and praises to the Great God." Local news continued to be reported in reverential context, as in this coverage of a storm:

The Water flowed over our Wharfs and into our streets to a very surprising height. They say the Tide rose 20 Inches higher than ever was known before. . . . Let us fear the GOD of heaven, who made the sea and the dry land.

In 1727, colonists felt an earthquake's "horrid rumbling" and "weighty shaking. . . . The strongest Houses shook prodigiously and the tops of some Chimneys were thrown down." Aftershocks over the next nine days "mightily kept up the Terror of it in the People, and drove them to all possible needs of Reformation."

Until the 1730s, no editor after Benjamin Harris took the risk of criticizing officials, but pastors during the first three decades of the eighteenth century introduced new ideas to their congregation. Minister Ebenezer Pemberton argued in 1710 that "kings and royal governors must govern themselves by unalterable Principles and fixed Rules, and not by unaccountable humors or arbitrary will. They take care that Righteous Laws be Enacted . . . as are necessary for the Safety of the Religion & Liberties of a People. [Rulers] that are not skillful, thoughtful, vigilant and active to promote the Public Safety and Happiness are not Gods but dead Idols."

The *New York Weekly Journal* in the 1730s reflected those views. The editor, John Peter Zenger, played the organ each Sunday in a Dutch Reformed church. He listened to sermons and then printed criticism in his newspaper of William Cosby, New York's royal governor. Cosby clearly thought he was above the law. When a farmer's cart slowed down Cosby's coach, the governor had his coachman beat the farmer with a horsewhip until he nearly killed him. When Cosby desired some land owned by Indians, he stole their deed and burned it. When Cosby granted new lands to those who applied legally, he demanded and received bribes often amounting to one-third of the estates.

Zinger sent a message in the second issue of his newspaper by publishing a piece that differentiated an absolute monarchy from one based on biblical principles of fixed law and limitations on power. In an absolute monarchy, the article argued, the "Will of the Prince" was over all, and "a Liberty of the Press to complain of Grievances" was impossible. In a limited monarchy, however, "Laws are known, fixed, and established. They are the straight Rule and sure Guide to direct the King, the Ministers, and his Subjects." Law (applying biblical principles) was above the king, not under him, just as the Bible itself was over all human royalty.

An essay in the *Journal* pointedly asked, "If we reverence men for their power alone, why do we not reverence the Devil, who has so much more power than men?" The article concluded that respect was due "only to virtuous qualities and useful actions," and it was therefore "as ridiculous and superstitious to adore great mischievous men as it is to worship a false god or Satan in the stead of God." Subjects had the right to evaluate their king; obedience was not guaranteed. Governmental authority must be limited, and such limitation is possible only if individuals are free to speak the truth to those in power. Biblical principles restrained power: "Power without control appertains to God alone, and no man ought to be trusted with what no man is equal to."

Cosby brought a charge of "seditious libel" against Zenger and threw him into jail. Journalists at that time had little defense against such accusations; if they proved their statements were true, they might be even worse off. (Under English law, truth made the libel worse by making it more likely the statements would decrease public support for the king and his officials. A common legal expression was "the greater the truth, the greater the libel.") Jurors were only to determine whether the accused had actually printed the objectionable publication. If they agreed he had, judges decided whether the statements in question were critical and deserved punishment.

At Zenger's trial in 1735, however, defense attorney Andrew Hamilton placed Zenger in the line of Martin Luther, John Foxe, John Stubbes, Marchamont Nedham, Increase Mather, and others. Zenger was one more victim of "the Flame of Prosecutions" by a government filled with "arbitrary Attempts of Men in Power." Hamilton argued: "If a libel is understood in the large and unlimited sense urged by Mr. Attorney . . . Moses, meek as he was, libeled Cain; and who is it that has not libeled the devil?" Hamilton said Zenger was merely following the lead of Isaiah, who attacked corrupt leaders as "blind watchmen" and "greedy dogs that can never have enough."

Zenger's defense, essentially, was that if God's authors produced such a critique, so could he. Judges in red robes and white wigs were ready to convict Zenger for his criticism of the royal governor, but the jury included "common People" among whom Zenger's newspaper had "gained some credit." A packed courtroom sympathetic to Zenger kept the judges from silencing Hamilton when he turned directly to the jurors and suggested they declare Zenger innocent even though he admitted to printing the material in question and was thus guilty under British law. Hamilton argued Zenger deserved support because he had been "exposing and opposing arbitrary power by speaking and writing Truth." The jurors agreed. They delivered a verdict of "not guilty." Royal officials decided not to provoke a riot. Zenger went free.

The verdict meant little, legally. A runaway jury had disobeyed English law and gotten away with it. But the verdict reverberated through the colonies and through England itself, encouraging Christian editors and discouraging officials from trying printers for seditious libel. No official brought a case of that sort anywhere in America after 1735. The year after the Zenger case, *Virginia Gazette* editor William Parks exposed corruption, including the stealing of sheep by a member of Virginia's legislature. Threatened with prosecution, Parks used the Zenger defense of truth-telling. When he produced court records showing the accusation was accurate, officials dropped the case against him.

By the 1750s, most American newspapers were independent of governmental control and free to provide, as *Maryland Gazette* editor Jonas Green promised his readers, not just "a Weekly Account of the most remarkable Occurrences, foreign and domestic," but also an examination of "whatever may conduce to the Promotion of Virtue and Learning, the Suppression of Vice and Immorality, and the Instruction as well as Entertainment of our Readers." When England and France went to war in 1754 and fighting commenced in America, the *New York Gazette* reported that guns furnished to troops by corrupt officials were out-of-date and practically useless.

Samuel Adams became America's most influential columnist in the 1760s. He was not handsome or rich, but he had a strong

Christian and classical education and the ability to write at any time under almost any conditions. Adams typically composed his columns after evening prayers, but his wife would sometimes wake in the middle of the night, hear only the sound of her husband's quill pen scratching on and on, and contentedly go back to sleep. He could also write amid the shouting of political meetings at local taverns. Adams's columns in the *Boston Gazette* came out every Monday afternoon, and a crowd often awaited its issues hot off the press. Contemporaries called him "a strict Calvinist. . . . No individual of his day had so much the feelings of the ancient Puritans."

Adams is a model for today's Christian reporters in four ways. First, observing that "mankind are governed more by their feelings than by reason," Adams emphasized appeals to the whole person, not just to a disembodied intellect. He took emotions seriously, for the "fears and jealousies of the people are not always groundless. . . . People in general seldom complain, without some good reason." Adams argued that ordinary citizens could "distinguish between realities and sounds; and by a proper use of that reason which Heaven has given them, they can judge, as well as their betters, when there is danger of slavery."

Second, Adams's biblical sense of human nature underlined his emphasis on investigative reporting. He favored tracking activities of those who are "watching every Opportunity to turn the good or ill Fortune of their Country, and they care not which, to their own private Advantage. Such Men there always have been & always will be, till human Nature itself shall be substantially meliorated." He praised exposure of leaders who "having gained the Confidence of their Country, are sacrilegiously employing their Talents to the Ruin of its Affairs, for their own private Emolument." Adams also understood that investigative journalists must be not only bold but thick-skinned. A writer investigates "at the Risk of his own Reputation, for it is a thousand to one [that the subjects of investigation] will give him the odious Epithets of suspicious, dissatisfiable, peevish, quarrelsome, etc."

Third, Adams argued that writers should pay careful attention to the connection between attacks on political rights and attempts to restrict religious rights. In one column that he signed "A Puritan," Adams described how he was pleased with attention paid to politics, but "surprised to find, that so little attention is given to the danger we are in, of the utter loss of those religious Rights, the enjoyment of which our good forefathers had more especially in their intention, when they explored and settled this new world." Adams, criticizing a new tax law that put newspapers and all documents under government control, wrote, "the Stamp Act itself was contrived with a design only to inure the people to the habit of contemplating themselves as the slaves of men; and the transition from thence to a subjection to Satan, is mighty easy."

Fourth, Adams defined the limits of protest. He showed a strong sense of lawfulness when reacting to demonstrations in 1765 that led to attacks on private homes such as that of Thomas Hutchinson, the royal governor. Adams favored peaceful demonstrations when legislative methods and petitions failed, but he criticized the "truly mobbish" assault on Hutchinson's home. Adams wanted America to remain within the British empire, but with more self-rule, including the opportunity to select leaders and decide how to be taxed. When Adams and his colleagues demonstrated for self-rule in 1773 by throwing some boxes of highly taxed tea into the Atlantic Ocean, they made it clear nothing except tea was to be destroyed, and replaced one accidentally broken padlock.

Adams did not favor overthrowing the British government. He saw both communism and absolute monarchy as wrong, and wrote that "Utopian schemes of leveling, and a community of goods, are as visionary and impracticable, as those which vest all property in the Crown. . . . What property can the colonists be conceived to have, if their money may be granted away by others, without their consent?"

Other writers came to similar conclusions. A columnist in the *Pennsylvania Evening Post* declared that "resisting the just and lawful power of government" was unrighteous rebellion, but resisting "unjust and usurped power" was not. When King George III and his officials continued to usurp power and refused to give the colonies any self-rule, tensions ratcheted up year by year until war tragically came in 1775.

KEY TERMS

news sermons

STUDY QUESTIONS

1. What are the positives and negatives of pastors moonlighting as correspondents?
2. Why did John Zenger get out of prison?
3. Can revolutions be moderate?

FOR FURTHER READING

Perry Miller, ed., *The American Puritans: Their Prose and Poetry* (Columbia University Press, 1982).

Daniel T. Rogers, *As a City on a Hill* (Princeton University Press, 2018).

Marvin Olasky, *Fighting for Liberty and Virtue* (Crossway, 1995).

Ira Stoll, *Samuel Adams: A Life* (Free Press, 2009).

Thomas Kidd, *American Colonial History* (Yale University Press, 2016).

24

Developing and Defending
Christian Journalism

WHEN THE AMERICAN Revolution ended successfully in 1783, its leading general, George Washington, could have become King George I of America or a tyrant without that title—but instead, he went home, grew crops for six years, and came back into office in 1789 as a president strictly limited both in tenure and power. No other major revolution in world history—French, Russian, Chinese, or even Cuban or Cambodian—has had a leader who freely gave up power and helped to bring about a constitution that strictly limited executive authority.

As noted in chapter 1, the writers of the U.S. Constitution, understanding our sinful tendencies to lord it over others, created a system of decentralized government. If the executive, legislative, and judicial branches joined forces against the citizenry, they hoped state legislators would stand up in their capitals and say "No." They had other lines of defense as well. Civil society—what today we refer to as nonprofit organizations and NGOs, along with churches—had power and influence. But what if the central government succeeded in bossing around all these groups?

Journalism was the last line of defense. The second president of the United States, John Adams, noting the Constitution stipulated the election of key leaders, asked: "How are their characters and conduct to be known to their constituents but by the press?" In Alexandria, Virginia, the *Gazette* also saw journalists with an essential role in limiting governmental power, for in newspapers "public men and measures are scrutinized. Should any man or body of men dare to form a system against our interests, by this means it will be unfolded to the great body of the people, and the alarm instantly spread through every part of the continent."

Nevertheless, the rise of French revolutionary ideas in the 1790s led to attempts to crack down on press freedom, as Adams and others feared the potential arrival of guillotines in America. That didn't happen, but spiritual change among some editors did. One typical editor, Nathaniel Willis, born in 1780, loved French revolutionary ideals and from 1802 to 1807 edited a radical newspaper, the *Eastern Argus*. He was happy to "spend Sabbaths in roving about the fields and in reading newspapers," but one Sunday he went to hear what he thought would be a political speech by a minister. He was surprised to hear a clear presentation of the gospel. "Much interested," Willis eventually came to believe "that the Bible is the Word of God—that Christ is the only Savior, and that it is by grace we are saved, through faith."

Applying that understanding to his occupation, Willis decided good journalism required biblical analysis of issues and an awareness of sin. Believing that those invested with power would work to increase it and oppress others while offering honeyed words, Willis in 1816 began publishing a newspaper, the *Boston Recorder*, which emphasized individual responsibility rather than grand societal solutions. *Recorder* columns argued that civil government has strictly limited jurisdiction and should be turned to only for defense or punishment of crime. Family, church, and charity groups were to take leadership in dealing with social problems.

Willis pushed for news stories that showed the consequences of sin and the need for Christ. For example, an article in 1819 headlined "Shocking Homicide," reported a man had killed his own son after being "for a long time troubled with irreligious fears, and a belief that his sins were too numerous to be pardoned." An 1820 article criticized U.S. Admiral Stephen Decatur for fighting a duel for fear of being declared a coward. He forgot "that there is no honor, which is valuable and durable, save that which comes from God."

Willis declared that all kinds of stories provided "occasion to record many signal triumphs of divine grace over the obduracy of the human heart, and over the prejudices of the unenlightened mind." The *Recorder*, he wrote, was a record of "these quickening influences of the Holy Spirit." Christian-run newspapers in other cities had similar formats and success. The *Baltimore Chronicle*, in its international coverage, described the troubles of one warlike king:

> The agitated monarch sees nothing but mangled limbs and bleeding bodies. . . . If Divine Providence had intended to have produced a living instance of the worthlessness of human grandeur, could a more awful example have been afforded?

Willis was not shy about reporting bad news. The *Recorder's* coverage of an earthquake in Syria in 1822 included a first-person account of destruction. Reporter Benjamin Barker wrote that he was racing down the stairs of a crumbling house when another shock sent him flying through the air, and his fall was broken when he landed on a dead body. He saw

> men and women clinging to the ruined walls of their houses, holding their children in their trembling arms; mangled bodies lying under my feet, and piercing cries of half buried people assailing my ears; Christians, Jews, and Turks, were imploring the Almighty's mercy in their respective tongues, who a minute before did not perhaps acknowledge him.

The sensational scene included "hundreds of decrepit parents half-buried in the ruins, imploring the succor of their sons," and "distracted mothers frantically lifting heavy stones from heaps that covered the bodies of lifeless infants." Sounds included "the crash of falling walls, the shrieks, the groans," but also many persons "falling on their knees and imploring the mercy of God." The *Recorder* treated the earthquake as Jesus did the fall of the Siloam tower: all of us, standing "on the brink of eternity, and liable by a thousand means as fatal to life as an earthquake, to be hurried into eternity, [should] seek the Lord while He may be found."

The number of newspapers in the United States shot up from 37 in 1775 to 359 in 1810 and then to 1,265 in 1834—and, as one contemporary observer noted, "Of all the issues of the press three-fourths are theological, ethical, and devotional." Ninety of these newspapers were dailies. The *New York Christian Advocate* became the weekly with the largest circulation in the country, with 30,000 subscribers in 1830. The *Lexington Western Monitor*, a Kentucky newspaper, was typical in its summary of one major role of the press: "to strengthen the hands of virtue and to rebuke vice." The *New York American* vowed to be "FREE from all control but that of religion and morality, INDEPENDENT of any influence but the good of our country and mankind."

These newspapers also covered international news in line with their theological concerns. They praised American missionaries who went to India, China, and other Asian countries. They blamed British and other European governments for putting money ahead of evangelism. One editor said the British government would "sponsor the worship of Beelzebub if the state could make money off of it." The *Columbian Phoenix* complained that British leaders thought "the Religion of the Most High God must not be suffered to interfere with the arrangements of the British government." Sensational stories about India's "Juggernaut festival"—in which people prepared for sacrifice to local gods were "crushed to death by the wheels" of a moving tower, while onlookers shouted with joy—led into reports that British agents were collecting a "Juggernaut tax."

The American daily newspaper with largest circulation in the early 1830s was the *New York Sun*, edited by George Wisner, a Christian who understood that it is neither accurate nor stimulating to pretend that all is well in the world. He wrote of how news stories "must generally tell of wars and fighting, of deeds of death, and blood of wounds and heresies, of broken heads, broken hearts, and broken bones, of accidents by fire or flood, a field of possessions ravaged, property purloined, wrongs inflicted." Wisner explained that "the abundance of news is generally an evidence of astounding misery, and even the disinterested deeds of benevolence and philanthropy which we occasionally hear of owe their existence to the wants or sorrows or sufferings of some of our fellow beings."

Wisner's practice followed his principles. He ran moral tales concerning the consequences of seduction, adultery, and abandonment. Knowing that specific detail won readers and made his product morally useful, he listed names of all criminal offenders, with the goal of inhibiting others inclined to vice:

> Much complaint has been made from a certain quarter, and emanating from a particular class of individuals, against the publication of the names of persons who have been arrested [but] such publications have a tendency to deter from disorders and crimes, and to diminish the number of criminals.

A typical story shows that Wisner was not afraid to shame offenders:

> Patrick Ludwick was sent up by his wife, who testified that she had supported him for several years in idleness and drunkenness. Abandoning all hopes of reformation in her husband, she brought him a suit of clothes a fortnight since and told him to go about his business, for she would not live with him any longer. Last night he came home in a state of intoxication, broke into his wife's bedroom, pulled her out of bed, and pulled her hair, and stamped on her. She called a watchman and sent him up [to jail].

Following the Reformed view that the heavens display the glory of God and the streets show the sinfulness of man, Wisner told stories to make his points, and also displayed a sense of humor. For example, he opposed dueling, but once accepted a challenge from a seller of quack medicines whom he had criticized. Given his choice of weapons, Wisner argued for syringes filled with the doctor's own medicine, at five paces. Amid laughter, the salesman called off the duel.

The most articulate journalistic writer on politics and morality during the 1830s was William Leggett of the *New York Evening Post*.

Leggett's major political principle was support for "equal rights," by which he meant the law should not discriminate among citizens, benefiting some at the expense of others. (With this position, Leggett was following Exodus 23, which commands us to show partiality neither to rich nor to poor in their disputes.)

Leggett believed it was unfair for government to be "offering encouragements and granting privileges" to those with political power. He set about to expose any governmental redistribution of income, whether through taxes, tariffs, or government aid to individuals, businesses, or labor groups.

Leggett foresaw problems whenever "government assumes the functions which belong alone to an overruling Providence, and affects to become the universal dispenser of good and evil." He especially did not want government to become "the greater regulator of the profits of every species of industry," and in that way to "reduce men from a dependence on their own exertions, to a dependence on the caprices of their Government." He complained some already were beginning to insist that "because our government has been instituted for the benefit of the people, it must therefore have the power to do whatever may seem to conduce to the public good."

Leggett in his columns reported the attempts of "designing politicians, interested speculators, or crack-brained enthusiasts" to turn the federal government into a "disguised despotism . . . the capricious dispenser of good and evil, without any restraint, except its own sovereign will. It holds in its hand the distribution of the goods of this world, and is consequently the uncontrolled master of the people."

Christian newspapers in the United States through the mid-nineteenth century attempted to look at all aspects of life from a biblical worldview. One Ohio newspaper declared in 1858 that the Christian newspaper should be a provider of not "merely religious intelligence, but a news paper, complete in every department of general news, yet upon a religious, instead of a political or literary basis." Another, the *Northwestern Christian Advocate*, proclaimed in 1860:

> Let theology, law, medicine, politics, literature, art, science, commerce, trade, architecture, agriculture—in fine, all questions which

concern and secure the welfare of a people—be freely discussed and treated, and this, too, for God, for Jesus Christ, and the advancement of the Redeemer's kingdom among men.

Overall, many early Christian journalists showed an awareness of how the Bible uses bad news to show us the wages of sin and to prepare us for understanding the necessity of the Good News. The journalists knew general statements about man's corruption were far less gripping than coverage with specific detail of the results of sin and misery.

That Christian consensus did not last. Beginning in the 1830s, intellectuals who became known as transcendentalists turned against Christ. Ralph Waldo Emerson, the most celebrated American thinker of that decade, complained Christianity speaks "with noxious exaggeration about the person of Jesus" instead of emphasizing "the moral nature of man, where the sublime is." Humanity, Emerson proclaimed, "is drinking forever the soul of God" and becoming godlike itself.

Starting in the 1840s, some American ministers began to proclaim that humans are not inherently sinful, and that if man's environment changed, man himself could become perfect. A host of panaceas, ranging from diet change (don't eat meat) to the abolition of private property, became popular as ways of purportedly changing mankind. Many proposals for change emphasized opposition to property rights. One prominent pastor, William Ellery Channing, attacked Calvinism, called avarice the greatest sin, and said the solution was to establish "a community of property."

Channing and a French philosopher, Charles Fourier (whose "utopian socialism" was attacked by Karl Marx), influenced three American journalists: George Ripley, Albert Brisbane, and Horace Greeley. All three favored the establishment of communes that would banish private property, establish "free love," and allow each member to be free to work when and where he wanted. Brisbane argued economic and sexual communism would create "a humanity worthy of that Cosmic Soul of which I instinctively felt it to be a part." Many communes formed, and Greeley financially supported several.

Greeley in 1841 founded a newspaper, the *New York Tribune*, and gave Brisbane and Ripley columns in it. He understood journalism and demanded from his reporters "vigor, terseness, clearness, and simplicity." He emphasized comprehensive news coverage, and described how an editor should make sure nothing "of interest to a dozen families occurs, without having the fact daily, though briefly, chronicled." He also emphasized shorter sentences than were typical of the time and an easy-to-read typeface.

Greeley attracted to his staff young people who also thought they knew better than their forefathers. The *Tribune* became the place to work. As competing editor E. L. Godkin noted, "To get admission to the columns of the *Tribune* almost gave the young writer a patent of literary nobility." One *Tribune* reporter recalled the furnishings were poor, but "ill-furnished and ill-kept as the *Tribune* office was in those days, it harbored a moral and intellectual spirit that I met nowhere else during my thirty-five years of journalistic experience. Every member of the force, from reporter to editor, regarded it as a great privilege to be on the *Tribune* and to write for its columns."

The *Tribune's* superior reporting gave Greeley the freedom to make his newspaper a proponent of social revolution without unduly alienating subscribers.

One of the young journalists Greeley hired, Henry Raymond, became a key *Tribune* editor. Greeley wrote he never saw "a cleverer, readier, more generally efficient journalist." But Raymond believed in God, left Greeley to edit another newspaper, and in 1846 challenged Greeley to a verbal duel. The two newspapers agreed to publish twelve articles from each editor on how society can change.

Raymond started with a statement of his fundamental position: only the "personal reform of individual men" through Christianity will lead to social progress. He argued that reformers should seek "personal, moral transformation," and "when that is accomplished, all needed Social Reform will either have been effected or rendered inevitable." Greeley disagreed and argued that life without property would turn "the young and plastic" into "agreeable and useful" commune members.

Greeley's belief that there is no human nature, so man can be molded into almost anything, prefigured twentieth-century Marxism's attempts at human engineering. Raymond agreed with Greeley about "the existence of misery, and the necessity of relieving it," but he did not believe that "to furnish some with good dwellings, all must abandon their houses and dwell together under a common roof." Nor did Raymond believe "the whole fabric of existing institutions, with all its habits of action and of thought, must be swept away."

Raymond also pointed to the role of Christian charity and praised "individuals in each ward, poor, pious, humble men and women," who daily visited the sick and helped the poor. He said,

> Members of any one of our City Churches do more every year for the practical relief of poverty and suffering, than any Phalanx [commune] that ever existed. There are in our midst hundreds of female "sewing societies," each of which clothes more nakedness, and feeds more hunger, than any "Association" that was ever formed.

Greeley argued that all of man's problems "have their root in that isolation of efforts and antagonism of interests on which our present Social Order is based." He said journalists should fight for revolutionary change: "'Relieving Social Evils' is very well; we think eradicating and preventing them still better, and equally feasible if those who have power will adopt the right means, and give them a fair trial." Raymond replied by emphasizing that spiritual problems and individual corruption, rather than social oppression, were the root of most social ills.

The last three exchanges showed even more clearly the conflict of two faiths. Greeley believed that if we give our desires free play, "universal happiness must be the result." If we "create a new form of Society in which this shall be possible . . . then you will have a perfect Society; then will you have the Kingdom of Heaven." Raymond responded:

> This principle is in the most direct and unmistakable hostility to the uniform inculcations of the Gospel. No injunction of the New Testament is more express, or more constant, than that of

self-denial; of subjecting the passions, the impulses of the heart to the law of conscience.

Raymond concluded by arguing that

> the principles of all true REFORM come down from Heaven. . . . The CHRISTIAN RELIGION, in its spiritual, life-giving, heart-redeeming principles is the only power that can reform Society: and it can accomplish this work only by first reforming the individuals of whom Society is composed. Without GOD, and the plan of redemption which he has revealed, the *World* is also without HOPE.

American journalism was on its way to describing the world as hopeless, unless radical social change occurred. But what kind of change? Raymond agreed with Greeley that social problems were great: "Far from denying their existence, we insist that they are deeper and more fundamental in their origin." But Raymond saw himself as arguing for "a more thorough and radical remedy"—the change of heart that acceptance of Christianity brings.

KEY TERMS

equal rights
transcendentalism
communes

STUDY QUESTIONS

1. In the early years of the American republic, what were the lines of defense against governmental oppression?
2. Why did Nathaniel Willis and other earlier editors move from radicalism to Christian understanding, and what effect did that have?
3. How did William Leggett and similar journalists understand "equal rights"?

FOR FURTHER READING

Michael Schudson, *Discovering the News* (Basic, 1978).
Alexis de Tocqueville, *Democracy in America* (many editions).
Ellen Wayland-Smith, *Oneida* (Picador, 2016).

25

When Societies Break Down

CIVIL WAR AND anarchy are terrible things. Christian publications should strive to be truth-tellers, but also peacemakers, whenever possible. That dual role in the United States became harder as Americans argued about slavery throughout the eighteenth and early nineteenth centuries. In the 1830s, New York columnist William Leggett called slavery "a deplorable evil and a curse," and said Americans should push for "the speedy and utter annihilation of servitude and chains." Many in the Northern states agreed. Many in the Southern states disagreed.

Leggett had faith that Americans, in both North and South, would eventually answer no to questions he posed:

> Have their ears become so accustomed to the clank of the poor bondman's fetters that it no longer grates upon them as a discordant sound? . . . Can the husband be torn from his wife, and the child from its parent, and sold like cattle at the shambles, and yet free, intelligent men, whose own rights are founded on the declaration of the inalienable freedom and equality of all mankind, stand up in the face of heaven and their fellow men, and assert without a blush that there is no evil in servitude?

Many journalists and pastors believed newspapers could help to convince both Northerners and Southerners to end slavery. For example, Elijah Lovejoy completed his theological training in 1833 at Princeton Theological Seminary (then a stronghold of Calvinist thought) and moved to St. Louis in 1834. There he received ordination as a minister and began editing a Christian newspaper, the *St. Louis Observer*. When he saw a slave, Francis J. McIntosh, burned at the stake, he became an abolitionist and ran into massive opposition.

Lovejoy stayed in St. Louis as long as he could, but when a proslavery mob wrecked his printing press in July 1836, he moved across the Mississippi River to Illinois, which had abolished slavery. There he established the *Alton Observer*, but proslavery men three times smashed his printing press. Lovejoy did not fight back, but he and twenty of his armed supporters stood guard over a new press when it arrived in November 1837 for temporary storage in a warehouse.

At nighttime, members of a proslavery mob, most of them drunk, hurled rocks at the warehouse windows. The defenders threw back earthenware pots they had found in the warehouse. Soon gunshots came from both sides. When the mob put up a ladder at the building and one of its members began climbing to the roof with a smoking pot of pitch in order to set fire to the building, Lovejoy and a friend rushed out to overturn the ladder. One mob gunman fired his double-barreled shotgun at Lovejoy. Five bullets hit him, and he died.

When Lovejoy's disheartened associates laid down their weapons and left, the mob broke the press into pieces and dumped the broken parts into the Mississippi. His friends buried Lovejoy on November 9, his thirty-fifth birthday. After the Civil War, Alton citizens erected a monument to him. It stands to this day on a hill overlooking the Mississippi, with a plaque introducing Lovejoy as "Minister of the Gospel, Moderator of Alton Presbytery," and explaining in Lovejoy's own words what befell him: "If the laws of my country fail to protect me I appeal to God, and with Him I cheerfully rest my cause. I can die at my post but I cannot desert it."

Eight years later and 300 miles to the east, another editor faced similar persecution. Cassius Clay of Lexington, Kentucky, saw slavery as a sevenfold evil: "morally, economically, physically, intellectually, socially, religiously, politically." He advocated emancipation for over a generation, and in 1845 (at age thirty-five) began publishing the *True*

American, "a paper devoted to gradual and constitutional emancipation." With the words "God and Liberty " as his newspaper's motto, Clay advocated a constitutional convention designed to state "that every female slave, born after a certain day and year, should be free at the age of 21." Clay argued that over time this plan "would gradually, and at last, make our state truly free."

This moderate program gained both support and furious opposition. Clay soon had the joy of printing letters to the editor such as this one: "C. M. Clay: You are meaner than the autocrats of hell. . . . The hemp is ready for your neck. Your life cannot be spared. Plenty thirst for your blood and are determined to have it." But Clay kept at it, arguing that the elimination of slavery would help the South to prosper economically, spiritually, and socially.

In one article, he even commented on a rise of divorce in the South and urged Southern women to

> put away your slaves. . . . If you want to drink, go to the pump or to the spring and get it; if to bathe, prepare your own bath, or plunge into the running stream; make your own beds, sweep your own rooms, and wash your own clothes. . . . Then you will have full chests, glossy hair, rosy complexions, smooth velvet skins, . . . eyes of alternate fire and most melting languor, generous hearts, sweet tempers, good husbands, long lives of honeymoons, and no divorces.

Clay, expecting attempts to destroy his press, turned his three-story redbrick newspaper office into a fort. With six loyal friends, he prepared for a siege. Familiar with the story of Lovejoy's death, they lined the outside doors and window shutters of the building with sheet iron to prevent burning. Clay purchased two small brass cannons at Cincinnati, loaded them to the muzzle with bullets, slugs, and nails, and placed them breast high on a table at the entrance. His friends stockpiled muskets and Mexican lances.

Those measures forestalled the attack for a time, but Clay came down with typhoid fever. He eventually had to give up and watch as slaveholders packed up his press and shipped it out of town. That was the last time he was helpless. In 1847, Clay resumed his antislavery writing and speaking, had to fight numerous duels, and survived. Once, facing a hostile crowd, Clay held up a Bible and said, "To those who respect God's word, I appeal to this book." Then he held up a copy of the U.S. Constitution and said, "To those who respect our fundamental law, I appeal to this document." Then he took out two pistols and his Bowie knife and said, "To those who recognize only force . . ."

Clay, although ready to defend himself, believed that nothing good would come from aggression. He demanded free speech in the hope of convincing his neighbors, but he did not want to go to war with them. He stressed the power of personal transformation through God's grace, which would lead to societal reformation:

> We recommend less haughtiness and indifference on the part of the rich towards the poor, and less invidiousness toward the rich on the part of the poor. Let true Christianity prevail, and earth will become the foreshadowing of Heaven.

Clay, unlike Lovejoy, managed to survive many assassination attempts. Defenders of slavery knifed and beat him. Once, gushing blood from a lung wound, he even lost consciousness and dramatically gave as his last words, "I died in the defense of the liberties of the people"—but he did not die. He kept speaking out against slavery in the 1840s and helped to form the Republican Party in the 1850s.

By then, Horace Greeley's utopian socialist movement had largely died out, as communes failed and disappeared. Reliance on a noble human nature, so attractive in the abstract, showed its weakness in practice. Commune members often neglected their work. "Free love" proved not to be so free, as disputes raged.

Greeley's colleague Albert Brisbane believed the communes failed, not because there was too much forced community, but because there was too little:

> Unless associative life is completely organized, so that all the sentiments and faculties of the soul find their normal development

and action therein, it cannot stand. In fact, it will be discovered one of these days that, according to a law which governs the spiritual or passional nature of man, there must either be the complex harmony of a perfect organization, with a high order of spiritual activity, or man must remain in his little isolated, individual state.

Socialism in one community was insufficient. Control over much more terrain was necessary, and Brisbane recommended to his adherents that they begin a long march through the institutions of American society, with "years of patient, careful propagation" that would, decades later, result in "complex harmony." The goal became one of building a strong central government, so that the entire nation could be socialized.

Greeley began his own long march by placing in *Tribune* editorial positions many of his commune associates, who in turn hired others on the left—including Karl Marx, as the *Tribune's* European correspondent. Greeley himself concluded, "The whole relation of Employer and Laborer is so full of antagonism, inequality and injustice, that we despair of any reform in it but a very thorough and radical one."

Greeley became ever more ardent for social change as his personal life disintegrated. Horace and Mary Greeley believed children were sinless, so they kept their son Arthur (Pickie), born in 1844, isolated from playmates or other means by which corruption could enter into him. At age five, Pickie's hair had never been cut, less that constrict his freedom, and he still wore baby clothes, to give him freedom of movement. Pickie was to be a beautiful combination of intellect and nature, equipped with "choice" thoughts and language.

One day, though, the five-year-old stood up before a commune meeting and starting complaining that his mother was "so particular, particular, particular, particular." When she reminded him that she had saved him from corruption, he shrieked at her, "Don't you dare shut me up. . . . I want fun." The Greeleys did not change Pickie's regime, but he died shortly after, during a cholera epidemic.

Greeley turned his attention to the battle against slavery. In the early 1840s, Greeley's commune enthusiasm had led the *Tribune* into expectation of utopia around the corner. In the 1850s, he thought the North could eradicate slavery by using its superior numbers and industrial capacity to eradicate part of the South. He had never traveled in the South, and he employed correspondents who preached against slavery, but did not report what white Southerners actually thought.

Greeley came to believe that only a few wealthy Southerners, along with a handful of politicians along for the ride, were truly pro-slavery. He ran a report from Alabama that said whites there were "divided into two classes, the rich and the poor," and the poor would readily unite with Northern workers to "create a new system of Truth, Equality, Justice." He quoted a Memphis correspondent who thought only "an insignificant clique" favored secession, but "the masses are heart and soul for the union," so the North should not be concerned with "threats, or predictions of disunion."

Karl Marx, peering across the Atlantic with a dialectical telescope, helped to convince Greeley's assistant, Charles Dana, that slavery had weakened the South so much that it would be unable to mount a war effort. The North, he thought, could push hard without losing much blood. With social revolution so near and slavery the only large obstacle, Greeley became a proponent of terrorist means to gain antislavery objectives. With Kansas soon to vote on whether it would allow slavery, Northerners and Southerners flocked there, and the *Tribune* always depicted Northerners as peace-loving citizens brought to conflict by Southern terror.

That wasn't the case, as the events of May 24, 1856, showed. That night in Kansas, John Brown and seven other men invaded the homes of several farming families: the Doyles, the Wilkinsons, and the Harrises. These families had done no one any harm. They did not own slaves. They were simply from the South. They were also trusting. When William Doyle opened his door in response to a request for directions, John Brown's men grabbed him and took him 200 yards from the cabin. John Brown then placed a revolver against Doyle's forehead and pulled the trigger, killing him instantly.

The massacre continued. Brown's men stabbed Doyle's twenty-two-year-old son William in the face, slashed his head, and shot him in the side. Drury Doyle, 20, had his fingers and arms cut off and his head cut open. A stab in the chest killed him. Brown's men would have murdered a third son, fourteen-year-old John, but the mother, Mahala Doyle, clutched him and screamed, "Not him; oh God, not him." John Brown let him live.

Brown, four of his sons, and other followers then moved on to the Wilkinson home, took the husband away from his wife and small children, and cut his throat. They then went to the Harris cabin, occupied that night not only by James Harris and his family, but also by three other men who had stopped by. One had come to buy a cow. The door was unlocked, because the region until then had been safe. Harris and two of the men turned out to be Northerners, and Brown allowed them to live. The Southerner died from saber slashes. One blow severed his left hand, raised in self-defense. Others split open his skull, and he fell into the river. The murderers washed their swords and walked away as the cold water carried away part of the dead man's brain.

The goal of the massacre was terrorism, pure and simple: kill those who sided with a hated system, focus attention on what became known as "bleeding Kansas," and raise tensions so high that warfare capable of destroying the hated system would become more likely. Terrorists need press publicity, preferably somewhat sympathetic, and John Brown and his associates got it. The *Tribune* called Brown's terrorism a self-defense strike needed to disrupt the Southern horde of Kansas settlers. Greeley advocated shipment of more arms to Kansas and dispatched a military expert to advise John Brown. *Tribune* correspondent James Redpath wrote that because there would be no peace as long as slavery existed, he would "fight and kill for the sake of peace."

The *Tribune* also publicized books, pamphlets, and plays on Kansas, and even serialized a novel depicting Kansas Southerners as "ruffians, half-tipsy, with hair unkempt and beards . . . squirting tobacco juice in every direction, and interlarding their conversation with oaths and curses" aimed at defenseless folk. One of the poor sufferers was the heroine, gentle Alice, who took to her sickbed in fright and remained sorrowful until she had a vision of freedom in

Kansas. Then "the thin lips of Alice quivered tremulously. It was her last smile on earth."

Greeley went at it again after John Brown's raid on Harper's Ferry, an attempt in 1859 to set off a slave rebellion. During the month following the raid, the *Tribune* ran twenty-six columns and fifteen editorials on Brown. The *Tribune* correspondent was consistently pro-Brown and anti-Southern; he generalized about the South, "Everything shows how far this region is behind the age." He was also sarcastic about particular Southerners, such as prosecutor Charles Harding, whose "face is a vindictive as well as a degraded one," and who "has a way of expressing profound contempt by ejecting saliva aloft, and catching it on his chin, which he practices with great success."

Greeley displayed extreme arrogance during this crisis, and knew exactly what he was doing. In a letter to his associate editor, James S. Pike, Greeley wrote that he was in the "position of the rich old fellow, who, having built a church entirely out of his own means, addressed his townsmen thus: 'I've built you a meetinghouse, / And bought you a bell; / Now go to meeting / Or go to hell!' One of Greeley's competitors, the *New York Herald*, saw Greeley's support for John Brown as a continuation of his embrace of "all the isms and ultras of the day," including "Fourierism, atheism, community of property socialism, every species of wild and extravagant thought and doctrine."

How else could slavery have been fought? Henry Raymond and his *New York Times* opposed slavery fervently, but with an eye to the difficulty of altering an imbedded institution. Raymond, unlike Greeley, did not see antislavery agitation as a step toward class warfare, and did not sanguinely look to blood as the answer to social problems. He was not fooled by those who said the outbreak of civil war would lead to a Southern social revolution that would spread north. *Times* reporting from Kansas and Harper's Ferry bemoaned the provocations and appealed for calm.

An explicitly Christian newspaper, the *New York World*, suggested that Republican celebration over the election of Abraham Lincoln in 1860 "be tempered with manly generosity." Southerners said Lincoln's election made war inevitable, but the *World* insisted it wasn't "if the press and orators of all parties will drop the vituperative style in which they are wont to indulge, and practice a reasonable courtesy and magnanimity. "

The *World* criticized many Northerners for attempting to excommunicate the South, and criticized Southern slaveholders for engaging in "the separation of families, the taking of the parent from the child and the child from the parent, ignoring the marriage tie, withholding even that amount of education which would enable the colored man to read God's oracles."

The *World* quoted Matthew 5:9—"Blessed are the peacemakers, for they shall be called the children of God"—and asked Christians of both sides "to humble themselves, and confess before God that they have disparaged our common Lord and Redeemer." It favorably covered proposals for gradual emancipation and publicized suggestions to smooth the way by payments from the North: "That would test the northern conscience, and put us right under a reformed constitution."

The *World* criticized rule by subjectivity, decrying the "journalistic firebrand who decided to "erect his own judgment or his own happiness, into a tribunal."

Greeley was the chief culprit, according to the *World*. Southerners who read his work saw him as representing not just New York, but Northern hatred of the South, particularly because the *Tribune* sent 200,000 copies of a weekly edition to readers from Maine to Minnesota. The *Tribune* prophesied that America was faced with an either/or decision: "It may be that a new era of religion of Justice and Brotherhood between man and man is commencing; or it may be that this is only a fresh spasm, to be followed by a more palpable moral lifelessness. Which shall it be?"

The decision: war. In the rapture of the moment, even those few newspapers that had realistically counted the costs of war jumped on the bandwagon. In January 1860, the *Richmond Dispatch* had offered an accurate prediction:

> It is impossible to exaggerate the horrors and sufferings which for years would follow a dissolution of the Union. . . . It would be war from the start, war to the knife and knife to the hilt. The widely extended border between the North and South would be a line of

fire and blood. Every accessible bay and inlet of every river would be entered, and, ever and anon, large masses of men hurled upon the capitols and important points of Southern States. But the horrors of ordinary warfare would be far transcended by the barbarities of this cruel strife.

In January 1861, though, the *Dispatch* strongly called for secession, and did not mention the costs. One Georgia newspaper reported that "the tone of the Northern press . . . should convince all Southern men that the hour for dissolution is come." Greeley's *Tribune*, confident in February 1861 that the radical upheaval to come could eliminate oppression, added to its masthead the words, "NO COMPROMISE! / NO CONCESSIONS TO TRAITORS!" Soon the cannons were roaring.

KEY TERMS

fundamental law
Fourierism

STUDY QUESTIONS

1. How would you assess Cassius Clay's Christian witness?
2. What is Horace Greeley's legacy?
3. Was John Brown a terrorist?
4. Was the *New York World* right in trying to avoid a Civil War?

FOR FURTHER READING

Jason Phillips, *The Looming Civil War* (Oxford University Press, 2018).
Jay Sexton, *A Nation Forged by Crisis* (Basic, 2018).
Shelby Foote, *The Civil War* (Random House, 1974).
Hans J. Morgenthau and David Hein, *Essays on Lincoln's Faith and Politics* (University Press of America, 1983).

26

Pro-Life Journalism, Socialist Journalism

THE U.S. CIVIL War was a miserable experience for Americans, with more than 600,000 dying from battle and disease, but it did conclude with slaves gaining their freedom—although it took many more decades before they received equal treatment.

One other positive result of the war's death toll was a greater appreciation of human life in all its stages: adult, child, and not-yet-born. Abortion was officially illegal, but nevertheless rampant in New York City from the 1840s through the 1860s. Editorials in Henry Raymond's *New York Times* complained that the "perpetration of infant murder . . . is rank and smells to heaven." But little was being done about it until the *Times* in 1871 sent one of its reporters, Augustus St. Clair, to carry out an undercover investigation of Manhattan's abortion businesses.

For several weeks, St. Clair and "a lady friend" visited the most advertised abortionists in New York, posing as a couple in need of professional services. The result was an August 23, 1871, story, headlined "The Evil of the Age," that began on this solemn note: "Thousands of human beings are murdered before they have seen the light of this world, and thousands upon thousands more adults are irremediably robbed in constitution, health, and happiness."

St. Clair then skillfully contrasted powerlessness and power. He described the back of one abortionist's office: "Human flesh, supposed to have been the remains of infants, was found in barrels of lime and acids, undergoing decomposition." He described the affluence of a typical abortionist: "The parlors are spacious, and contain all the decorations, upholstery, cabinetware, piano, book case, etc., that is found in a respectable home."

St. Clair also listed leading abortionists by name and noted their political connections. "You have no idea of the class of people that come to us," one abortionist said. "We have had Senators, Congressmen and all sorts of politicians, bring some of the first women in the land here." St. Clair concluded with a call for change:

> The facts herein set forth are but a fraction of a greater mass that cannot be published with propriety. Certainly enough is here given to arouse the general public sentiment to the necessity of taking some decided and effectual action.

The *Times* aroused public interest by laying out the basic facts, but a specific incident galvanized readers. Tragically for a young woman, providentially for the antiabortion effort, an ideal story of horror arrived within the week. St. Clair published his exposé on August 23; on August 27, a *Times* headline at the top of page 1 read: "A Terrible Mystery."

The general facts of the story were miserable enough: a railroad station baggage worker discovered the nude body of a young woman inside a trunk that had begun to smell. An autopsy showed she had died from an infection caused by abortion. The *Times* provided evocative detail:

> This woman, full five feet in height, had been crammed into a trunk two feet six inches long. . . . Seen even in this position and rigid in death, the young girl, for she could not have been more than eighteen, had a face of singular loveliness. But her chief beauty was her great profusion of golden hair, that hung in heavy folds over her shoulders, partly shrouding the face. . . . There was some discoloration and decomposition about the pelvic region. It was apparent

that here was a new victim of man's lust, and the life-destroying arts of those abortionists.

The *Times* played out details of the exciting "trunk murder" detective story during the next several days, as police searched for the perpetrator. Meanwhile, the *Times* reminded readers every day that this particular incident showed what went on "in one of the many abortion dens that disgrace New York, and which the *Times* had just exposed as 'The Evil of the Age.'" The police arrested one of the abortionists whose advertisements St. Clair had quoted, and the *Times* followed with an editorial, "Advertising Facilities for Murder." An editorial quoted St. Clair's article, discussed the death of the "golden-haired unfortunate," and asked whether "the lives of babes are of less account than a few ounces of precious metal, or a roll of greenbacks."

The *Times* also printed a superbly written follow-up by St. Clair. "A Terrible Story from Our Reporter's Note-Book" revealed how St. Clair, in his undercover research for the exposé, had visited several weeks earlier the accused abortionist's Fifth Avenue office, with its "fine tapestry carpet" and "elegant mahogany desk." St. Clair described one of the patients he had seen:

> She seemed to be about twenty years of age, a little more than five feet in height, of slender build, having blue eyes, and a clear, alabaster complexion. Long blonde curls, tinted with gold, drooped upon her shoulders, and her face wore an expression of embarrassment at the presence of strangers.

St. Clair then quoted the abortionist's reply when he asked what would happen to the aborted infant:

> Don't worry about that, my dear Sir. I will take care of the result. A newspaper bundle, a basket, a pail, a resort to the sewer, or the river at night? Who is the wiser?

On his way out, St. Clair glimpsed once again the beautiful young woman he had seen on his way in. This time, as a fitting conclusion to his story, he drove the point home: "She was standing on the stairs, and it was the same face I saw afterward at the Morgue."

That abortionist received a seven-year prison sentence. *Times* editors and reporters showed a willingness to be controversial in battling sin. One *Times* antiabortion editorial stated,

> It is useless to talk of such matters with bated breath, or to seek
> to cover such terrible realities with the veil of a false delicacy. . . .
> From a lethargy like this it is time to rouse ourselves. The evil that
> is tolerated is aggressive.

The editorial concluded that "the good . . . must be aggressive too."

The campaign against abortion, which other newspapers joined, was the last crusade of the Christian journalism that had dominated the early nineteenth-century press. Biblically-directed reporters showed the universality of sin and the need for repentance, but the Bible did not remain dominant in American journalism. Instead of seeing sinful man and a society reflecting that sinfulness, Horace Greeley and his followers believed that man, naturally good, was enslaved by oppressive social systems—and they developed the rationale for journalists to become advocates of secular liberalism.

Following the traumatic Civil War, even editors of some Christian publications succumbed to intellectual trendiness. For example, editor Lyman Abbott of *Christian Union*, a large-circulation weekly newspaper of the 1870s, decided the Bible was fable rather than fact. He became known for attacking God's sovereignty in the name of Charles Darwin. With the support of others who were similarly swayed, Abbott eventually took Christianity out of the magazine's title as well as its pages, with the name becoming *Outlook* in 1893. By that time, other anti-Christian doctrines—Marxism, Freudianism, and a general emphasis on "science" as mankind's savior—had kicked in also, or soon would.

As those trends gained power, a counterinfluence developed. The period of great advances for anti-Christian thought also was a great era of revivals. During the last two-thirds of the nineteenth century, God used great evangelists such as Charles Finney and Dwight

Moody to expound the gospel of grace to millions. Many were saved through their preaching. Many also learned, as Proverbs 1:7 notes, that "the fear of the LORD is the beginning of knowledge" and wisdom. They thus were kept from believing in evolutionary or Marxist scriptures.

Revivalism, though, did not particularly help Christian journalism. The great revivalists' focus on evangelism tended to be specifically individualistic. They did not stress worldview and applying biblical wisdom to general news coverage. Furthermore, many Christians began to believe the general culture would inevitably become worse and worse. They thought little could be done to stay the downward drift. Christian publications should cover church news, they thought, and ignore the rest of the world.

The anti-Christian trend and the separatist Christian reaction combined to minimize Christian presence in newsrooms. As journalists who had embraced materialism and/or pantheism advanced in newspaper and magazine work, Christians who embraced separatist revivalism retreated. Some Christian newspapers may have died after being overrun, but many abandoned the social realm without ever engaging the invading forces. A sense of "Whew! Glad I'm saved!" often replaced a strong sense of God's sovereignty over all areas of human life.

The general result of the two underlying movements was that Christians neglected the Reformation idea of Christ as Lord of all of life. A gap emerged between ministry and laity, and between sabbatical and general church activities. John Calvin and other leaders of the Protestant Reformation had argued that good work outside the pulpit glorified God as much as the activities of the ministry proper. But as views of inevitable cultural decay began to grip nineteenth-century American Protestantism, some editors began to consider journalism inferior to preaching. The editor of one Ohio newspaper said "the work of a Christian minister" was far more important than the work of an editor.

As Christian publications became less significant, the selection of editors became more haphazard. Often those who could, preached, while those who could not, edited—and the latter knew they were considered second-class Christians. One minister thrown into an editor's chair in Cincinnati wrote, "I had never seen a newspaper made up. . . . I was stunned by the cry of 'Copy!' 'Copy!'" That newspaper ceased publication when a follow-up editor took a vacation and never came back. The editor of the *Southern Christian Advocate* proclaimed it was better to "wander through the earth on foot, preaching Christianity, than to be the editor of a religious newspaper."

Those who styled themselves "Christian socialists" gained authority in the late nineteenth century. Professor Richard Ely, who founded the American Economic Association in 1885, strove to apply principles enunciated by Horace Greeley to all of American society. Demanding that all unite behind the "coercive philanthropy . . . of governments, either local, state, or national," he received favorable coverage from journalists who fulsomely praised a gospel of salvation through government action.

One much-quoted book of that era, William H. Fremantle's *The World as the Subject of Redemption*, asserted that government alone "can embrace all the wants of its members and afford them the universal instruction and elevation which they need." Fremantle praised the worship of governmental power as a furtherance of Christian worship of God:

> We find the Nation alone fully organized, sovereign, independent, universal, capable of giving full expression to the Christian principle. We ought, therefore, to regard the Nation as the Church, its rulers as ministers of Christ, its whole body as a Christian brotherhood, its public assemblies as amongst the highest modes of universal Christian fellowship, its dealing with material interests as Sacraments.

It is hard to know how much of this journalists absorbed and believed, but these notions did begin receiving favorable press. It was easier to attribute problems to social maladjustments than to innate sinfulness; if personality was a social product, individuals were not responsible for their vices. Crime reporting began to change as journalists attributed "antisocial action" to the stress of social factors beyond an individual's control. Editorial pages began calling for new government action, not merely to redistribute income, but as a means to achieve a cooperative commonwealth in which men and women could become godlike.

Journalistic pioneers such as Joseph Pulitzer popularized such ideas. Pulitzer's New York newspaper, the *World* (no relation to the Christian newspaper that tried to forestall the Civil War), combined easy-to-read, gripping stories with economic envy. Typical *World* headlines were like a dragon's fire: "Death Rides the Blast," "Screaming for Mercy," "Baptized in Blood," "A Mother's Awful Crime," "A Bride but Not a Wife," and "Victims of His Passion." Readers who paid a penny to read the details of these horrific stories would encounter, on inside pages, Pulitzer's political agenda: tax large incomes, tax corporations, tax inheritances, redistribute income.

Pulitzer's *World* juxtaposed current horror with future social salvation. It transmitted a message of hope through science and material progress, evenly distributed by benign government agents. Features like "Experimenting with an Electric Needle and an Ape's Brain" showed scientific transformation of man's thought patterns was just around the corner. Stories like "Science Can Wash Your Heart" suggested immortality was possible. In the meantime, however, monstrous crime and terrible scandal bedeviled mankind.

In one sense, Pulitzer was merely imitating the methodology of the Puritan press two centuries before: emphasize bad news, so the need for the good news becomes even greater. But the message was totally changed. Instead of pointing readers toward man's corruption and God's grace, the *World* portrayed itself as battling against systemic oppression, and proposed running over anyone (including business owners in America, Spaniards in Cuba, and Boers in South Africa) who stood in the way of "progress."

The *World's* circulation rose from 60,000 in 1884 to 200,000 in 1886 to one million during the Spanish-American War in 1898. For journalists yearning to transform society and have fun and profit, the *World* became the New York workplace of choice, much as the *Tribune* had been at mid-century. The *World's* full-time workforce numbered 1,300 in the mid-1890s, and the growing arrogance of what had become a major institution soon was apparent: "The *World* should be more powerful than the President," Pulitzer argued, since presidents are stuck with four-year terms, but the *World* "goes on year after year and is absolutely free to tell the truth."

Eternal life plus absolute knowledge of good and evil: Pulitzer believed he had feasted from both of Eden's trees, but he found no joy. By 1900, Pulitzer was spending most of his time on his yacht, with seventy-five employees catering to his whims. As one biographer put it,

> The yacht represented the logical end toward which the eccentric despot, so concerned with democracy, had been working for decades. It gave him *complete control*. It was an absolute monarchy.

A second major editor-publisher of the period, William Randolph Hearst, took Pulitzer's insights and spread them across the nation through a mighty newspaper chain. One reporter described his excitement upon going to work for Hearst:

> At last I was to be the kind of journalist I had dreamed of being. I was to enlighten and uplift humanity. Unequaled newspaper enterprise, combined with a far-reaching philanthropy, was to reform . . . the whole United States. The printing press, too often used for selfish ends, had become a mighty engine for good in the world, and I was to be a part of the directing force. Proudly I was to march under the banner of William R. Hearst, helping to guide civilization's forward strides.

Hearst, owner of the *San Francisco Examiner* and the *New York Journal*, starting in the 1890s, ordered his editors to "make a great and continuous noise to attract readers; denounce crooked wealth and promise better conditions for the poor to keep readers. INCREASE CIRCULATION." Pulitzer and Hearst offered not only big headlines and exciting stories, but a class-based attack on the wealthy (other than themselves).

Hearst's editorial writers worked hard to press issues into a class-struggle mold. Classic *Journal* editorials portrayed

> the horse after a hard day's work grazing in a swampy meadow. He has done his duty and is getting what he can in return. On the horse's flank you see a leech sucking blood. The leech is the trust. The horse is the labor union.

Hearst's ostentatious sympathy for workers made readers think he cared about them. Calls for socialism came next. Hearst wrote in one signed editorial that socialism was the key to advancement, since folding small businesses into massive combinations would create industrial progress: "We are advancing toward a complete organization in which the government will stand at the head and to be the trust of trusts. It is ridiculous to attempt to stop this development."

One way to bring about political and social change was to emphasize the evil of the present. Hearst built a chain of American newspapers that emphasized sensationally tragic incidents, with headlines like "He Murdered His Friends" or "He Ran Amuck with a Hatchet." A woman, already in jail for beating a man senseless with a beer bottle, stabbed her jailer with a hat pin. A maidservant poisoned her mistress's soup. In New York, a boy shot and killed his father, who was beating his mother. Another woman told "How She Horsewhipped Husband." An eleven-year-old drank a bottle of acid because she "did not want to live."

Hearst newspapers also tried to promote change by forecasting a much improved future, if resources now used for "barbaric" displays of wealth would fight "distress and misery." Science (actually, pseudoscience) would help. The *San Francisco Examiner* reported one professor had produced "solidified air," and another had discovered that what a woman eats determines the gender of her baby.

The third ingredient for change was to create cults of personality by making leaders seem godlike. Hearst instructed his reporters and editors to praise him at every opportunity. He posed as a benefactor of the poor, sending pale children on jaunts to the beach. A reporter sent to cover one expedition, however, later wrote she was given only one container of ice cream to be dealt out on a beach trip:

When at last I placed a dab on each saucer, a little fellow got up and declared that the *Journal* was a fake and I thought there was going to be a riot. I took away the ice-cream from a deaf and dumb kid who couldn't holler and gave it to the malcontent. Then I had to write my story beginning: "Thousands of children, pale-faced but happy, danced merrily down Coney Island's beaches yesterday and were soon sporting in the sun-lit waves shouting, 'God bless Mr. Hearst.'"

Hearst overreached when his *New York Journal* editorialized that "if bad institutions and bad men can be got rid of only by killing, then the killing must be done." When an anarchist assassinated President William McKinley in 1901, police found the killer had a copy of the *Journal* in his coat pocket. Citizens hanged Hearst in effigy, and the new president, Theodore Roosevelt, criticized "reckless utterances of those who, on the stump and in the public press, appeal to dark and evil spirits." Congressman John A. Sullivan called Hearst the Nero of American politics for his attempts to incite class conflict.

But others promoted Hearst. Best-selling author Upton Sinclair, who funded the establishment of a commune that he called "an industrial Republic in the making," declared in his book *The Industrial Republic* that a bright socialist future would not be far off if Hearst became president. Sinclair also confused holiness and hatred, eventually declaring that Jesus had been an anarchist and agitator whose vision of violent upheaval was covered up by church institutions. One prominent liberal columnist, Herbert Croly, wrote that Hearst's ambition was to bring about a "socialistic millennium."

KEY TERMS

the Evil of the Age
coercive philanthropy

STUDY QUESTIONS

1. What led to the marginalizing of Christian journalism in the late nineteenth century?
2. What impact did revivals have on journalism?
3. How did Joseph Pulitzer's *New York World* gain popularity?

FOR FURTHER READING

Marvin Olasky, *The Press and Abortion, 1838–1988* (Erlbaum, 1988).

Marvin Olasky, *Abortion Rites: A Social History of Abortion in America* (Crossway, 1992).

Joshua Muravchik, *Heaven on Earth: The Rise and Fall of Socialism* (Encounter, 2002).

Thomas C. Leonard, *Illiberal Reformers* (Princeton University Press, 2016).

27

Slouching toward Socialism and Postmodernism

KARL MARX FAMOUSLY said, "The philosophers have only interpreted the world, in various ways. The point, however, is to change it." Many of his followers over the years have turned to journalism as the way to promote change, and many Americans have seen themselves as agents of change. Let's pick up from chapter 26 the saga of publisher William Randolph Hearst, who said the press had the power to "so exert the forces of publicity" that radical change would result.

Hearst gained election to Congress in 1904 and said,

> We have won a splendid victory. We are allying ourselves with the workingman, the real Americans. This is just the beginning of our political actions. Our social aspirations have a greater chance than ever to be realized.

Popular journalist Lincoln Steffens wrote a sympathetic profile of Hearst and said the publisher "was driving toward his unannounced purpose to establish some measure of democracy, with patient but ruthless force."

Hearst failed in his attempt to become governor of New York and then president of the United States. He settled back into newspaper publishing and gave up on socialism, but his emphasis on oppression spread around the country, aided by such national magazines as *Munsey's, McClure's, Cosmopolitan, Everybody's,* and *The Arena,* which provided an outlet for freelancing radicals during the twentieth century's first decade. *The Arena,* for example, pushed its 100,000 readers to "agitate, educate, organize, and move forward, casting aside timidity and insisting that the Republic shall no longer lag behind in the march of progress."

One of the most prominent magazine writers, David Graham Phillips, compared Karl Marx to Jesus Christ, not unfavorably:

> Both labor leaders—labor agitators. The first proclaimed the brotherhood of man. But he regarded this world as hopeless and called on the weary and heavy-laden masses to look to the next world for the righting of their wrongs. Then—eighteen centuries after— [Marx] said "No! not in the hereafter, but in the here. Here and now, my brothers. Let us make this world a heaven. Let us redeem ourselves and destroy this devil of ignorance who is holding us in this hell!"

President Theodore Roosevelt in 1906 criticized Phillips and others he called "muckrakers." Roosevelt explained that

> In Bunyan's *Pilgrim's Progress* you may recall the description of the Man with the Muck-rake, the man who could look no way but downward, with the muck-rake in his hand; who was offered a celestial crown for his muck-rake, but who would neither look up nor regard the crown he was offered, but continued to rake to himself the filth of the floor. In *Pilgrim's Progress* the Man with the Muck-rake is set forth as the example of him whose vision is fixed on carnal instead of on spiritual things. Yet he also typifies the man who in this life consistently refuses to see aught that is lofty, and fixes his eyes with solemn intentness only on that which is vile and debasing.

Roosevelt added,

> It is very necessary that we should not flinch from seeing what is
> vile and debasing. There is filth on the floor, and it must be scraped
> up with the muck-rake; and there are times and places where this
> service is the most needed of all the services that can be performed.
> But the man who never does anything else, who never thinks or
> speaks or writes, save of his feats with the muck-rake, speedily
> becomes, not a help to society, not an incitement to good but one
> of the most potent forces for evil.

That criticism did not end the influence of socialism-promoting
journalists. Upton Sinclair said the muckrakers' "revolt against capitalism" would continue, and the muckraker, "as forerunner of a revolution . . . will be recognized in the future as a benefactor of his
race." But journalists who stayed on the left became more aggressive
in considering how change could come. Liberal journalists like Ray
Stannard Baker had found socialism attractive because of the "high
and unselfish ideals" and "community spirit of service" they found
among socialists they knew. But some press leaders came to scorn
such spirit in the way Marx, Lenin, and Mao came to scorn those who
thought a revolution could be a garden party.

For example, E. W. Scripps, a publisher whose chain of newspapers rivaled Hearst's, started out calling his socialism-promoting
editorials the "teaching department, the statesmanship department
and the spiritual department." He wrote, "I do not believe in God,
or any being equal to or similar to the Christian's God," and prided
himself on "leveling my guns at the employer class." But he also read
and believed Charles Darwin's teachings about what became known
as "survival of the fittest," and worried that socialism had "no practical
plan for the elimination of the unfit and for the dominance of the fit."

While some were dismayed by the murderous results of
the Bolshevik Revolution, Scripps wrote an essay in 1921 titled
"Wanted—a Tyrant." He argued that "as Lenin has striven and is still
striving to seize and hold power of dictator in Russia, so may we have
to depend on some coming strong man." Scripps left to posterity the

news service that became United Press International and also a maxim for never-ending revolution: "Whatever is, is wrong."

Another example is the prominent magazine writer Lincoln Steffens. He became a radical while studying at the University of California during the 1880s. He said his professors "could not agree upon what was knowledge, nor upon what was good and what evil, nor why." Steffens thought he figured out the why. Once, discussing the biblical fall in the garden of Eden, Steffens said the culprit was not Adam, or Eve, or even the snake: "It was, it is, the apple." A bad environment corrupted good people, Steffens thought. He hoped to change the environment by working to eliminate capitalism, which he saw as the twentieth-century equivalent of the apple.

When reactions to the Bolshevik Revolution divided American socialists, the hard-line Communists at first thought Steffens soft, a playful child of the despised bourgeoisie "wandering among the social battlefields." But Steffens proved himself by turning on a fellow Marxist and former friend, Max Eastman, who was honest enough to report accurately on Soviet repression during the 1920s and early 1930s. Steffens went the other way, writing propagandistic pieces praising Lenin and Stalin. One of his contemporaries remembered him "talking revolution and blood and sucking the guts out of a chocolate eclair impaled on an upright fork."

Steffens even argued that "treason to Communism" would be a "sin," for "Russia is the land of conscious, willful hope." He wrote on the last page of his autobiography, "I have been contending with all my kind, always against God." Political imperatives changed him from an apostle of man's reason as the glory of existence to a propagandist who said in 1932, "There comes a time to close our open minds, shut up our talking, and go to it."

Steffens praised Stalin's purges when they began in 1934, writing that Stalin was killing other Communists because he wisely realized "that the job was not yet done, that security was not yet secured." Later the constant lying got to him, and Steffens at one point contemplated suicide, but he stayed on the path he had chosen, writing shortly before his death in 1936 that "poetry, romance—all roads in our day lead to Moscow."

One more example is Walter Duranty. Covering the Soviet Union for the *New York Times* during the 1920s and 1930s, he was the father of all those who covered and praised the rise to power of Mao in the 1940s and Castro in the 1950s. Duranty received a Pulitzer Prize—America's top journalism award—in 1932 for his work's "scholarship, profundity, impartiality and exceptional clarity, and an example of the best type of foreign correspondence." Historical hindsight is not so kind, nor were the few among Duranty's journalist colleagues who were not tied to the left.

Duranty's clarity was actually false analogy. He said the Russian people were antirevolutionary only because they "are in the position of children at school, who personally might sooner be out at play and do not yet realize that they are being taught for their ultimate good." He equated Josef Stalin's opponents with the Ku Klux Klan, America's worst racist group, and wrote that "the peasants by and large at last have begun to realize the advantages offered by the new system, just as a plebe at West Point comes later to admire what at first he found so rigorous."

(Those first-year students at the U.S. military academy were not being murdered, but neither were those who resisted Stalin, according to Duranty. Rather, they could redeem themselves by working in Gulag lumber camps, those "communes" where "the labor demand exceeds the supply" and prisoners have the satisfaction of working "for the good of the community.")

Duranty intensified his defense of Soviet Communism when a worldwide depression began in the 1930s and some were praising Soviet "full employment"—true in that Stalin enslaved an entire nation. In 1930, discussing Stalin's Five Year Plan, Duranty acknowledged minor problems, but "what does count is that Russia is being speeded up and fermented—and disciplined—into jumping and making an effort." He portrayed Stalin as a harsh but kindly teacher, trying to "stir the people up, force new ideas into their heads and make them talk and think and learn despite themselves."

Duranty equated Stalin's Five Year Plan with the biblical exodus from Egyptian slavery: "Moses and Aaron can become Lenin and Trotsky, Joshua becomes Stalin." In 1932 and 1933, though, the Soviet countryside neared collapse in famine. About five million persons died in the manner later described by Victor Kravchenko: "Everywhere we found men and women lying prone, their faces and bellies bloated, their eyes utterly expressionless."

Stalin needed Duranty's help because the Soviets were shipping grain to the West to get cash to buy machinery for the steel industry. Coverage of the famine might have led to protests that could have stopped the big deals. Duranty aided Stalin by writing, "There is no actual starvation or deaths from starvation." He also wrote that reporters who wrote anything to the contrary were concocting a "big scare story."

Such was the prestige of Duranty and the ideological mood of the times, that honest reporters often had trouble with their editors when they described the reality that Fedor Belov captured: "The people were like beasts, ready to devour one another. And no matter what they did, they went on dying, dying, dying." Alexandr Solzhenitsyn later wrote that "long lines of [peasants] dying of famine trudged toward the railroad stations in the hope of getting to the cities . . . but were refused tickets and were unable to leave—and lay dying beneath the station fences in a submissive heap of homespun coats and bark shoes."

Duranty knew what he was doing. Malcolm Muggeridge, then also a Moscow reporter, remembered Duranty acknowledging the famine in conversation, but saying "you can't make an omelet without breaking eggs." Some say Duranty was bribed or compromised by the Soviets, but it was just as likely that he had made an idol of the Soviet Revolution. Duranty's favorite expression was, "I put my money on Stalin."

At the end of Duranty's tour of duty in Moscow, he said it had been a tour of love: "Looking backward over the fourteen years I have spent in Russia, I cannot escape the conclusion that this period has been a heroic chapter in the life of Humanity." Duranty's Pulitzer Prize led to other honors, along with a well-fed retirement in Southern California, during which he continued to worship capital-H "Humanity" rather than capital-G "God." His time on earth concluded with a well-attended funeral in the mid-1940s.

Most U.S. journalists did not follow in the paths of Scripps,

Steffens, and Duranty, but these press leaders influenced them, and many lost the confidence to stand up against atheists and socialists because of a revolution in journalists' thinking. Instead of believing they could convey an accurate view of reality, more came to agree with Henry Luce, founder of *Time* magazine, who said, "Show me a man who thinks he's objective and I'll show you a man who's deceiving himself." Ivy Lee, a journalist who became known as the founder of public relations, said it was "humanly impossible" to state a fact: "All I can do is to give you my interpretation of the facts."

The Luce and Lee statements were part of the journalistic revolution, discussed briefly in chapter 4, that arose early in the 1920s and 1930s as reporters influenced by Marxism and Freudianism redefined "objectivity." Marx had argued that much of what was called objectivity actually was class subjectivity, with one class-bound vision of the world up against another's, thesis versus antithesis. Freud contended that much of what affected individuals was unknown, even to the individuals themselves, so it could not be assumed judgments were unimpaired.

Walter Lippmann, probably the most influential American newspaper columnist of the twentieth century, was a Marxist in his early years and an admirer of Freudian thought. He used those ideas in the 1920s to become a philosopher of journalism as well. Lippmann was sarcastic about reporters' claims to objectivity, arguing that "for the most part we do not see first, then define; we define first and then see." Lippmann viewed the typical reporter as akin to the traveler who liked trains and did not think it proper to give porters tips: "His Odyssey will be replete with . . . train escapades and voracious demands for money."

The three L's—Lippmann, Luce, and Lee—had departed from the premodern American and European belief that truth was out there and journalists should seek it, generally with wisdom gained from reading the Bible. They were pioneers in going beyond the modernist belief that whatever truth there is should be sought through man's wisdom. Their assertion that there is no such thing as objective truth pointed to postmodernism.

Influenced by the three L's, journalists began to redefine the

meaning of objectivity, so it came to mean a balancing of subjectivities, a recitation of several subjective views in a way that appeared
evenhanded. As opposed to a standard dictionary definition of
objective—"existing independent of mind; emphasizing or expressing
the nature of reality as it is apart from subjective experience"—the
outcome of new "objectivity" might be neither truthful nor accurate,
but who knew what accuracy, let alone truth, really was?

The Society of Professional Journalists concretized this in its
code of ethics, proclaiming that "Truth is our ultimate goal," but
"Objectivity in reporting the news is another goal, which serves as
the hallmark of an experienced professional." Since objective truth
did not exist, objectivity and truth were in two separate compart-
ments. Specific detail A, which points a reader in one direction,
should be balanced by specific detail B, which points the reader in
another. A pro-something statement by Person X is followed by an
anti-something statement from Person Y.

Postmodernism was most common in covering national and
international news. Full-fledged journalistic postmodernism—the
belief that each reporter is a god unto himself, obliged not to report
but to create his own reality—has developed least rapidly on local
newspapers. Local reporters trying to create their own reality run
into opposition when the story concerns something about which the
reader has personal experience. A sports reporter, for example, cannot
stray too far when describing a game witnessed by millions.

Journalistic postmodernism has developed furthest among feature
writers with a descriptive flair, or among those reporting from foreign
climes that few of their readers comprehend. Postmodernism gives
journalists not only the freedom to construct whatever they choose,
but a rationale for deconstruction. They see knowledge, morality, and
law as social constructs, alongside truth claims that form the basis
of many of our institutions. Journalists used to voice concern about
increasing public cynicism in some areas, but now, since every conservative establishment purportedly exists behind a façade of rational-
ity, thoroughly postmodern journalists have one response to virtually
everything: "Bah, humbug."

Here's an alternative: even though much is false, find out what is true, and stick with it. Gain journalistic freedom from cynicism by regaining a Christian understanding of the nature of man, the nature of God, and the nature of man's tasks and hopes. That biblical way is not based on confidence in man—we all naturally distort and lie—but confidence in the objectivity of God. Just as a person assessing the strengths and weaknesses of his house is wise to consult the builder, so a person who wants to describe accurately the world God created should get information from its builder.

The biblical way is based on man's ability, with God's grace, to study the Bible and apply it to everyday situations. Biblical objectivity is the God's-eye view of things. Human beings cannot attain it, but in many realms the Bible is clear and we can come close enough to God's objectivity so as to know what is right to do and what is wrong. *Right* and *wrong* are not popular words among postmodernists, but they will be around long after postmodernism has given way to an understanding that will be new because it is so old.

KEY TERMS

muckrakers
the apple
capital-H Humanity
journalistic postmodernism

STUDY QUESTIONS

1. Why would anyone want a tyrant?
2. Who was the least-deserving recipient of a Pulitzer Prize?
3. What are the challenges and opportunities that postmodernism presents to Christian journalists?

FOR FURTHER READING

Linda Lumsden, *Black, White, and Red All Over* (Kent State, 2014).
Lincoln Steffens, *The Autobiography of Lincoln Steffens* (Harcourt, Brace, 1931).

S. J. Taylor, *Stalin's Apologist: Walter Duranty* (Oxford University Press, 1990).

Anne Applebaum, *Red Famine* (Doubleday, 2017).

Yuri Slezkine, *The House of Government* (Princeton University Press, 2017).

28

Ideological Battles

WHEN LINCOLN STEFFENS and Walter Duranty praised Communist leaders, other American journalists applauded—in part because the United States wallowed in economic depression during the 1930s. When Franklin Roosevelt became president in 1933, he proposed new laws that gave him power over banks and other institutions. The U.S. Congress cemented into law Roosevelt's wishes without debate or amendment, and in some cases without even reading them.

Popular support for Franklin Roosevelt was great. One congressman compared him to Jesus Christ, not unfavorably. A poll among New York schoolchildren showed God running a poor second to him. Representative John Young Brown of Kentucky said he would "as soon start a mutiny in the face of a foreign foe as start a mutiny today against the program of the President of the United States." Forty-one popular songs trilled his praises.

The centerpiece for Roosevelt's great leap forward, which he called "the New Deal," was the National Recovery Administration (NRA), empowered to set wages and prices for the entire country. *Business Week*, a magazine that represented the thinking of business leaders, approved of such dictatorship: "The wolves of depression have to be shot, and without the delay inherent in deliberative procedure." Many thought competition was bad and government control of the economy would improve life—as it purportedly improved life in the Soviet Union.

Imitation of the Soviets included mass mobilization. The NRA's symbol was a blue eagle, and 8,000 children stood in formation at a San Francisco baseball park to form an eagle. In Boston, 100,000 children assembled in the city's major park and recited a pledge: "I promise as a good American citizen to do my part for the NRA. I will buy only where the Blue Eagle flies. I will help President Roosevelt bring back good times." Four young ladies had eagles tattooed on their backs. NRA chief administrator Hugh Johnson said of his eagle, "May God have mercy on the man or group of men who attempt to trifle with this bird."

Few reporters were willing to trifle. The San Francisco press club publication *Scoop* said, regarding press and president, "The nation's reporters will smile contentedly as long as F. R. sits on the throne." Joseph Medill Patterson, who published the nation's most-read newspaper, the *New York Daily News*, promised in 1933, "Whatever President Roosevelt does or doesn't do, we're going to be for him." Popular columnist Mark Sullivan said Roosevelt "could recite the Polish alphabet and it would be accepted as an eloquent plea for disarmament."

Frank Kent (1877–1958), a *Baltimore Sun* writer and syndicated columnist, was one of the rare journalists who pushed back. He complained, "A tremendous propaganda emanated from Washington. . . . Anyone who did not fall in line was regarded as 'rocking the boat,' or 'pulling back on prosperity.'" Kent muttered in one of his columns about

> government propaganda . . . never has anyone seen anything like it. . . . The publicity men are so numerous that they stumble over each other. . . . The making of favorable news is one of the principal Administration activities, and more real efficiency is there shown than in any other department.

Kent voted for Roosevelt in 1932, only to be appalled by the "fine fake game" the president's administration played as it flooded the country with puff pieces and articles designed for newspaper publication:

"Much of the publicity is so arranged that it has the appearance of entirely spontaneous and wholly untainted news, but it is all thought out and planned with the utmost care." When Kent analyzed the NRA legislation in 1933, he saw price-setting as a retreat to medieval guilds with "competition eliminated, prices raised, profits assured."

The NRA created seven hundred codes based on 11,000 federal administrative orders and seventy presidential executive orders. It classified every business transaction from Automobile Manufacturing and Cotton Textiles to Lightning Rod Manufacturing and Corn Cob Pipes. Four hundred codes allowed for the fixing of prices. Business owners learned about "codes, supplemental codes, code amendments, executive orders, administrative orders, office orders, interpretations, rules, regulations"—and they could be fined and jailed for getting something wrong.

Kent protested all this and was willing to offend powerful people. When one senator responded to a Kent attack by saying, "Your friends in the Senate regret that," Kent replied, "Who said I want friends in the Senate?" Government propagandists called Kent and other NRA opponents "corporals of disaster." Kent in turn was sarcastic about those whose job was to proclaim that the NRA was "succeeding beyond expectation, that everything is lovely and the goose hangs high."

By 1934, it was apparent that the NRA was not working. Employment was not increasing. Small businesses were in a straight-jacket. According to another dissident journalist, John T. Flynn, NRA enforcers

> roamed through the garment district like storm troopers. They could enter a man's factory, send him out, line up his employees, subject them to minute interrogation, take over his books on the instant. Night work was forbidden. Flying squadrons of these private coat-and-suit police went through the district at night, battering down doors with axes looking for men who were committing the crime of sewing together a pair of pants at night.

By 1935, small businesses were beginning to openly defy the NRA codes. Kent reported the pushback, and rejoiced in May 1935 when the U.S. Supreme Court unanimously declared the NRA unconstitutional. The federal government would not be allowed to control every aspect of private enterprise, and the movement toward socialism in America stopped. That same year the Communist Party USA developed a new slogan, "Communism is twentieth-century Americanism," but that was just propaganda. Americans were accepting a larger federal government, but did not want socialism.

Nevertheless, as one brilliant journalist, Whittaker Chambers, wrote,

> The New Deal was a genuine revolution, whose deepest purpose was not simply reform within existing traditions, but a basic change in the social, and, above all, the power relationships within the nation. It was not a revolution by violence. It was a revolution by bookkeeping and lawmaking. In so far as it was successful, the power of politics had replaced the power of business. This is the basic power shift of all the revolutions of our time. This shift was the revolution.

Chambers wrote for *Time*, the leading American news magazine, and published at mid-century a best-selling autobiography, *Witness*. He was also a Communist Party USA member who spied for the Soviet Union during the 1930s and then became a Christian. He pointed out that Communism

> is not new. It is, in fact, man's second oldest faith. Its promise was whispered in the first days of the Creation under the Tree of the Knowledge of Good and Evil: "Ye shall be as gods." It is the great alternative faith of mankind. . . . The Communist vision is the vision of Man without God . . . redirecting man's destiny and reorganizing man's life and the world.

Chambers and Alger Hiss, who had been an important aide to President Roosevelt, were the two major figures in a big story of the late 1940s. Chambers charged Hiss had been a spy, and produced microfilm and other evidence to back up his accusations. Washington reporters could not understand why someone like Hiss—handsome, successful, and well-connected—would become a traitor. Nor did they understand how the grace of redemption propelled Chambers to leave a comfortable and coveted position at *Time* to become a witness against communism.

Chambers cast doubt, not only on the integrity of Hiss, but also on the management of the federal bureaucracy generally. He wrote,

> When I took up my little sling and aimed at Communism, I also hit something else. What I hit was the forces of that great socialist revolution, which, in the name of liberalism, spasmodically, incompletely, somewhat formlessly, but always in the same direction, has been inching its ice cap over the nation for two decades.

Chambers tried to teach the reporters. He told them of the true evil of communism (not just mistake, or misfortune, or trying too hard to make progressive changes, but satanic evil). He described the true grace of God (not just existing in some abstract form, but actively changing men's hearts and creating the opportunity for new lives). His first statement to the press, shortly before appearing at a congressional hearing, was that he had left the Communist Party because "it was an evil." He continued to use such blunt words throughout his public agony.

Chambers consistently stressed religious presuppositions. He criticized "the great alternative faith of mankind," the Communist vision of "Man without God . . . man's mind displacing God as the creative intelligence of the world." Chambers testified he had been consumed by that sinful vision also, until God had changed his heart through free grace. Reporters could not understand Chambers's story unless they understood something about sin and grace—and few did.

He wrote,

> Many of my colleagues at *Time*, basically kind and intensely well-meaning people, seemed to me as charming and as removed from reality as fish in a fish bowl. To me they seemed to know little about the forces that were shaping the history of our time. To me

they seemed like little children, knowing and clever little children, but knowing and clever chiefly about trifling things while they were extremely resistant to finding out about anything else.

Chambers had also been a clever child, but when God touched him,

what I had been fell from me like dirty rags. The rags that fell from me were not only Communism. What fell was the whole web of the materialist modern mind—the luminous shroud which it has spun about the spirit of man, paralyzing in the name of rationalism the instinct of his soul for God, denying in the name of knowledge the reality of the soul and its birthright in that mystery on which mere knowledge falters and shatters at every step.

To reporters who approved the socialist tendencies of the New Deal, it made no sense that officials with impressive resumes should become traitors—but it made perfect sense, given an awareness of original sin. It made no sense that a liar such as Chambers should now be trusted—but it made perfect sense if there is a God who so transforms hearts that those who once loved lying now find false witness abhorrent.

Many reporters thought that when Chambers testified to how God had saved him, he was saying he was better than them, but Chambers said he could not "explain why God's grace touches a man who seems unworthy of it." They could also understand a hunger for money, power, or fame influencing Chambers, if he thought the Communist tide was receding, but he thought the opposite: "I am leaving the winning side for the losing side." (He added, "It is better to die on the losing side than to live under Communism.")

If Chambers had come to faith through long study at a seminary, maybe journalists would have understood his change, but he described a major shift based on observing his baby daughter:

My eye came to rest on the delicate convolutions of her ear—those intricate, perfect ears. The thought passed through my mind: "No, those ears were not created by any chance coming together of atoms in nature (the Communist view). They could have been created only by immense design." (Up until then, he had seen abortion as a "mere physical manipulation." Afterward, it "now filled me with physical horror.")

A jury in January 1950 believed Chambers and found Hiss guilty of perjury. Hiss was lying about his spying. Careful historians have no real doubt that the jury verdict was correct. Yet, when I had five of my journalism students read 1950 coverage of the Hiss trial only in the *Washington Post*—then, as now, a newspaper devoted to expanding the power of national government—they concluded Hiss was innocent. That's because *Post* reporters downplayed evidence against Hiss that was irrefutable in the courtroom: microfilm of stolen documents, other documents retyped on his typewriter.

Instead, *Post* reporters emphasized the personal battle between "tall, lean, 44-year-old Hiss," who had character references from Supreme Court justices, and "short, fat-faced" Chambers, with his "customary air of complete emotionless detachment." In *Post* pages, Chambers wore a "supercilious expression," while Hiss "calmly strode to the stand" and was always "sure of himself, answering the barrage of questions without hesitation, showing no uneasiness or equivocation."

By comparing *Post* coverage with that of a then-conservative newspaper, the *Chicago Tribune*, we can learn a lot about how reporters affect readers by choosing specific detail. On June 2, 1949, Chambers testified that Alger Hiss had furnished government secrets to the Soviets, and also admitted having himself lied while a Communist during the 1930s. The following day, the *Post* headline emphasized Chambers's past derelictions: "Lies Admitted by Chambers." The *Tribune*, though, spotlighted Hiss's activity: "Hiss Aided Reds: Chambers." Each newspaper also described the emotional state of Chambers as he was testifying. The liberal *Post* reported "Chambers seemed to be showing discomfiture," while the conservative *Tribune* noted Chambers "never lost his composure."

One lesson from that is that reporters should not be swayed by appearances, but should look at the facts. Here's one more example:

Fidel Castro in 1957 was hiding in Cuba's mountains until a *New York Times* reporter, Herbert Matthews, wrote a fawning story about him. Castro had marched his small band in circles several times to make Matthews think he had a large following, and Matthews told the world that Castro's force was strong. Matthews described Castro's program as "a new deal for Cuba, radical, democratic, and therefore anti-Communist."

More articles by Matthews in 1958 stated that Castro would hold free elections. Americans came to favor his takeover. Even half a year after Castro came to power in 1959, Matthews insisted that Castro is "not only not Communist but decidedly anti-Communist." Cuban poet Armando Valladares knew that wasn't true, and his opposition to Castro led to twenty-two years in prison. In the 1980s, after an international campaign, Castro let him go to the United States, where he became chief of the United States' Delegation to the United Nations Commission on Human Rights.

In 1988, he told that group:

> Perhaps I am the only delegate in this Commission who has spent such a long time in prison, although there are several persons here who have known in their own flesh the meaning of torture. I do not care about their political ideology, and I offer to you my embrace of solidarity, from tortured to tortured. . . . They kept me in a punishment cell, naked, with several fractures on one leg which never received medical care; today, those bones remain jammed up together and displaced. One of the regular drills among the guards was to stand on the steel mesh ceiling and throw at my face buckets full of urine and excrement.

Here's one more paragraph:

> For me [prison meant] eight thousand days of hunger, of systematic beatings, of hard labor, of solitary confinement, of cells with steel-planked windows and doors, of solitude. Eight thousand days of struggling to prove that I was a human being. Eight thousand days of proving that my spirit could triumph over exhaustion and

pain. Eight thousand days of testing my religious convictions, my faith, of fighting the hate my atheist jailers were trying to instill in me with each bayonet thrust, fighting so that hate would not flourish in my heart.

In 1997, on the fortieth anniversary of the Castro-Matthews interview, the Cuban government erected a monument on the spot where the *New York Times* reporter had lionized the would-be dictator and condemned Cuba to decades of despair.

KEY TERMS

Blue Eagle
man's second oldest faith

STUDY QUESTIONS

1. Why did most leading reporters offer enthusiastic support to President Franklin Roosevelt?
2. What did Chambers-Hiss coverage show about the *Washington Post* in the mid-twentieth century, at a time when it was often seen as promoting objectivity?
3. How did Fidel Castro come to power, and what did he do to his opponents?

FOR FURTHER READING

Whittaker Chambers, *Witness* (Random House, 1952).

James William Crowl, *Angels in Stalin's Paradise* (Rowman and Littlefield, 1981).

Tom Kelly, *The Imperial Post* (William Morrow, 1983).

Russ Braley, *Bad News: The Foreign Policy of the New York Times* (Regnery, 1984).

Lian Xi, *Blood Letters* (Basic, 2018).

29

The Recent American Journalistic Tilt

I COULD GO decade by decade through recent American journalistic history, but the story gets repetitive, so I'll come at it in a different way. The great British writer C. S. Lewis, author of *Mere Christianity* and *The Screwtape Letters*, also wrote seven novels for children that are collectively known as *The Chronicles of Narnia*.

One of the great moments of book four, *The Silver Chair*, comes when the evil Queen of Underland tries to lull the heroes into sleepiness. The queen's main tool is a mandolin she plays with "a steady, monotonous thrumming that you didn't notice after a few minutes. But the less you noticed it, the more it got into your brain and your blood. This also made it hard to think."

We've heard a similar kind of thrumming from most of America's Goliath Media during the twenty-five years I've been writing *World* columns. We heard, for example, that the Democratic presidential candidate in 2000, Al Gore, was apparently an intellectual giant. *Newsweek's* Bill Turque described what Gore "really loves: thinking about complexity theory, open systems, Goethe, and the absence of scientific metaphors in modern society." *U.S. News* senior writer Timothy Noah fitted him out as a major thinker: "Gore's commitment to the world of big ideas is no pose. . . . Gore is truly engaged in the life of the mind." There was no focus on Gore's pro-abortion positions or the economic disaster that his hyper-environmentalism would bring. Thrum, thrum.

I could present thousands of examples of adulation regarding the successful Democratic candidate in 2008, Barack Obama. To *Time*'s Joe Klein, he was

> the political equivalent of a rainbow—a sudden preternatural event inspiring awe and ecstasy. . . . He transcends the racial divide so effortlessly that it seems reasonable to expect that he can bridge all the other divisions—and answer all the impossible questions— plaguing American public life.

ABC's Terry Moran gushed that Obama was "the thrill, the hope. . . . Is he the one?"

In 2008, MSNBC's Chris Matthews gained notoriety for describing what he felt whenever Obama spoke: "this thrill going up my leg." In 2010, he said again, "I get the same thrill up my leg, all over me." He said Obama was "the perfect American," a person who has "never done anything wrong." Newsweek headlined an inauguration cover "The Second Coming." ABC's Lara Spencer even called him "a baby whisperer": "Watch as the First Lady tries to quiet down the fussy little friend. . . . She then hands the bawling baby to the big man and, presto, the tot is simply transfixed." As were leftist reporters. Thrum, thrum.

Hillary Clinton, whom Obama beat out for the presidential nomination in 2008, was a favorite until she lost her presidential campaign to Donald Trump in 2016. CBS's Diane Sawyer crooned about her "political mastery," and *Time*'s Lance Morrow swooned, "I see a sort of Celtic mist forming around Hillary as a new archetype . . . at a moment when the civilization pivots, at last, decisively— perhaps for the first time since the advent of Christian patriarchy two millenniums ago—toward Woman."

Time ran this about the 2016 version of Clinton: "Her decades in our public life must not blind us to the fact that she represents new realities and possibilities. Indeed, those same decades have conferred upon her what newness usually lacks: judgment, and even wisdom." ABC's Cokie Roberts said of Clinton,

> She does have a new message out from the last time, which is the grandmother message, and she's using it very well. On climate change for instance, when she says, "Everybody says I'm not a scientist." She says, "I'm not a scientist either, I'm just a grandmother with two eyes and a brain." That's brilliant.

Sure it was, until Clinton lost.

The United States does not have the great British parliamentary tradition, Prime Minister's Questions, where the government head has to respond to hostile questions from political opponents—so in America reporters sometimes take on that role. The process, though, does not sharpen Democratic presidents or educate the public, because press questioning of Democrats is almost always soft.

In the 1990s, for example, President Bill Clinton received criticism for using the famed Lincoln Bedroom in the White House as an enticement to big donors. Here's the question from the *Washington Post*:

> There's been a lot of talk lately, as you know, printed and so forth, about the Lincoln Bedroom and the people who stay here. And obviously a lot of them are your friends. And I don't think anybody would begrudge somebody having guests in their own house. Some of them, though, it seems apparently you didn't know quite as well. And we're wondering if you might feel let down a little bit by your staff or by the DNC [Democratic National Committee] in their zeal to raise funds?

Thrum, thrum.

President Barack Obama regularly received softball questions like this one from Bob Schieffer of CBS:

> You had a tough summer. We saw the rise of ISIS, the outbreak of Ebola, trouble in the Ukraine, illegal immigrants coming across

the border. Did you ever go back to the residence at night and say, "Are we ever going to get a break here?". . . . You came here talking about hope and change. Do you still hope? Is change, was it harder than you thought it would be?

Schieffer was one of the Washington reporters whom his CBS colleague, Bernard Goldberg, cited as evidence that charges of liberal bias in the media were "blatantly true. . . . We don't sit around in dark corners and plan strategies on how we're going to slant the news. We don't have to. It comes naturally to most reporters." Schieffer responded, "People are just stunned. It's such a wacky charge. . . . I don't know what Bernie was driving at. It just sounds bizarre."

Some reporters had a tinge of shame about their lapdog tendencies with Democrats. *CBS This Morning* cohost Norah O'Donnell was interviewing new network darling Sen. Elizabeth Warren (D-Mass.) and became embarrassed about a query that had just come out of her mouth: "That was a softball of a question, wasn't it?" Cohost Charlie Rose had fewer scruples. He told Warren, "She just teed it up for you. Go." When CNN's Piers Morgan had a chance to question Iranian leader Mahmoud Ahmadinejad, he asked how many times the autocrat had been in love. Ahmadinejad said, "I'm in love with all of humanity," and Morgan responded, "That might be the best answer I've ever heard to that question." Thrum, thrum.

Goliath Media also have bad guys, of course. In the 1990s, *New York Times* columnist Maureen Dowd said Republicans concerned about national debt were "cannibals. . .vampires. . . zombies." Republican leaders criticizing Bill Clinton's character in the House of Representatives were like Ku Klux Klan "night riders," according to *Newsweek*'s Eleanor Clift: "All they were missing was white sheets." A *New York Times* story about the Clinton impeachment trial opened with an analysis by psychotherapist Ellen Mendel of how she "feels the same despair that she did as a girl in Nazi Germany."

President George W. Bush came under hostile fire in 2001, especially when he announced his intention to pursue to Afghanistan the planners of the September 11 terrorist attack. Clift declared, "There's nothing this administration won't do under the guise of battling terrorism." *Newsweek* editor Allison Yarrow called Vice President Dick Cheney "one of the most evil people in the world." MSNBC's Keith Olbermann announced the Bush administration is "more dangerous to our liberty than is the enemy it claims to protect us from."

Goliath Media's attack on the GOP did not just begin with the ascendency of Donald Trump. *New York Times* columnist Charles Blow said 2012 Republican candidate Mitt Romney "does not have a soul . . . not even a heart." The *Boston Globe*'s Charles Pierce labeled Speaker of the House Paul Ryan a "zombie-eyed granny-starver." The *Washington Post*'s Harold Meyerson observed, "Today's Republican Party is not just far from being the party of Lincoln: It's really the party of Jefferson Davis. . . . It is the lineal descendant of Lee's army, and the descendants of Grant's have yet to subdue it."

New York Times columnist Joe Nocera wrote, "Tea Party Republicans have waged jihad on the American people" and wear "suicide vests." His fellow *Times* columnist Paul Krugman said Republicans have "a state of mind that takes positive glee in inflicting further suffering on the already miserable. . . an almost pathological mean-spiritedness." He then said in an interview, "As a *Times* columnist, I can't do endorsements, so you have no idea which party I favor in general elections." Thrum, thrum.

Chris Matthews regularly ranted, as in this questioning of Republican National Committee Chairman Michael Steele, who is black:

> You go to a Democratic convention. . . and black folk are hanging together and having a good time. . . . You go to a Republican event, you get a feeling that you are all told. . . "Don't get together, don't crowd, you'll scare these people." . . . Did you fear that if you got together with some other African-Americans, these white guys might get scared of you?

Steele replied, "No! What are you talking about?"

Christians were usually the objects of greatest scorn. Bonnie Erbe of PBS, reporting from the GOP national convention, said Republicans were trying to be "pro-woman, pro-minorities, [but] this is in sharp contrast to the delegates on the floor, 60 percent of whom are self-identified as conservative Christians." Goliath Media repeatedly depict conservative Christians as anti-minority and anti-woman, in part because they oppose abortion, even though black babies are far more likely than white babies to be killed before birth, and even though abortion is more popular among men than among women.

Mediacrats regularly displayed ignorance of Christianity. NBC's Bryant Gumbel asked former president Jimmy Carter,

> You write that you prayed more during your four years in office than basically at any time in your life and yet . . . you are consistently viewed as one of the more ineffective presidents of modern times. . . . What do you think, if anything, that says about the power of prayer?

Gumbel apparently equated prayer with getting what you ask for. Thrum, thrum.

When George W. Bush appointed John Ashcroft to his cabinet, *Newsweek* pointed out that Ashcroft had said, "We have no king but Jesus," and asked, "Can a deeply religious person be Attorney General?" A decade later, PBS host Tavis Smiley thought Muslim dissident Ayaan Hirsi Ali was wrong on the roots of Islamist terrorism when he said, "The idea got into their minds that to kill other people is a great thing to do and that they would be rewarded in the hereafter." Smiley objected, "But Christians do that every single day in this country." Ali asked, "Do they blow people up every day?" Smiley said, "Yes."

Goliath Media leaders also refused to comprehend Communism's enormity. Newt Gingrich was just "like Lenin," according to ABC's Sam Donaldson: "They both made a revolution by shooting people—Newt shot Democrats, Lenin shot everybody—and then they didn't have enough sense to stop shooting once they won." Republican congressional leaders, according to Robert Scheer in the *Los Angeles Times*, "would rather kill people than raise taxes."

Reporters often knew little about American history, but they did know the 1950s were "the McCarthy years," and that was bad. They did not understand the threat that prompted Sen. Joseph McCarthy's exaggerations and lies. The *New York Times* complained that

> the war on terrorism was starting to look suspiciously like the great American campaign—against Communism. . . . The McCarthy years in some ways were eerily similar to the present moment. . . . Communists were often conceived as moral monsters whose deviousness and unwavering dedication to their faith made them capable of almost anything.

Sadly, some Communists were indeed highly dedicated moral monsters capable of almost anything.

In their ignorance, some journalists became propagandists. Ray Suarez on the *PBS NewsHour* spoke of communist Cuba's "impressive health outcomes. . . no doctor shortage. . . care that's both personal and persistent." Right. In reporting from Havana in 2004, I talked with doctors serving as cab drivers and bellhops to get money for their families. Some churches hosted illegal clinics because parishioners couldn't get help through official channels. A pharmacy's shelves were mostly empty. A hospital had a BYOX policy: Bring your own X-ray film.

CBS This Morning cohost Jane Robelot reported, "Under Cuba's communist form of government, a Cuban family's basic necessities, housing, education, health care, and transportation, are provided by the state for free or at very little cost." Right. I once carried to Havana fifty pounds of powdered milk, because the state was handing out a very watery variety. Paul Haven of the Associated Press reported Cuba was allowing some small businesses to develop, and the likely result would be "a society of haves and have-nots in a land that has spent half a century striving for an egalitarian utopia." Thrum, thrum.

ABC's Diane Sawyer even became an apologist for North Korea. Reporting from a school there, she said, "It is a world away from the unruly individualism of any American school. . . . Ask them about their country, and they can't say enough." The clip showed a North Korean girl saying in English, "We are the happiest children in the world." Later, Sawyer said to the class: "You know *The Sound of Music?*" Children's voices chorused, "Yes." Sawyer then sang with the class: "Do, a deer, a female deer. Re, a drop of golden sun . . ." Anchor Charles Gibson intoned, "A fascinating glimpse of North Korea"— and of a country when one wrong word can send whole families to slave labor camps.

Chris Matthews once turned a U.S. train derailment into an advertisement for the Chinese government. He said,

> In communist countries like China, they just draw a straight line, whether it goes through your house or not. . . . [Amtrak] doesn't go in a straight line. In this case, it tried to make a turn and turned over, because there's so many turns on that route. How do you get rid of the turns?

The answer is simple: ride roughshod over anyone who gets in the Communist Party's way—but Matthews did not connect the dots. Thrum, thrum.

Goliath Media mainstays not only treat their subjective opinions as objective, but also say what's not so and declare it "fact." Because I follow poverty statistics, I looked into this statement by MSNBC's Martin Bashir half a dozen years ago: "We know today that more people were collecting food stamps under George W. Bush than are under President Obama." Just plain wrong. More than 46 million Americans were on food stamps at the end of 2011, a figure 40 percent higher than at any time during the Bush years.

Sometimes the incorrect statements aren't statistical. Eleanor Clift stated about the killings in Libya that became a campaign issue, "Ambassador [Chris] Stevens was not murdered. He died of smoke inhalation." Maybe, and eighty years ago Walter Duranty of the *New York Times* won a Pulitzer Prize for coverage of the Soviet Union. As a Communist-imposed famine killed millions, Duranty said no one was dying of starvation. True, they died because their weakened organs stopped working.

When *Washington Post* business reporter Zachary Goldfarb reported that "with his 2015 budget request, Obama will call for an end to the era of austerity that has dogged much of his presidency," he was stating a fact—Obama did call for that—but not leaving a truthful impression. Federal government debt during the Obama years doubled from $10.6 trillion when he took office. It's a good thing we had austerity.

Predictions of the coming apocalypse require frequent recalibrating. Josh Elliott opened one episode of ABC's *Good Morning America* by announcing it was "deadline day. Hours, now, until massive government cuts go into effect that could impact every American: jobs vaporizing, flights delayed, even criminals walking free." Nothing much happened. Savannah Guthrie four days later on NBC's *Today* explained the sequester is "not a poison that kills you overnight. Apparently it's a slow, rolling poison."

Sometimes mediacrats offered not just purported facts, but counterfactuals. *USA Today* asked what would have happened if "prescient" 1972 Democratic nominee George McGovern had been elected, and then answered, "The Cold War would have ended in the '70s rather than in the '90s." That may be true; the United States would have lost. *Newsweek* acknowledged its manufacturing of role models in a cover story about demagogue Al Sharpton: "If he didn't exist, we might, in fact, need to invent him." (Goliath Media did.)

CBS Early Show cohost Jane Clayson, though, called counterfactuals off-limits in one discussion of abortion. What great inventions and songs and books would have emerged had abortion not killed tens of millions of children? Clayson said, "We're not here to debate the right and wrong."

In the late twentieth century, journalists would often claim a lack of bias. For example, Dan Rather said,

> Most reporters don't know whether they're Republican or Democrat, and vote every which way. . . . Most reporters, when you get to know them, fall in the general category of kind of commonsense moderates. . . . I don't think "liberal" or "conservative" mean very much anymore.

Thrum, thrum.

But journalists' defenses against charges of bias often showed how deep the bias goes. NBC's Tom Brokaw said he didn't see "a liberal agenda. It happens that journalism will always be spending more time on issues that seem to be liberal to some people: the problem of civil rights and human rights, the problem of those people who don't have a place at the table with the powerful." Those issues are not liberal. Liberals have kept the poor semi-enslaved on government plantations, and compassionate conservatives have tried to free them. That Brokaw thought those are liberal issues showed his agenda.

Some journalists during the pre-Trump years acknowledged the tilt. In 2006, the *Washington Post's* Tom Edsall acknowledged that the proportion of Democrats to Republicans in "mainstream media" is "probably in the range of 15 to 25:1 Democrat." That is probably low now, but Edsall's analysis of the effects of the tilt was good:

> There is a real difficulty on the part of the mainstream media being sympathetic, or empathetic, to the kind of thinking that goes into conservative approaches to issues. I think the religious right has been treated as sort of an alien world.

Even *ABC News* political director Mark Halperin acknowledged the dominance of the left in journalism "tilts the coverage quite frequently, in many issues, in a liberal direction. . . . It's an endemic problem."

When some journalists like *Time's* Jay Carney became White House press secretaries or nabbed other administration positions, cynics saw crass job-hunting at work. Chris Matthews may have panted too hard during Obama's first term when he interviewed two pro–Hillary Clinton journalists and said, "If you're watching, Madam Secretary, all three of us have brilliant ideas." *New York Times* correspondent Mark Landler had a more typical approach at a press conference when, instead of asking a question, he expressed adulation for Obama's bringing about a trade deal. The president's reply rewarded him: "I think that's a great example."

MSNBC host Lawrence O'Donnell, interviewing Michigan governor Jennifer Granholm during the Obama years, was typical in his offering of talking points to Democrats. O'Donnell stated,

The Republican Party is saying that the President of the United States has bosses, that the union bosses this president around. Does that sound to you like they are trying to consciously or subconsciously deliver the racist message that, of course, a black man can't be the real boss?

Granholm replied, "Wow, I hadn't thought about the racial overtones."

Maybe, though, the tilt originates in neither ambition nor ideology, but theology. When Jill Abramson became editor of the *New York Times*, she said her rise was like "ascending to Valhalla. In my house growing up, the *Times* substituted for religion. If the *Times* said it, it was the absolute truth." Some American conservatives have responded to this leftist movement by engaging in distortions of their own or getting hysterical. Christians, though, should remember that the sky isn't falling, because God holds up the sky.

KEY TERMS

> thrumming
> mediacrats
> watchdog
> Goliath Media
> BYOX

STUDY QUESTIONS

1. What is the American alternative to Britain's "Prime Minister's Questions," and what are the limitations of that alternative?
2. Why do some liberal reporters still claim that leading media outlets, with rare exceptions, are not liberal?

FOR FURTHER READING

Brent Baker, *How to Identify, Expose, and Correct Liberal Media Bias* (Media Research Center, 1994).

Marvin Olasky, *Standing for Christ in a Modern Babylon* (Crossway, 2003).

Alister McGrath, *The Twilight of Atheism* (Doubleday, 2004).

Paul Marshall, Lela Gilbert, and Roberta Green Ahmanson, *Blind Spot: When Journalists Don't Get Religion* (Oxford University Press, 2008).

30

Factual Accuracy and Humble Sowing

I OFTEN WORK with younger journalists and am excited to see their strong faith in Christ—but their faith isn't strong enough if they think that God needs our public relations help.

Here's a paragraph about how a Christian volunteer in the United States received permission to teach a Bible study in the classroom of a government-run school, and then attracted students by offering them free food of a kind beloved in America:

> The boxes of pepperoni pizzas entice curious students into classroom 413, where 20 students regularly study the Bible. When newcomers hear the words "free pizza" and enter the classroom, only to realize they have come to a Bible Club, the volunteer invites them to stay and makes sure to add a short gospel presentation to his teaching—and most of the students make the decision to profess Christ. Next time they bring friends.

Since that paragraph seemed more like a sweet story than trustworthy reporting, I challenged the writer:

> Are you describing what you saw on the Tuesday you visited? Are you describing what took place earlier in the year? If the latter, how

do you know what happened then? If this happened before, did the newcomers have no idea that this was a Bible Club? Did most make a decision to profess Christ? What exactly did this decision consist of? Did the kids say anything? Did they raise their hands when asked if this made sense to them? How many of these kids did you interview? If this is what you saw happening, how do you know they returned with friends another time?

My conclusion:

> We're reporters, not public relations people. Are you relying on the volunteer's account of other meetings? People often exaggerate the success of efforts. Do you have the testimony of two or more witnesses? Tell me what the kids told you, or what several parents who were present saw.

As always, we need to be eyewitnesses, or at least we need consistent testimony from witnesses with no reason to exaggerate.

Secular reporters in the U.S. often speak of a conflict between religious faith and journalistic skepticism. They offer an old journalistic joke—"If your mother says she loves you, check it out"—and conclude that reporters can't take anything on faith, so Christians should not be reporters. But that ignores the Bible's teaching that if our heavenly Father says he loves you, check it out. Why else would Luke stress at the beginning of his gospel that he relied on eyewitnesses, that he had "followed all things closely for some time," and that his goal was to offer the recipient of his letter, Theophilus, "certainty concerning the things you have been taught"?

Why else are we instructed in Psalm 107 to "give thanks to the LORD, for he is good"? The psalm explains how God delivered from distress those who "wandered in desert wastes," those who "sat in darkness and in the shadow of death," those who "went down to the sea in ships" and, amid storms, "reeled and staggered like drunken men." The psalm gives the experience of deliverance that millions have had, and concludes, "Whoever is wise, let him attend to these things."

That appeal is not for blind faith, but for attending to the lessons of experience that emerge throughout the Bible. For example, we can continue thumbing through the Psalms and note 116:1, "I love the LORD, because he has heard my voice and my pleas for mercy." Or Psalm 118:5, "Out of my distress I called on the LORD; the LORD answered me and set me free." Or Psalm 119:65, "You have dealt well with your servant, O LORD, according to your word."

The Bible also offers the evidence from Israel's history to explain why we should have faith in God. In Joshua 24:7, God tells the Israelites, "Your eyes saw what I did in Egypt." In Acts 7:36, Stephen tells of how Moses showed God's power by "performing wonders and signs," not only in Egypt, but also "at the Red Sea and in the wilderness for forty years."

Yet what of the famous words in John 20:28? Jesus asked the apostle who became known as Doubting Thomas, "Have you believed because you have seen me? Blessed are those who have not seen and yet have believed." Those sentences are sometimes taken, out of context, as signifying that faith and evidence are opposed.

The context is important. The other disciples have told Thomas, "We have seen the Lord." Thomas was doubtful, because he did not trust the eyewitness evidence others provided, and it's in this sense that those who believe without seeing for themselves are blessed. They are not so self-centered or solipsistic that they refuse to accept the testimony of anyone other than themselves.

Journalists also must rely heavily on what others say—and what reporter will not go to press when ten people say the same thing, even if he has not seen it himself? Doubting Thomas, despite the name, is not a model for journalists; he's the model for a reporter who will always be scooped.

I could go on, but it's evident that the Bible does not favor blind faith. Instead, the Bible regularly appeals to personal experience, just as journalists do. The canyon between Christianity and today's mainstream journalism is large, but it does not have an evidentiary river running through it.

Here's what the Bible does emphasize: humility. Paul told the Christians in Philippi,

Do nothing from selfish ambition or conceit, but in humility count others more significant than yourselves. Let each of you look not only to his own interests, but also to the interests of others. Have this mind among yourselves, which is yours in Christ Jesus, who, though he was in the form of God, did not count equality with God a thing to be grasped, but emptied himself, by taking the form of a servant, being born in the likeness of men. (Phil. 2:3–7)

I once put the words "journalistic humility" into a major U.S. electronic retrieval system for newspaper and magazine stories. I asked for all the articles over the past year that included the term. The reply message was: "No documents were found for your search. You should edit your search and try again."

A generation or two ago, the reportorial ethic came as close to emphasizing humility as it ever has. A California friend of mine remembers that at her local newspaper she enjoyed being "a fly on the wall," listening to a variety of views and then presenting them fairly, rather than imposing or even insinuating her own. Columnists (like liberal Supreme Court justices) could flaunt their opinions, but reporters were to be strict constructionists in their reports. They did not legislate from their notepads.

This was journalism still based on statements of faith, such as "The Journalist's Creed" quoted in chapter 1: "The public journal is a public trust; that all connected with it are, to the full measure of their responsibility, trustees for the public." The Creed emphasized reporting that "fears God and honors man . . . self-controlled, patient, always respectful of its readers."

How many reporters followed that creed, let alone the Apostles' Creed, is hard to tell. Movies throughout the twentieth century tended to emphasize journalistic cynicism and rudeness, but some reporters saw themselves as public servants, not puppet masters. Others, though, decided "fly on the wall" humility was less important than nailing to the wall the hides of those considered reactionary.

Now in America, as New York University professor Jay Rosen puts it, "Journalism is itself a religion." Rosen describes "the priesthood of the journalism profession in the United States, especially those at top news organizations in New York and Washington." They think everything is a matter of opinion, and it's their opinion that counts. Christians could push back by asserting that their opinions should take precedence, but the better approach is to show the world we value God's counsel highly enough to live by it, even when it hurts, and to interpret the world in accordance with it.

We learn God's counsel best through careful Bible study. It's important to ask about any Bible passage, "What does it say?" and then, "What does it mean?" In other words, we should first look at what the passage itself says, and then examine the context and the way it fits with or against other passages—for Scripture (unlike, say, the Talmud) does not ultimately argue with itself. A key principle is that Scripture interprets Scripture, which means we use clearer passages to interpret murky ones, and that we don't rest key doctrines on obscure passages or play "here a verse, there a verse."

Furthermore, since the Bible is primarily a true story of how God saves sinners, we do not treat it like a textbook. We distinguish between descriptive and prescriptive passages and acknowledge that in some areas, even after conscientious study, we still see through a glass darkly. Helps in this process include creeds of the early church and confessions developed by later church leaders who did careful biblical study following *sola scriptura* principles (for example, the Westminster Confession and the Heidelberg Catechism). Those creeds and confessions must always be checked against Scripture, but they still allow a third question—"How has the church applied the passage?"—to come after "What does it say?" and "What does it mean?"

Sola scriptura, applied properly, helps us not to overuse the Bible or to underuse it. If we overuse it by saying the Bible says certain things it does not say, we feed our human tendency to make up rules that supposedly will help us save ourselves, or at least allow us to think ourselves better than others. That error feeds into many others, including the legalism that has pushed many of my Christian students into animosity toward denominations of their youth.

If we value the *sola scriptura* principle, with its emphasis on scriptural clarity on essential matters, then biblical objectivity makes sense and other approaches have logical flaws. After all, if the Bible is

God's Word, can any other words trump his? Since only God knows the true, objective nature of things, doesn't his book, the Bible, present the only completely objective and accurate view of the world? Shouldn't our goal be to see the world as much in biblical terms as our fallen and sinful natures allow?

That understanding underlies *World*'s mission statement: to provide "Biblically objective journalism that informs, educates, and inspires." We know that, given our human limitations, along with our fallenness and sinfulness, we can never fully achieve that biblical objectivity, but by following the Bible's teachings, we try to come closer than we otherwise would, showing humility before God.

That's what biblical objectivity means. We don't merely cover all the sound and fury in the world, and then present people's lives as tales told by idiots, signifying nothing. Nor do we cover only the good and uplifting parts of life, so as to provide sugary stories. Biblical objectivity emphasizes, like Stephen's speech in Acts 7, God's holiness and man's sinfulness. *World* stories over a typical month try to show how terrible man is, yet how wonderful, created in God's image. Our articles, we hope, accurately describe the world God has made and reflect his view of how his creatures mess up and sometimes get things right.

Journalists are sowers. In the parable of the sower, three-fourths of the seed lands by the road, on stony ground, or amid thorns. Three-fourths of the sower's work is wasted. That parable, like so many that Jesus presented, is not a happy story to put listeners in a cozy, receptive mood. Jesus told iceberg parables, not icebreakers.

In 1912, the builders and owners of a huge ship, the *Titanic*, advertised it as "unsinkable." It left England on its first voyage, hit an iceberg, and sank, with more than 1,500 people dying. Many non-Christians think of themselves as unsinkable, but many of us who have been Christians for a long time also start thinking of ourselves in that way—until an iceberg penetrates our hulls.

Jesus ratcheted up the tension in his penetrating parables. In his fictional feature stories, a young man turns his back on home and learns a hard lesson—will he return to his father? A woman loses a coin and desperately searches for it—will she find it? A man trades all he has for one thing more precious—has he acted with discernment? Jesus brings us a wake-up call, not a snooze button.

In the United States, internet stories with no larger purpose than to attract attention have gained the label "clickbait." While good journalists want to write stories their audience will read, stories that merely attract attention are equivalent to the seed that lands by the road, on stony ground, or amid thorns. We should aspire to write stories that joyfully show us how entertaining the world around us is, or stories that wake us from the slumber in our souls. Journalists can remind us that we live in an amazing world, where a mustard seed that could be eaten by birds becomes a tree in which birds take shelter.

A story is more than information. Information does not save. The best-remembered stories pierce us. Sometimes journalists can be God's servants in cutting open chests prior to his bringing about a heart transplant. To assist in such an operation is the highest honor there is—but we have to decide whether we are willing to be assistants, rather than gods unto ourselves.

Moses before the burning bush told God the people of Israel would demand to know his name. God told Moses to say, "I AM has sent me to you." "I AM," of course, means God is neither past nor future, but everlasting, making every moment throughout eternity the present one, always focused. The contrast with his human creations forces a question: do I care most about God's I AM or my own "I am"? The human "I am" stands for the unholy trinity of me, myself, and I. The A is for ambition: magnify *my* name. The M stands for money: maximize it.

Self-magnification and maximization get us nowhere, though. We ascend only through the grace of Jesus Christ, whom the apostle Paul called the second Adam—but we live by working, following what God set forth for the first Adam. God's pronouncement to Adam that he would sweat to earn his daily bread was a punishment, yes, but also a severe mercy. When we don't need to serve others by working, we typically start obsessing about ourselves. With our sinful natures, it's harmful for poor human beings to live on welfare and rich human beings to live on trust funds for which they did not work.

Lamentations 3 displays the contrast between "I am" thinking and "I AM." The first part of the chapter describes the individual reflecting on his own afflictions. He is in darkness without any light, he is walled about so he cannot escape, he wears heavy chains, he is on crooked paths, a bear and a lion are ready to attack him, he is torn into pieces, his kidney has become a pincushion for arrows, he is drinking wormwood, his teeth grind on gravel, he is cowering in ashes. It's the march of a million groaning metaphors.

In the next part of the chapter, nothing in the author's troubled situation has changed, but he has moved from "I am" to "I AM": "The steadfast love of the LORD never ceases; his mercies never come to an end; they are new every morning; great is your faithfulness." The goal of life is to move from the baby's first cry of "I am" to the wise maturity of allegiance to I AM. Our human "I am" emerges from fear: my position and my bank account give me a haven in a harsh world. God's I AM requires trust, which is very hard for those of us who grew up amid suspicion and worry—but if it were easy, we wouldn't need a Redeemer.

KEY TERMS

> journalistic humility
> strict constructionist journalists
> Scripture interprets Scripture

STUDY QUESTIONS

1. How is Doubting Thomas both a positive and a negative role model for Christian journalists?
2. What factors should an aspiring Christian journalist bear in mind when deciding whether to work in mainstream secular media or in Christian media?

FOR FURTHER READING

Mitchell Stephens, *Beyond News* (Columbia University Press, 2014). John G. West, *Darwin Day in America: How Our Politics and Culture*

Have Been Dehumanized in the Name of Science (Intercollegiate Studies Institute, 2014).

Timothy Sandefur, *The Permission Society* (Encounter, 2016).

Marvin Olasky, *World View: Seeking Grace and Truth in Our Common Life* (New Growth, 2017).

Epilogue:
Beyond Shimei Journalism

ARISTOTLE SAID, "MAN without society is either beast or God." Communist-turned-Christian Whittaker Chambers offered a striking corollary: "Man without God is a beast, and never more beastly than when he is most intelligent about his beastliness." American media have largely abandoned their Christian background and become beastly.

In *Prodigal Press* (1988; second edition, 2013), I showed how American journalism, a prodigal son of Christianity, still showed no desire to return home. Many major media, having abandoned biblical wisdom, have become "progressive" propagandists, and in the process lost much of their audience. Secular journalists sometimes make a contribution by pointing out problems, but have few alternatives to offer.

Reporting of problems is useful, even when Christians are the objects of reportorial wrath. Puritan author Jeremiah Burroughs wrote, "If you hear others report this or that ill of you, and your hearts are dejected because you think you suffer in your name, your hearts were inordinately set on your name and reputation." Sometimes we should have lower self-esteem. In the Old Testament, David reacted properly to Shimei, who cursed him, threw stones at him, and flung dust at him, because David discerned that Shimei actually was God's instrument. I've been to many Washington and New York wine-and-cheese parties where journalists whine and share cheesy complaints. It would be better to listen to criticism and not overstate our plight.

Today, America's Shimei journalists can remind us that a generation ago many white members of Christian churches harassed blacks, and that racial prejudice remains. A Shimei can show that some members of affluent churches have turned their backs on the poor. That's no surprise—Christians know "all have sinned and fall short of the glory of God"—but we need to repent. (And repentance means not only feeling sorry because we're caught, but realizing that we have offended God and must pray for the grace to change our ways.)

A Shimei journalist can also remind us that talking *at* non-Christians rather than reasoning *with* them is usually unproductive. Proselytizing styles may grate; Christians need to remember that God's action, not our strategy or intensity, changes lives. Many journalists speak privately of their experience with evangelicals who, not taking no for an answer, pushed even harder when rejection was apparent. (That impoliteness may stem from a lack of confidence in Christ, because this year's no is never a final answer from those he calls.)

But bias and ignorance lead many leading U.S. publications to lump evangelical Christians in with repressive forces in other cultures that have little in common with them. For instance, some journalists see how those they label "Islamic fundamentalists" engage in terror, and they imply that "Christian fundamentalists" are no different. That practice began soon after terrorists on September 11, 2001, hijacked planes and flew them into New York City's tallest buildings and the Pentagon, the U.S. government's largest building.

Here's one example from among thousands: Less than a month later, on October 7, the *New York Times* labeled the new war on terrorism "a religious war—but not of Islam versus Christianity and Judaism. Rather, it is a war of fundamentalism against faiths of all kinds that are at peace with freedom and modernity." The definition of fundamentalism: "The blind recourse to texts embraced as literal truth, the injunction to follow the commandments of God before anything else, the subjugation of reason and judgment and even conscience to the dictates of dogma." Among the blind subjugators of reason, according to the *Times* are fundamentalist Christians.

Are leading American journalists not so much biased against Christianity as ignorant of it? Studies have certainly documented that ignorance, and sometimes it comes out in humorous ways. For example, the *New York Times* reporter in Jerusalem described "the vast Church of the Holy Sepulcher marking the site where many Christians believe that Jesus is buried." But surveys have shown that more than 90 percent of American professors worry evangelicals are trying to suppress others by "merging church and state."

That is not useful Shimei criticism, because such fear shows ignorance. Most American Christians have not had to receive instruction from the outside about separating church and state, because that division is a biblical creation. Moses was the lawgiver, Aaron the priest. Saul was king, Samuel was prophet. Ahab tried to become a dictator, Elijah opposed him. Representatives of both priesthood and kingdom, each assigned to keep the other honest, watched over contributions to the Temple building fund.

Much later, when Christians had political power in Europe, popes and emperors, or bishops and kings, checked and sometimes balanced each other. Did churches in ancient and medieval times sometimes overstep their bounds? Of course, but defining Christianity in terms of the sins committed in its name is like defining electricity solely in terms of the development of electric chairs used in executing murderers. The key question now in American society is not whether church will overawe state, but whether the state will take away religious liberty.

Christian parents with boys—my wife and I have raised four—learn the question to ask when meditating on the proper punishment for a transgression: "Is it sin or is it boy?" By nature, boys can be impetuous and adventuresome, which gets them into trouble. Parents need to help their charges become more responsible, but should not assume the malice of sin unless they witness direct disobedience. The Christian response to secular liberal reporters should be similar: "Is it ignorance or malice?"

Among journalists, is misreporting of Christians the product of ignorance or malice? Most journalists who have grown up in non-biblical homes will naturally see people with biblical perspectives as weird, and will report from some combination of ignorance and malice. But in my experience, patient explanation can at least educate some reporters to the point where they can begin to think logically about Christianity. Some can even begin to see that beyond either ignorance or malice lies a third factor: fear.

We live in an age of phobias. These days, when we turn tail and run, we are no longer supposed to admit we are cowards. We say we are merely acting in accord with our phobias. The Bible describes a true phobia—fear of God and his angels—that truly is a consuming fire for many. Virtually every angel in the Bible needs to say to men and women, quivering in the presence of the supernatural, "Fear not." That's because we are all sinners and have good reason to fear a holy God, until he graciously tells us, "Fear not," and even more graciously provides a way to escape his wrath. If we run from Christ, we fear him all the more, since deep down we know we are throwing away our only realistic hope.

What are the alternatives? How many people in Russia or China wish to resurrect the Communist experiments of Lenin and Mao? British socialist H. G. Wells wrote science fiction novels, but also *The Outline of History*, which portrays mankind "at first scattered and blind and utterly confused, feelings its way slowly to the serenity and salvation of an ordered and coherent purpose." He thought government could bring about "harmonious cooperation" that would leave behind "narrow, selfish, and contradicting nationalist traditions." That hasn't worked.

Some, sickened by collectivism, have proposed individualism. Many U.S. schools of education have embraced the philosophy of Lawrence Kohlberg, who proclaimed ethical stages through which he thought people should move: from following the law to "social duty" and perhaps to "autonomous ethical thinking," wherein a person makes up his own principles. Kohlberg argued such ethical autonomy should be the goal of human existence—even though in this stage humans are in some ways the most selfish, virtually inventing a world, totally apart from God.

Many American journalism students and journalists I've talked with display faith in their own autonomous judgment. Here are some typical responses: "I make my decisions based on what I feel is right."

"The bottom line is I believe in me." "My governing belief is the only person you can really trust in life is yourself." "I believe in taking bits of pieces from several religions and in that way making up my own, personal religion."

Kicking off the new millennium, the *Washington Post* in 2001 praised those who "write their own Bible. They fashion their own God . . . turning him into a social planner, therapist or guardian angel." The *Post* told the story of Ed and Joanne Liverani, who decided to "build their own church, salvaging bits of their old religion they liked and chucking the rest." They ended up with a god who "cheers them up when they're sad, laughs at their quirks." Lynn Garrett, a religious book tracker for *Publishers Weekly*, called this "an eclectic approach. People borrow ideas from different traditions, then add them to whatever religion they're used to." Having "A Self-Made Deity," as the subtitle to the *Washington Post* story put it, is popular now, particularly among journalists.

Faith in God logically requires assent to the proposition that God is wiser than we are. Long ago Augustine said, "If you believe what you like in the gospel, and reject what you don't like, it is not the gospel you believe, but yourself." But as ABC's Ted Koppel acknowledged, it doesn't make sense for the Ten Commandments to become the Ten Suggestions. If they really come from God, we should follow them. Mockers know that, but psychologist Lawrence Kohlberg became prominent for suggesting that "autonomous thinking" is the seventh and highest stage of human intellectual development.

It would make more sense to think in terms of three stages, with faith in ourselves flipped from top to bottom. The first and lowest stage is purported autonomy, also known as I'm-the-center-of-the-world self-glorification. The second is the stage where we are loyal to something outside of and bigger than ourselves: perhaps a nation, perhaps a concept. The real hope is to move by grace to the highest stage, where we act to bring glory to God the Creator, and not to ourselves or other creatures (although in the course of glorifying God, we may bring honor to ourselves and to our nation).

The previous chapter showed how some American journalists saw Barack Obama as a new messiah in 2008. Eight years of leftward movement during the Obama presidency led to a reaction that put Donald Trump into the presidency in 2017. Leading newspapers and most networks demonized him, and one network, Fox News, became a Trump administration organ.

Prodded by journalists and politicians, the United States became a polarized country. Now, as one old American hymn put it, "Nothing but the blood of Jesus" will save us. I'm applying that to a nation, but the prime meaning is for individuals. As an elder of the Presbyterian Church in America, I had sometimes served communion to church members gathered in a semicircle, giving them bread and wine one-by-one and saying, "This is Christ's body, broken for you. This is Christ's blood, shed for you." And on a reporting trip to Ethiopia in 2008, I saw a parallel kind of communion.

That perception came one afternoon at the opening of a Christian hospital's "cleft clinic," a program for children and adults with holes in their faces and their throats. I watched as twenty patients, usually brought by their parents, came to Paul Lim, an American plastic surgeon of Chinese ancestry who had sacrificed security and a colossal income to move with his young family to Addis Ababa, the East African country's capital.

God's mercy is evident in both the Lord's Supper and the way most of us are born with faces with the right number of holes. At six to eight weeks of gestation, our faces usually fuse. For some reason, in some children, the parts don't fuse. They have extra holes between their noses and their lips. They need additional grace.

"We'll make his nose better," Lim (through a translator) told one mother holding her baby. "We'll make his lip better. Jesus brought us, brought me, here for him."

Then a twenty-three-year-old who was very pretty except for her malformation came in, looking ready to cry. She had unskilled surgery as a child and is now a teacher, with students who sometimes hoot at her. Lim said, "We'll make your nose better. Jesus brought me here for you." She walked out, dazed—would this miracle come to pass?

A teenage mom walked in holding a one-month-old with a completely cleft lip. She sat, gazed at her baby, and smiled—no, *glowed*. She was in love with her baby. The father, a few years older, wearing a Michael Jordan NBA shirt, was unsmiling. When Lim said, "We will fix his lip," the mom beamed even more broadly, but the father remained stern. Then Lim said, "Jesus brought me, brought us, here for him." The man suddenly smiled, as if just getting it, and enthusiastically shook the doctor's hand.

A thirteen-year-old girl slipped in, holding up her scarf to cover her mouth. She uncovered her mouth only when seated before Lim—and her reason for hiding behind her scarf was immediately obvious. Lim maintained his composure, examined her, and said to the translator, "Tell her that she will need more than one operation. We will do everything we can to help. Jesus brought us here, brought us all here, for her."

A twelve-year-old came in with his mouth frozen in a grimace. Malnourishment had provided the base for an infection when he was five. Now he was missing a lot of tissue, skin, and part of his mouth. He had wanted to commit suicide, but Lim said, "We can help you. Jesus brought me, brought us here, for you." The grimace did not, could not (for now) change—but it would.

A father arrived from fifty miles away with his baby, who was dehydrated and shaking. The baby would get immediate help, and the operation would come later. Lim said, "By God's grace we have an expert here on feeding children with cleft lip. Jesus brought us here for your son. That's why we are here."

Luke 22 tells us that at the first Communion, Jesus "took bread, and when he had given thanks, he broke it and gave it to them, saying, 'This is my body, which is given for you.'" Communion with St. Paul Lim in Addis Ababa: telling a seven-year-old in a Yao Ming NBA shirt, "We will take care of this. Jesus brought me here for you."

Two millennia ago, some Jews asked Jesus why a man was born blind. He responded: "that the works of God might be displayed in him" (John 9:3). Why are some born with a cleft palate? The answer could be similar: so that God will be glorified through the works of those he calls to help. Why was a reporter present as Lim offered words of life? So God will be glorified as others hear of this doctor and aspire to display the grace of God.

Appendix:
Journalism in China

by June Cheng

PART ONE: HISTORY

AS IN MANY countries, the imperial court originated the first written mass dissemination of information in China. The handwritten *dibao*, an official gazette, was first issued during the Han dynasty (206 B.C.–A.D. 220). It reached a larger audience with the invention of woodblock printing in the Song dynasty (960–1279) and remained a vital source of information until the late Qing dynasty.

Officials and gentry-scholars scattered across China read the *dibao* to stay informed about the emperor's edicts and official news. Yet during the Song dynasty, an unofficial press called the *xiaobao* also began popping up. Established by local representatives, the *xiaobao* provided more timely political news, since the *dibao* was sent from the palace and could take weeks to reach far-flung cities. Private reporters gathered news, local gossip, and even some commentary, according to Xiantao Zhang's *The Origins of the Modern Chinese Press*. Because the *xiaobao* strayed from the official line, the government tried repeatedly to shut it down.

The first modern Chinese newspapers began after Protestant missionaries brought the idea of newspapers to China in the 1800s. Because China banned direct missionary activity, early missionaries published gospel tracts, Chinese-language Bibles, books, and periodicals. Missionary presses disseminated biblical truth as well as a greater knowledge of the West, introducing the concept of spreading news independently of the government.

As noted in chapter 1, missionary Robert Morrison published the first Chinese periodical, the *Chinese Monthly Magazine*, in August 1815 in Malacca, a port city in Malaysia that enjoyed greater freedom. Editor William Milne described the mission of the periodical simply: "To promote Christianity was to be its primary object; other things, though, were not to be overlooked. Knowledge and science are the hand-maids of religion, and may become the auxiliaries of virtue."

Printed with traditional Chinese woodblock, the magazine included portions of the New Testament as well as articles explaining Christian doctrines and articles comparing Christianity with traditional Confucian values. It also discussed astronomy, Western technology like the steamboat, world history, geography, poetry, and current events. Each month, five hundred copies of the magazine circulated among Chinese residents and the Chinese diaspora.

The magazine ran until 1821, when Milne fell seriously ill. Other missionaries from the London Missionary Society followed in his footsteps. In 1823, W. H. Medhurst published *A Monthly Record of Important Selections* from Batavia, Dutch East Indies, which lasted for three years. In 1828, Samuel Kidd established *The Universal Gazette in Malacca*. The newspaper, which focused more on European and Chinese news than Christianity, ended after a year. Often publications shut down as missionaries became preoccupied with other aspects of their missionary work.

The first periodical established on Chinese soil was Prussian missionary Karl Gutzlaff's *Eastern Western Monthly Magazine*, which published its inaugural issue in Canton in August 1833. After traveling through China, Gutzlaff found that Chinese people largely viewed Westerners as "barbarians." He said he created the magazine to counter that idea and help the Chinese get "acquainted with our arts, sciences, and principles." Christianity played a smaller role in this publication. Instead, it included translated articles from foreign magazines, news from the official *Peking Gazette*, and commentary.

After England defeated China in the Opium War, the Treaty of Nanking handed Hong Kong over to the British, allowing missionary presses to run freely. Medhurst in 1853 created the *China Serial*, the first newspaper to have advertisements. He focused on domestic news, such as reports on the Taiping Rebellion, while continuing to introduce the Chinese readers to Western history, geography, and sciences. The paper lasted for three years, and in its last issue editor James Legge said he believed the paper had met his goal "to stir the Chinese mind from its apathy, and circulate among the people the lesson of universal history and the accumulations of Western knowledge."

As Shanghai opened up to foreigners, the missionary press moved north to the port city. In 1857, the London Missionary Society Press established the *Shanghai Serial*, which included news, history, and science. The next decade saw new missionary newspapers flourishing alongside commercial newspapers by local Chinese.

Young John Allen, an American missionary, founded the most influential missionary newspaper, *Wanguo Gongbao*. Originally called *Church News* in 1868, the newspaper initially targeted the Protestant community, but the amount of religious material in the paper quickly dropped from about half of the content to a fifth. As Allen become more interested in promoting reform in China, he renamed the newspaper *Wanguo Gongbao—A Review of the Times*. While it included some Christian articles, it also translated Western articles and drew from existing Chinese newspapers. It had several sections: "Events and conditions in China," "Sino-Western relations," "The West and its institutions," and "Japan and its reform."

At the time, Westerners called China the "sick man of Asia," since its defeat by foreign forces had resulted in different nations claiming spheres of influence. Chinese scholars concerned about the future of their country called for radical reforms from the Qing court, believing China needed to modernize. Allen, who agreed with these sentiments, made sure the magazine did not just explain scientific developments, but urged the Chinese to create more railroads, coal mines, and a telegraph system. It criticized China's education and exam systems, with its focus on classics and resistance to Western subjects.

Government officials, merchants, and scholars, including lead reformers Kang Youwei and Liang Qichao, read *Wanguo Gongbao*. The magazine also drew from Chinese voices. Five hundred Chinese writers from fifty cities contributed to the newspaper over its thirty-nine-year run. Many of these contributors ended up starting their own newspapers, for *Wanguo Gongbao* popularized the practice of using the press to spread ideas about political reform in China. By the time of the Xinhai Revolution and the establishment of the Republic of China in 1911, there were five hundred newspapers and periodicals in China.

This proliferation of newspapers ended once the Chinese Communist Party (CCP) established the People's Republic of China in 1949. The CCP silenced the independent press and gave all official media one goal: to serve the Communist Party and its agenda. "Your job is to educate the masses, to enable the masses to know their own interests, their own tasks, and the Party's general and specific policies," said Chairman Mao Zedong. Mao himself had written for and edited different newspapers, including *Xinhua*, beginning in 1919, according to William A Mulligan's *The Chinese Press: Journalism under Mao*.

Journalists spent a third of their time in political study sessions. Newspapers propagated whatever the Party wanted, did not cover the mass starvation during the Great Leap Forward, and extolled the country's gains, whether they existed or not. Those who fell out of line gained the label "Rightists," lost their job and CCP membership, and ended up in reeducation camp.

The writings of one jailed journalist and writer, Lin Zhao, reveals the voices and talents that Mao stifled. Lin, who became a fierce critic of the CCP, was born in Suzhou in 1932. Baptized at a Methodist high school, she embraced communism and joined the Communist Party in 1948 at the age of sixteen. Attending the party-run South Jiangsu Journalism Vocational School and then writing for the *Changzhou People's News*, Lin's passion to "obey the [party] organization in all matters" was apparent in her writing. Yet her family's bourgeois background and her own refusal to obey party leaders kept her from rising in the ranks, according to *Blood Letters*, by Lian Xi.

In the aftermath of the 1956 Hundred Flowers Movement, Lin lost faith in the CCP. Started by Mao, the movement encouraged writers to freely express their thoughts and even challenge him. Liu Shaoqi, who was then Vice Chairman, encouraged news agencies to follow international journalism standards, publishing both negative and positive news. Yet after a year, Mao retracted his position and started the Anti-Rightist Movement to imprison those who dared to criticize him. More than 1.2 million people received a "Rightist" label.

Lin, then a student at Peking University, watched police cart her friends off to labor camps for their writings. In 1958, officials named Lin a Rightist, and she felt she "naturally had no choice but to opt firmly for resistance." She refused to make self-criticisms and returned to church and the faith of her youth. Collaborating with Lanzhou University students, she wrote anti-Mao poems in an underground publication called *A Spark of Fire*. That led to her imprisonment in 1960. Behind bars, she penned letters, diary entries, a play, and poetry protesting the enslavement of the Chinese people under Mao, writing with her own blood when prison guards took away her pen.

In 1965, she wrote a 137-page letter to the *People's Daily*, calling the CCP a form of "tyranny and slavery," critiquing the cult of personality around Mao, and arguing that the CCP cared about nothing but "the terror of centralization. It has long lost any trace of democracy!" Her defiance and moral integrity were rooted in her faith in God, as she followed "the line of a servant of God, the political line of Christ." After eight years in prison, Lin was executed.

None of her letters were sent, but public security officials didn't dare to throw them away. They remained in her case file until 1981, when the Shanghai High People's Court posthumously commuted Lin's death sentence, declared her innocent, and returned her writings to her family. Eventually, friends and family privately printed the collection of her work and posted her letter to the *People's Daily* online. Liu Xiaobo, the late Nobel laureate, called Lin "the rare one who stood upright in an era when the entire country prostrated themselves."

Amid the atrocities during Mao's reign, one positive was the rise of the literacy rate from below 20 percent to 66 percent as education became available for people of all classes. This made newspapers accessible to the common man. In 1954, the *People's Daily* had a circulation of 710,000, according to *The Yearbook of Chinese Journalism 1982*.

Press restrictions were not relaxed during Mao's last years. In 1972, the New China News Agency signed a news exchange agreement with the Associated Press, but change began only after Mao's death in 1976. Deng Xiaoping's market reforms meant journalism was no longer fully subsidized by the government. For many newspapers, survival depended on subscriptions and advertisements, so publications needed to attract readers while still obeying the directives of the propaganda department. Officials censored stories that went too far into the "sensitive" zone, yet for the first time, journalists could diversify their content, writing human interest stories, investigative pieces, and economic news.

In the 1980s, city-level propaganda offices increased the number of evening newspapers. Unlike the official mouthpieces like the *People's Daily*, these newspapers covered topics that typical Chinese people could relate to: local crime, sports, health, and celebrity gossip. As long as they didn't touch on national politics, journalists had room to roam. The popularity of this new type of paper made Shanghai's *Xinmin Evening Newspaper* the second most widely circulated newspaper after the *People's Daily* in 1993, according to Emily Chua's *Writing for the Masses after Mao: News-Production in Contemporary China*.

In 1987, then-Premier Zhao Ziyang introduced the concept of newspapers informing the Party of corruption in businesses and lower-level officials, which he termed in Chinese "supervision by public opinion." Zhao, who had a more liberal bent, encouraged newspapers to start investigations and increase reporting on critical news. The Tiananmen Square massacre cut short this reform; Zhao lost his position and was put under house arrest. Investigative journalism didn't take off until 1992, when Deng pushed for greater market reforms.

Many journalists consider the decade that followed to be the golden age of journalism in China. Salaries were high, and widely read newspapers had the resources and prominence to attract top talent. At Guangzhou's *Southern Weekly*, the most liberal and outspoken newspaper in China, investigative journalists wrote about corruption in the police system, migrants cheated out of their land, and other social problems. Chinese journalists desired professionalism in their craft, working within the restraints and often pushing the envelope to create more space. Journalists felt they were speaking out for the marginalized in a way that had been impossible in the previous fifty years.

To get around censorship, the newspaper would report stories in other provinces, where propaganda departments didn't have control over them. Still, the central government allowed this watchdog journalism because it benefited from it. Stories informed the central government of low-level corruption that had grown out of the rapid economic reforms, and the coverage helped the government regain the public's trust. Although things were better than ever, authorities still stopped journalists from reporting on higher-level officials, nationwide policies, or problems with the political system itself.

State-run CCTV started to do investigative journalism as well. Its program *Focus* in 1994 included exposés on corrupt local officials, unresponsive bureaucracies, and issues like pollution. Common Chinese citizens and top government officials watched *Focus*, which attracted 300 million viewers and became the network's second most watched show, according to Ying Zhu's *Two Billion Eyes: The Story of China Central Television*. Yet a year later, *Focus* came under pressure from the higher-ups, who insisted each episode's topic be submitted to the head of the division. Only two critical stories were allowed each week, and by 1998, authorities required any negative reports to include follow-up segments on how the government solved the problem.

In 1996, CCTV started *News Probe*, a show like the American program *60 Minutes*, but it quickly felt pressure to move away from hot-button issues. Depending on the censorship climate, the show reported on nonexplosive issues like housing reform as well as corruption stories such as fraud on an irrigation project in the city of Yuncheng. But by 2006, the show's watchdog journalism gave way to "enlightenment" pieces that were light on criticism and instead focused on building up society.

The golden era sputtered out in the beginning of the new millennium. In 2005, the government made it illegal for journalists to cover topics outside of their province, closing the loophole for investigative reports. As investigative journalism lost its teeth, economic newspapers became fashionable, hoping to eschew political issues and focus on China's growing economy from a detached, technical viewpoint.

Journalism had a few bright spots in 2008, as journalists gained greater freedom covering the Olympics and the Sichuan earthquake, but censors scrubbed mention of the clampdown on Tibet and the poorly constructed schoolhouses in Sichuan that led to 5,000 deaths when the earthquake hit. Readers and viewers lost faith in the media, as they could no longer distinguish what was real from what was fake news.

Press freedom declined further when President Xi Jinping took the reins in 2013. The year started out with a strike at *Southern Weekly*, after the propaganda department rewrote a New Year editorial without the editor's knowledge. The original piece called for China to respect constitutional rights, while the altered article praised the CCP and included factual errors. In response, two hundred journalists and supporters protested outside the headquarters of Nanfang Media Group, the paper's owner.

Under Xi, press control reverted back to that of the Mao era, with only positive news about the CCP being allowed. "Supervision by public opinion" ended. When Shanghai's *The Paper* spent a year researching the social and environmental impacts of the Three Gorges Dam in 2015, and then published its report, censors pulled the story after just seven hours. In 2016, Xi visited major Party news outlets to urge all news media—including commercial newspapers—to take the surname of Party, making it part of their identity. Journalists can now get press cards only after passing exams in which they have to show knowledge of socialistic ideology to "guide the masses." Propaganda department officials run journalism schools.

Once again, those who stray from the party line receive punishment. It's a crime for journalists to report "state secrets, commercial secrets, and unpublished information." Reporter Gao Yu in 2015 received a five-year prison sentence for giving foreign media an internal Communist Party document. That same year, Wang Xiaolu reported a stock market drop in the economic magazine *Caijing*, and then had to make a televised confession about purportedly spreading "fake information on the securities and futures market."

Today, journalists may write only on a dwindling number of topics. Directives leaked online reveal the government censored articles on everything from air pollution, natural disasters, and Christmas-related news, to Google's AlphaGo beating Chinese prodigy Ke Jie at a go match in 2017. With more than one hundred journalists and bloggers currently detained, China was the fifth-worst country for violations of press freedoms in 2017, according to Reporters Without Borders.

Reporters are increasingly young and inexperienced. They see the job as a stepping stone to other careers. The turnover rate is high, as reporters in their thirties and forties move on to other professions that are more lucrative and less professionally stifling. "Being a journalist has no meaning anymore," an editor from one of China's leading news organizations told *The Guardian*, a London newspaper: "In recent years the industry's freedoms have reached their lowest ebb."

PART TWO: CHINESE CHRISTIANS IN SECULAR NEWSROOMS

When Gabriel Yu (name changed for security reasons) graduated with his master's degree in journalism in 2010, he hoped to seek truth and give a voice to the voiceless. He wanted to be a watchman for Chinese society, warning people when things go wrong and serving as a catalyst for change, even small ones.

Those ideals quickly gave way to Chinese journalistic realities, with government officials refusing to give interviews and threatening him if he covered hard topics. He would invest time in researching and writing groundbreaking stories, only to have the propaganda department nix it right before publication. "There are very important stories you can't write about," Yu explains. "When this happens more and more, you feel your work has no meaning."

As a Christian, he also faces conflicts between his faith and his conscienceless work environment. Receiving *hongbao*, or red envelopes stuffed with money, is normal practice. When he refuses them, his editor says it looks bad for the newspaper. Rather than write about what he observes, he can only regurgitate official statements or reports from *Xinhua*. His writing strays far from biblical values. Instead of looking at the root of problems and writing about issues that promote human betterment, his stories must focus on the false idols of wealth, fame, and success. "What secular media cares about is different from my value system," Yu says. "I spend too much of my energy on trivial topics to attract eyeballs, but the next day people forget all about it—it's like fast-food news."

In the past seven years, he's watched many of his coworkers leave journalism for jobs that are less taxing, higher paying, and more fulfilling. Yu has persevered, believing God has given him a passion and talent for journalism—yet in 2017, the media environment further deteriorated as the government prepared for the Nineteenth Party Congress in October. Stories on religion or local corruption that Yu had written in his earlier years could not get published today. Reporters must ignore negative news and write only positive stories about the Communist Party. Yu wonders whether he should stay in journalism—and whether he can reconcile his Christian faith with his work in modern-day China.

Perhaps you can relate to Yu's questions and concerns. Perhaps you also work at a secular publication and are unsure how to navigate the many contradictions of being a Chinese Christian journalist. President Xi Jinping has said media must "sing the main theme and transmit positive energy," but you'd rather report the truth and "sing praises to God while I have being." You're asking God, "Should I stay or should I go?"

That is a good question, and one this book cannot answer for you. Every person's situation is different, and everyone has a different calling from God, a different role to play in the kingdom of heaven. That's the beauty of the global church. We are not all called to be pastors or overseas missionaries, but we exist in every (non-sinful) profession: journalists, professors, janitors, politicians, factory workers, police officers, and stay-at-home moms.

Likewise, even though Christian media are legal in America, not all Christians working in journalism are called to them. We need

Christians in secular publications. If all Christians left secular papers, then printed articles would stray even further from biblical truth, and society would be worse off because of it.

Of course, in America newspapers still have freedom of the press and Christians have much more room to do good, honest journalism. But look at Christians in the film industry. Hollywood movies promote values contrary to the Bible—for example, premarital sex, illicit drug use, homosexuality, and a relativistic worldview—but many Christians still work on secular films. Why? Some actors say it gives them opportunities to talk about God with actors who most likely will never step inside a church. Others look for movies that have a redemptive arc, often implicit, and can reveal biblical truth, such as the need for a Savior.

Dean Batali, a writer and executive producer of *That '70s Show*, a crude sitcom that aired from 1998 to 2006, believes being the only Christian in the writer's room kept the show from becoming even worse. "We're called to be salt and light in this world," he told *Angulus News*, a Catholic magazine. "Salt can bring flavor, but sometimes, all salt does is stop the decay. . . . I think we as Christians are called to be salt to stop the decay of something, and that's why I think we as Christians go to places that are sometimes messy, within reason."

Working at the popular sitcom for seven years placed Batali in a position where he could pitch shows that better align with his faith, and Hollywood executives would listen. Still, during much of Batali's time on the show, he struggled with questions similar to Yu's: Make the content less bad by working in an industry that may be leading people away from God? Work for the enemy, yet stay true to God, like Daniel in Babylon? Batali often spoke with other Christians, including those working in ministries specifically aimed at the entertainment industry. They understood his dilemma and could help him think things through.

You too should talk and pray with others who understand your situation. Seek wise counsel from mature Christians who know you well. Like all major decisions in the life of a Christian, our greatest counsel comes from the Word of God. Pray that God would help you see why he has you in this particular newsroom, how you can follow his will where you are, and whether he is calling you to move on to a different job.

What could be the right decision for some may be the wrong one for others, so this book doesn't aim to convince you to go one way or the other. Instead, here are questions to consider as you decide whether or not to stay at a secular newspaper:

Am I Working in a Way That Is Honoring to God?

This question can be applied to any Christian at any job anywhere in the world. Before we consider external factors compelling us to leave or stay, we need to make sure we are working with integrity. Are we the image of model workers, doing good reporting and producing good stories, without cutting corners? This book looks at how to do quality reporting to please not only your human bosses, but also your heavenly Father. Colossians 3:23–24 says, "Whatever you do, work heartily, as for the Lord and not for men, knowing that from the Lord you will receive the inheritance as your reward."

This may mean pushing against commonly accepted practices in the newsroom, such as accepting *hongbaos*. Yu said he tries to refuse all *hongbaos*, and when he cannot refuse them, he immediately hands them to his boss to ensure that bribes do not influence his writing. This certainly means stepping away from stories where you may have a conflict of interest. It means always having proof to back up assertions. It means recognizing that plagiarism is stealing.

Our coworkers listen to what Christians say, but they also watch how we work, curious about whether Christianity makes a difference. We must be above reproach, so, if we are punished for our deeds, it is clear that we are blameless and the accuser is wrong.

Can I Communicate Truth in My Articles within My Current Constraints?

Even if you cannot write the stories you want, you can still find creative ways to relay gospel truths through your articles. When you interview business leaders, actors, or others for human interest profiles, you can focus less on worldly success and ask penetrating questions like "Does having money make you happy?" or "How is your family life?" Whatever the answer, it could cause both the readers and the interviewee to contemplate where they place their values.

Different types of publications will offer different levels of flexibility. For instance, China recognizes that severe demographic problems face the country. Relaxing the one-child policy was mainly an economic issue for the government, but Christians see it as a moral issue as well. God makes every human in his image, so abortion—which is the main way populations are controlled—is against his design and a heinous act. Many Chinese women who have had abortions feel the grief of losing unborn children. A Christian journalist can report on the topic and hint at these deeper truths through different interviews.

Christians reporting on foreign affairs can help others understand how Christian principles underlie democratic governments, scientific progress, and economic growth in the West. Because of the close ties between Western history and Christianity, the topic is unavoidable in examining the region. If we leave these stories to non-Christians to report, this could lead to greater misinformation, as most do not understand the faith.

Does My Presence Help Truth to Flourish in the Newsroom?

Other journalists will watch the way you do your work and live your life. By being a living example of a good journalist, you can encourage others to take the high road. You may gain respect, so others come to you for personal and professional advice. You can also be a mentor to younger Christians in the newsroom.

This leads to another way that God may be using you at your workplace: as a messenger bringing the gospel to fellow journalists. Our work product is not only what we create with our minds and our hands, but our contribution to the lives of people with whom we spend most of our waking hours. Especially in an environment as physically and emotionally taxing as a newsroom, many of your coworkers may feel hopeless. You can offer answers when they wonder, "What is the purpose of my life?" and, "What is truth?" You can point them to the gospel, bring them to church, and show them that Christianity isn't some strange, foreign cult—it brings good news to people everywhere.

The newsroom is a mission field that can have a huge impact on society, and an incubator for relationships with the thinkers, writers, and producers of mass media. When the time is right, you can share the good news with them.

If I Were to Leave This Newsroom, Would the Result Be Positive or Negative?

A newspaper with Christian journalists who are restricted in what they can write is still better than a newspaper without any Christians involved. If you were not there, what would be different about how the newsroom is run, the lunchtime conversations, the types of stories that are published, and how Christianity is portrayed in the newspaper? Perhaps censorship restricts much of what you want to write, but if you were gone, would articles lead readers even further astray? Let's not mourn days of small things, when God has put us in such a time. If you're an editor, can you take out a phrase that is untrue or add a sentence that points readers to the truth?

Dean Batali told *The Atlantic* in 2005 that while writing for *That '70s Show* he pitched storylines that stayed away from sex—and if he was instructed to write a sex scene, he'd make it less graphic. One time he wrote in a scene where the characters talked about God—although they were portrayed as high on marijuana at the time. "Does that change the culture and bring more people to the God of Abraham? No. But it's a tiny grain of salt," Batali said.

If absolutely nothing would be different if you were gone, this could also be a wake-up call that causes you to examine how Christlike your behavior is at your workplace. As Christians, we are called to be like Jesus in our everyday lives, witnesses to God's grace in a world that is cold and cutthroat. As a reporter, you have the opportunity to influence hundreds of thousands of people who read your writing, which is an incredible platform, no matter what country you're in. But if the platform doesn't allow you to say things that you agree with, it's worthwhile to think long and hard about whether to stay.

Conclusion

Your answers to the above questions don't definitively determine what you should do, but you can pray over these questions and listen to the guidance of the Holy Spirit inside of you. There are also many legitimate reasons to leave the profession, and sometimes your boss makes the decision for you. Here are some examples:

- If your boss forces you to participate in an unethical action.
- If the work environment is detrimental to your Christian life.
- If you are forced to renounce your faith.
- If you can no longer stand being muzzled about issues that are important to you.
- If there is no way to write anything of worth.
- If you feel convicted about contributing to lies or misinformation.
- If you feel God is calling you to a different profession or ministry.
- If the pay is not enough to support your family.

Even if you decide to stay, it's good to keep your eyes open for other opportunities, should nonnegotiable conflicts arise. With policies getting tighter and tighter, what was acceptable today may no longer be acceptable tomorrow, and Christians need to hold all things of this earth—journalism job included—lightly, as we hold fast to Christ and his coming glory. The Christians I have met in China are some of the bravest people I know, and I believe that by praying, reading the Bible, and carefully thinking through the pros and cons of your work, you can find direction for your career future.

PART THREE: CHINESE CHRISTIANS IN CHRISTIAN MEDIA

I have one last question to leave with Chinese Christian journalists. Right now your main concern is how to squeeze truth out of the tight constraints placed on your writing. But if one day China were to open up and grant publications press freedom, how could you excel as a Christian journalist in secular or Christian media? Reading this book has prepared you not just for what you do now, but the work you will do, God willing. So every time we keep going despite obstacles, we prepare ourselves for the future that, in God's timing, will one day come.

I interviewed more than a dozen people working in Chinese Christian media who described for me the challenges they face. The advent of the internet, and especially WeChat in 2011, opened up a whole new world for Christian media entrepreneurs who could instantaneously reach a wide audience without upfront costs outside of paying writers and designers. But despite the incredible benefits of WeChat, I still heard the same concerns coming up over and over again in the interviews:

- Money: How can I make a living off this? How can I offer a fair salary to pay writers and attract new talent?
- Talent: How do I find Christians who are good at writing?
- Faith: How do I find Christians with a mature faith who can look at issues from a Christian perspective?
- Censorship: How can I write about issues that are important to believers without being censored?
- Crackdown: What happens if the government shuts down my publication?
- Readership: How do I maintain a solid readership when so many WeChat channels are out there?

Some issues listed above are problems for Christians in America as well. Any new Christian publication struggles to attract readers, differentiate itself from other publications, raise the funding needed to pay freelance and staff writers, and find spiritually mature Christians who are also good writers.

Yet in China, the problems are much deeper and wider, as the publication will most likely not be legally registered with the government. Chinese censors scour the internet for sensitive words or topics and can quickly wipe out hours of hard work. Fund-raising and finding quality writers in the young Chinese church are more difficult. Editors face the additional risk of having their publication shut down and their writers detained.

Let us consider some of those concerns and give advice based on biblical principles as well as experiences from the American church. We'll look at what someone who plans to start his or her own Christian publication should consider—here, focusing on WeChat channels. We'll also offer tips to improve existing Christian media.

For Those Creating a Christian Publication

First things first. As in all ministry, the best place to begin is by examining your heart. Do you want to create a Christian WeChat channel because you want to help your fellow Christians, or because you have something to prove? Do you want yourself glorified and your stories widely read, or do you seek the glory of God? In a world obsessed with "likes" and page views, it's easy to find your identity in the approval of netizens, rather than from God. Take some time to pray, and allow the Holy Spirit to search your heart to see where you are placing your identity and whether you should pursue journalism.

Next, researching existing Christian publications is vital. What will set your publication apart from them? Have you seen other Christian channels overlook or gloss over a particular issue? Do you aim to focus on a certain group—such as homeschool stay-at-home moms—that you see as underserved? It's much easier to join an existing publication with a similar focus than to start one from scratch—and the money you are able to raise will go much further at a publication that already has a platform and a following.

After checking your heart and existing publications, say you decide to go forward with the new publication. The next step is finding a team of people to come alongside you in this endeavor. Do you know of others who are passionate about Christian journalism? Do they agree with theologian John Piper that "we ought not just be reflections of our culture, we ought to be constantly making assessments from God's perspective"? That's what biblically objective journalists do, taking great care because, as Piper says, Christian journalism is "good journalism, [looking] carefully, honestly, truthfully at what is happening and analyzing it from a biblical worldview."

Those who understand the importance of Christian journalism will make up your support base. That's where you'll find donors, writers, copy editors, promoters, and prayer warriors for your new publication. They will be the ones sharing your articles on WeChat, sending in suggestions, and encouraging you as you run into difficulties. If you can't find many of these people in your church, you'll need to cast a wider net by talking to friends of friends, connecting with journalist fellowships, or posting an open call on WeChat.

Next we look at one of the most important yet difficult issues: where will the money come from? How do you get enough money to pay writers, designers, and photographers, and have some to cover reporting trips? Budgeting is important to ensure that your publication lasts longer than just a few months—yet because the publication won't be registered, you can't rely on the typical revenue sources of subscriptions and ad sales. Instead, you'll need to rely on donations from churches, friends, family members, and kindhearted strangers who share your vision.

This brings us back to finding a team of like-minded Christians to support you long-term. You can also put together a pitch for your publication to present at churches and among potential donors. You'll need to explain winsomely why your publication is needed, how it will benefit the Chinese church, what they can get out of it, and how you will accomplish your plan. If you are able to get donors to feel a deep interest in the success of your publication, they'll take responsibility and remain supportive of you.

If you can't raise the money needed to run the publication, perhaps it's not yet time to start it. Some may say this type of thinking represents a lack of faith in God's ability to provide. Yet God has also provided us with minds to plan and structure sustainable businesses. In the United States, we see many editors eager to start Christian publications, yet without careful planning and budgeting, the papers quickly run out of steam and close.

Perhaps you are thinking, "But WeChat channels are free to start! All you would need is a few people willing to take turns writing articles, and we can quickly set something up without spending one yuan!" But a publication can't run on volunteer writers alone. People who are passionate about your cause and devoted to it still need to eat. Few will be able to write for long if they are not getting paid. Working for free also devalues the time and effort writers put into researching, interviewing, writing, and revising their stories. Without compensation, writing drops down on their priority list and is the first to go when life gets busy.

You likely won't be able to pay for full-time writers (but good for you if you can!). With effort, you'll probably be able to offer competitive freelance wages that could supplement your writer's income. Trained journalists have invested in their journalism education and want to get compensated for their work—so without a revenue stream, publications find it hard to attract new talent.

This brings us to the next question: how do you find good writers with enough spiritual maturity to write from a Christian perspective? This is a problem with no easy answer, yet as Christ is bringing people to himself in China every day, the supply of quality writers is growing. If we take steps now, the next generation of Christians will not face the same dilemma.

Around China, Christian and secular groups help aspiring writers hone their skills. Good writers become greater writers by reading voraciously and writing daily, even if the writings never get published. In addition to books about writing (like this one!), it is important to read classic literature, theology books, and modern paperbacks. They will teach you more about how language works and what sounds good. Ask friends whose writing you respect to read your work and be brutally honest in critiquing it. Only then will you grow in your writing.

If your church sees the necessity of staying up-to-date in world news, that will also help. Some pastors think they need to focus only on the Bible and leave the news for others to worry about, but John Piper has noted that if a certain news event is the topic of everyone's conversations on Sunday morning, yet a pastor goes on with his scheduled sermon without ever touching on the news, his congregation will think, "This man doesn't live in the world I'm living in; he is out of touch with reality."

Piper also said, "To be good, empathetic pastors we need to know what's going on, because our people are affected by what's going on." A wise pastor brings up the news while welcoming his congregation and visitors to worship. That comforts the weary and helps them make sense of the news that exists under the "glorious sovereignty of God." Pastors, Piper said, should think of "what is honoring to our sovereign God and helps people in their struggles." The late theologian Karl Barth put it this way: "Take your Bible and take your newspaper, and read both. But interpret newspapers from your Bible."

A pastor who understands the importance of journalistic work can create an environment in which parents encourage their children to become writers and reporters, speaking truth in a dark and broken world. These days a well-written article can travel further and faster than ever before, yet more useless content than ever before floats around in cyberspace. Christians who want to have their voices heard, their thoughts expressed, and the gospel message understood, must possess the ability to write in a way that stands out. They must be able to logically structure a story, get to their point, and cut out excess words.

Older Christians can and should help train up the young people in the church who may have an interest in writing. Take an aspiring younger writer under your wing and become his or her first editor. If enough people are interested, gather a group of Christian brothers and sisters and meet biweekly for a writing club. You can gather at a home or coffee shop, find some writing prompts, and do some timed writings. You should assign homework, such as profiling someone with an interesting testimony. All the people in the classes can bring their profiles to the next meeting, and you can go around the room reading, critiquing, and discussing.

It's best not to limit topics to overtly Christian ones. Writers interested in basketball, Tang dynasty poems, artificial intelligence, or fashion have much to contribute. How do Christian basketball players view the game differently from their teammates? How does a particular poem point to truth about the human condition, the beauty that God designed, or the need for salvation? What are the pitfalls to those who view AI as a cure-all for man's problems? What do current fashion trends reveal about modern-day values? There are so many ways to look at the things around us in the context of God's great story of redemption.

Once you have your budget and writers, then you can conduct

an editorial meeting, set a launch date, and send out story ideas and deadlines for your writers. It's important to consider how much you and your team can realistically do. Consistency is important in online publications, so you'll need to decide whether you'll be releasing two stories a week, one story a day, or five stories a day. Be realistic and remember that it's more important to have high-quality content than high-quantity content. Even if the latter can get you more views, it may not necessarily be edifying for Christians.

For Those with Existing Christian Publications

How should the quality of Christian WeChat channels be improved? Our goal should not be to make them like typical Christian publications in America. Many of those are mediocre. Some offer public relations for God, rather than real journalism, with less excuse for timidity than Chinese Christians have, because the U.S. government is not throwing Christian journalists in jail. In America, as in China, God does not need our public relations. We must tell the truth.

Christian WeChat channels often emphasize translated articles, transcriptions of sermons, and meditations—but the internet already has plenty of those. The translation of foreign articles and sermons is an easier form of journalism because it doesn't require coming up with new ideas. But China needs journalists who can write original articles and do interviews both locally and internationally with the help of video chat services like Skype. Chinese Christians have unique experiences and thoughts—more people need to hear them! You can distinguish yourself by creating original content.

Many writers, in both America and China, like to pen reflections or meditations. They will write a first-person account of how a certain passage touched them or their insights on a popular discussion. Some people really have a gift for this type of writing, yet huge amounts of it already exist online. Meditations are easier than hard journalism because you can write them without leaving the comfort of your room and you can use minimal references. But what's needed in Christian media is the type of original reporting that we've talked about throughout this book—the kind that leaves hands dirty and notebooks full.

The current restrictive climate in China, with online censorship limiting what can be reported, is a challenge that Western journalists do not (yet) face. Some Chinese Christians have learned to work around the censorship. Young journalists can learn from older ones how to see where the red lines are (even though they sometimes change day to day). Some Chinese Christians do find ways to work within the constraints without dampening the power of their reporting.

All Christians should work to set a high ethical standard. If you make a promise to pay a writer by a certain day, do all you can to keep your promise and maintain his trust in you. If you make a factual error in your reporting, have the humility to own up to it and make the necessary changes. Give credit where credit is due; don't copy articles from other sites without the consent of the writer and an attribution to him or her. If you want to quote from an interview in another publication, make it clear that you didn't talk to the person yourself. (For example, "'This case makes a mockery of justice,' Cheng told *China Daily*.") Some publications have taken quotations from another's WeChat post and restructured them so they appeared to interview the person directly, but here's how to use it honestly: "'This case makes a mockery of justice,' Cheng wrote on a WeChat post on Saturday."

Honesty with readers is important, not only for maintaining credibility, but because our God loves truth, as enshrined in the ninth commandment: "You shall not give false testimony against your neighbor." Even if a practice is common in journalism in China, this doesn't mean that it's right. As followers of the Bible, we are called to a higher standard than "this is what has always been done." Buying followers, plagiarizing articles, or using clickbait article titles that sensationalize news to get more views are activities that hurt Christian witness.

We should also avoid conflicts of interest in our reporting. Covering an organization run by a friend is a conflict of interest—friendship makes it harder to report negatives. If your friend's organization has done something newsworthy, have one of your coworkers develop the story, and tell your friend that the reporter will be writing a biblically objective story that will cover both positives and negatives.

No one wants to offend a friend by reporting negatives, but our calling is to report the truth.

Photographs are important. Take your own original photos as much as possible. Now that smartphones have high-quality cameras, reporters should take pictures while they're at an event or meeting with a source for an interview. If you don't have the skill and equipment, hire Christian photographers to help you. If you need to use photos from the internet, make sure you find ones from a free images website that doesn't violate copyright laws. Photos should be not merely eye-catching and interesting, but connected to the article and able to enhance the reader's experience.

Finally, it's important to have a contingency plan in the event that your WeChat channel gets shut down. How will you alert followers of a new way to access your work? Who will register for the new account? Even though none of us want this to happen, it's better to be prepared for the worst-case scenario than to be unprepared. Make sure that all involved with your publication understand the risks they take.

Our last word is: be prayerful and bold! God has placed you in this time and place for a reason, and given you the gift of reporting, writing, and editing. We also believe it's no accident that you have picked up this book. We hope it is helpful as you seek to glorify God by filling WeChat with high-quality, truth-filled journalism. May God bless your endeavors!

Glossary

5W1H. Who, what, when, where, why, how.

active voice. The subject of the sentence acts. For example, "They stormed the cemetery."

agenda-setting. Choosing what news to cover.

amoral journalism. Stories that portray lives as tales told by idiots, signifying nothing.

anecdotal lead. A specific mini-story introducing the reader to the theme of the overall story.

antinomianism. The belief that we make up our own rules.

apple, the. According to Lincoln Steffens, the reason Adam and Eve sinned.

AWK. Awkward.

biblical journalism. Stories based on an understanding of God's creation, man's fall, and redemption through God's grace.

biblical objectivity. Only God knows the true nature of objective reality. The Bible reflects his understanding, so as we follow the Bible, we come as close to objectivity as humanly possible.

biblical sensationalism. Stories that wake up the sleeping and remind us of the nature of God and man.

Blue Eagle. Symbol of the National Recovery Administration, which attempted to control prices and wages in every American industry.

BYOX. Bring your own x-ray film—a necessity at some Havana hospitals that officially offer free medical care to all.

capital-H Humanity. The alternative to capital-G God.

CAR. Computer-assisted reporting, also known as data or precision journalism.

Christian hedonism. The idea that God is most glorified in us when we are satisfied in him.

Christian religion. While we were yet sinners, Christ died for us.

chronological. Telling a story in time.

circular ending. The last scene brings back a central character or situation for a final look.

circular. Starting at one location or situation, explaining the story, and eventually returning back to the beginning.

class one rapids. The Bible is explicitly clear on an issue, so Christians can and should take a firm stand.

class two rapids. The biblical position is implicit, so Christians should take a stand, but perhaps not as strongly as one would with a class one issue.

class three rapids. Partisans on both sides quote Scripture, but careful study allows one to reach biblical conclusions.

class four rapids. The Bible does not explicitly or implicitly take a position, but a biblical understanding of human nature and the way that plays out in history allows Christians to come to solid conclusions.

class five rapids. We should not claim a biblical warrant for a particular position, but implications from history and human nature help us arrive tentatively at a Christian understanding.

class six rapids. No historical trail for the discerning to apply, no clear inferences from human nature, and not much else to mark our path. We look for truly expert advice, but stories in a Christian publication might end up as a balancing of subjectivities.

class objectivity. Each economic class has its own standards of right and wrong.

coercive philanthropy. A "Christian socialist" goal in the late nineteenth century.

communes. Utopian socialist attempts in the 1840s and 1850s to banish private property and, often, private marital relationships.

compassion. Suffering with a person in need, not just feeling sorry. What God showed in dying for us.

conventional objectivity (late twentieth century). A balancing of subjectivities.

corruption story. A macro-story based on understanding that all (including leaders) sin and fall short of the glory of God.

creation, fall, redemption, restoration. The plot of the Bible, which many stories follow.

descriptive lead. Presents a scene without characters or action, but creates a mood.

dictablanda. A soft dictatorship.

dictadura. A hard dictatorship.

directed reporting. Every reporter begins his research with a thesis directed by a worldview.

divine right. Kings claimed a right to rule and to control news.

DQ. Determination quotient.

DRAW. Discern, report, analyze, write.

dress-ups. Adjectives and adverbs that clutter sentences.

elder brother. One who is self-righteousness and fault-finding.

English Civil War. The 1640s battle between King Charles I and Britain's Parliament that ended with the king's head chopped off.

equal rights. The understanding of William Leggett and journalists like him that governmental power should not be used to benefit some citizens at the expense of others.

ESB. Electrical stimulation of the brain.

evangelism. The calling of Christians to spread the gospel of Jesus Christ to those who have not heard of his redeeming power.

Evil of the Age, the. Abortion, according to the *New York Times* in 1871.

exchange religion. You do something nice for God, and he does something nice for you.

existential subjectivity. Every person, a god in his own eyes, decides for himself what is right and wrong.

face. A person used by journalists to portray a massive trend. An individual whose experience or situation is similar to that of many people.

feature lead. Pushes the reader to read on.

Fourierism. A type of socialism popular in some mid-nineteenth-century circles.

fundamental law. The U.S. Constitution.

Goliath Media. An alternative term for mainstream newspapers that no longer represent the mainstream.

great cloud of Christian journalistic witnesses, the. Those who have gone before us.

high on the ladder. Emphasizing abstract theory.

inverted pyramid. Starting with the most important facts and letting the story trickle out paragraph by paragraph.

jeremiad. A furious critique.

journalistic humility. A rare commodity.

journalistic moralism. Stories that present smiling church people moving from one triumph to another.

journalistic postmodernism. The belief that each reporter is a god unto himself, obliged not to report, but to create his own reality.

journalistic ventriloquism. Finding an expert who will say what the writer believes.

ladder of abstraction. An analytical metaphor that illuminates the difference between suite-level and street-level reporting.

LA. Too high on the ladder of abstraction.

licensing. Government approval required to publish books and pamphlets.

linear. Telling a story in space.

low on the ladder. Using specific detail from observation.

macro-story. A major understanding that forms the basis for framing a news or feature story.

man's second oldest faith. Communism, as Whittaker Chambers analyzed it.

mediacrats. Liberal reporters.

metaphorical ending. Evoking a response by making a biblical reference or presenting the problem in a cultural context.

muckrakers. Investigative reporters who did good work, but sometimes overdid it.

multigrain. Melding various structures.

multi-vignette lead. Uses several real examples to display a similar problem.

nail-it-shut ending. A key individual states the story's theme.

native advertising. Sponsored content that tries to fool readers into thinking it's not advertising.

news sermons. Puritan preachers sometimes reported in their sermons news of war and peace, crime and punishment.

newspaper lead. Summarizes the news, making it easy to skip the rest of the story.

next-step ending. Telling what happened after the time span of the article.

nut graf. The essence of a story.

O&O. A macro-story favored by establishment revolutionaries that combines official and oppression stories, so politicians become liberators.

objective report. A report that stresses objective reality as distinguished from subjective experience or appearance.

official story. A macro-story that emphasizes trusting government and publishing what officials want published.

off-the-record. A standard of confidentiality that can mean different things.

oppression story. A macro-story that we are naturally good, but are harmed by external influences like corporations or churches.

pacing. Alternating between "medicine" and "sugar."

PAMO. Protagonist, antagonist, mission, obstacles. Every story at least implicitly has a protagonist, an antagonist or antagonism, a mission, and obstacles to overcome.

parallel. Cutting back and forth between scenes to contrast two sides of a story.

passive voice. The subject of the sentence is acted upon. For example, "The cemetery was stormed by them."

pounding the pavement. Leaving your desk and observing persons, places, and things.

profiling. Interviewing on steroids.

PROOF. Purpose, Road, Obstacles, Overcoming, Future.

Promised Land, the. A semi-Eden—ancient Israel—that God set aside for his people.

Protestant Reformation. Began in 1517, when Martin Luther published his Ninety-five Theses that criticized Roman Catholic Church policies.

puffitis. Doing public relations for an interviewee.

qualities of top reporters. Curiosity, willingness to work hard and long, desire to go beneath the surface, charm, integrity, thick skin.

quotosis. Overdosing with too many quotations.

rapids. A metaphor for helping Christian journalists avoid either underuse or overuse of the Bible.

salt. A tasty substance composed of two poisons, sodium and chloride.

Scripture interprets Scripture. Using clearer passages to interpret murky ones.

SD. Needs specific detail.

sensational facts, understated prose. Telling an exciting story without hyping it.

sensationalism. A journalistic emphasis on excited feelings, with stories that often produce more heat than light.

situation lead. Presents a problem that needs a solution.

soft despotism. When journalists are threatened, not by prison, but merely by criticism, and so they play it safe.

sola scriptura. The Bible alone.

stenographers. Journalists who merely take down words without asking hard questions.

street-level journalism. Stories with specific detail based on direct observation.

strict constructionist journalists. Those who are reluctant to legislate from their notebooks.

structural editing. Reorganizing a story's movement from start to finish.

subtracting versus adding. In Old Testament times, God's people were to keep Israel holy and push out/keep out unholy nations. In New Testament times, the goal is to bring into God's kingdom people from every nation.

suite-level journalism. Stories told from the official point of view, which often is more public relations than an accurate reflection of street-level reality.

TEK. This everybody knows.

testimony of two or more witnesses. The biblical standard for actionable evidence.

the "uns." The unborn, unschooled, unemployed, unfashionable.

thesis. An idea of what a story is about—which usually changes as honest reporters learn more.

third brother. How journalists can be helpful, by not pointing fingers, but by showing universal sinfulness and God's holiness.

thrumming. Lulling into sleepiness, as in C. S. Lewis's *The Silver Chair.*

transcendentalism. An early nineteenth-century religious-literary view that humans can become godlike.

watchdog. A role for high-DQ reporters who do not want to become lapdogs.

worldview. Everyone, whether religious or not, has one.

writing block. A poor excuse for not doing enough research.

younger brother. The prodigal son in the New Testament parable who wastes his inheritance in libertine living.

Select Bibliography

Alcorn, Randy. *The Grace and Truth Paradox: Responding with Christlike Balance*. Colorado Springs, CO: Multnomah, 2003.

Anderson, James. *What's Your Worldview? An Interactive Approach to Life's Big Questions*. Wheaton, IL: Crossway, 2014.

Applebaum, Anne. *Red Famine: Stalin's War on Ukraine*. New York: Doubleday, 2017.

Associated Press. *The Associated Press Stylebook*. New York: Associated Press, 2013, 2018.

Baker, Brent. *How to Identify, Expose, and Correct Liberal Media Bias*. Alexandria, VA: Media Research Center, 1994.

Baldwin, Jeff. *The Deadliest Monster: A Christian Introduction to Worldviews*. Eagle Creek, OR: Coffee House, 1998.

Bernays, Edward L. *Propaganda*. New York: H. Liveright, 1928.

Blanchard, John. *Does God Believe in Atheists?* Auburn, MA: Evangelical Press, 2000.

Blundell, William. *The Art and Craft of Feature Writing: Based on the Wall Street Journal Guide*. New York: Plume, 1988.

Boynton, Robert. *The New New Journalism: Conversations with America's Best Nonfiction Writers on Their Craft*. New York: Vintage, 2005.

Braley, Russ. *Bad News: The Foreign Policy of the New York Times*. Chicago: Regnery, 1984.

Brooks, Arthur C. *Who Really Cares: The Surprising Truth about Compassionate Conservatism*. New York: Basic, 2006.

Carroll, Vincent, and David Shiflett. *Christianity on Trial: Arguments against Anti-Religious Bigotry.* New York: Encounter Books, 2002.

Chambers, Whittaker. *Witness.* New York: Random House, 1952.

Christians, Clifford, Kim Rotzoll, and Mark Fackler. *Media Ethics: Cases and Moral Reasoning.* New York: Longman, 1983.

Chua, Emily Huiching. "Writing for the Masses After Mao: News-Production in Contemporary China." PhD diss., University of California, Berkeley, 2013.

Crowl, James William. *Angels in Stalin's Paradise: Western Reporters in Soviet Russia, 1917 to 1937, a Case Study of Louis Fischer and Walter Duranty.* Lanham, MD: Rowman and Littlefield, 1981.

Farley, William. *Gospel-Powered Humility.* Phillipsburg, NJ: P&R Publishing, 2012.

Farrar, Ronald T. *A Creed for My Profession: Walter Williams, Journalist to the World.* Columbia, MO: University of Missouri Press, 2013.

Flaherty, Francis. *The Elements of a Story: Field Notes on Nonfiction Writing.* New York: HarperCollins, 2009.

Foote, Shelby. *The Civil War: A Narrative.* Vol. 3, *Red River to Appomattox.* New York: Random House, 1974.

Foxe, John. *Foxe's Book of Martyrs.* Many editions available.

Geisler, Norman, and Frank Turek. *I Don't Have Enough Faith to Be an Atheist.* Wheaton, IL: Crossway, 2004.

Goodwin, Gene. *Groping for Ethics in Journalism.* Ames, IA: Iowa State University Press, 1983.

Graff, Gerald. *Clueless in Academe: How Schooling Obscures the Life of the Mind.* New Haven, CT: Yale University Press, 2003.

Hamburger, Philip. *Separation of Church and State.* Cambridge, MA: Harvard University Press, 2002.

Hart, Jack. *Storycraft: The Complete Guide to Writing Narrative Nonfiction.* Chicago: University of Chicago Press, 2011.

Hewitt, Hugh. *In, but Not Of: A Guide to Christian Ambition and the Desire to Influence the World.* Nashville, TN: Thomas Nelson, 2003.

Hunt, Angela. *Writing Lessons from the Front: The First Ten Books.* N.p.: Hunt Haven, 2014.

Keller, Tim. *The Prodigal God: Recovering the Heart of the Christian*

Faith. New York: Penguin, 2011.

———. *The Reason for God: Belief in an Age of Skepticism*. New York: Penguin, 2008.

Kelly, Tom. *The Imperial Post: The Grahams, the Meyers, and the Paper That Rules Washington*. New York: William Morrow, 1983.

Kidd, Thomas. *American Colonial History: Clashing Cultures and Faiths*. New Haven, CT: Yale University Press, 2016.

Kramer, Mark, and Wendy Call, eds. *Telling True Stories: A Nonfiction Writers' Guide from the Nieman Foundation at Harvard University*. New York: Plume, 2007.

Leonard, Thomas C. *Illiberal Reformers: Race, Eugenics, and American Economics in the Progressive Era*. Princeton, NJ: Princeton University Press, 2016.

Lin, Yutang. *A History of the Press and Public Opinion in China*. Chicago: University of Chicago Press, 1936.

Lippmann, Walter. *Public Opinion*. New York: Harcourt, Brace, 1922.

Lumsden, Linda. *Black, White, and Red All Over: A Cultural History of the Radical Press in Its Heyday, 1900–1917*. Kent, OH: Kent State University Press, 2014.

Marshall, Paul, Lela Gilbert, and Roberta Green Ahmanson, eds. *Blind Spot: When Journalists Don't Get Religion*. New York: Oxford University Press, 2008.

McGrath, Alister. *The Twilight of Atheism: The Rise and Fall of Disbelief in the Modern World*. New York: Doubleday, 2004.

Miller, Darrow. *LifeWork: A Biblical Theology for What You Do Every Day*. Seattle, WA: YWAM Publishing, 2009.

Miller, Perry, ed. *The American Puritans: Their Prose and Poetry*. New York: Columbia University Press, 1982.

Milton, John. *Areopagetica*. Many editions available.

Morgenthau, Hans J., and David Hein. *Essays on Lincoln's Faith and Politics*. Lanham, MD: University Press of America, 1983.

Mulligan, William A. "The Chinese Press: Journalism Under Mao." *Selected Papers in Asian Studies: Western Conference of the Association for Asian Studies* 1/42, 1992.

Muravchik, Joshua. *Heaven on Earth: The Rise and Fall of Socialism.* New York: Encounter, 2002.

Olasky, Marvin. *Abortion Rites: A Social History of Abortion in America.* Wheaton, IL: Crossway, 1992.

―――. *Central Ideas in the Development of American Journalism.* Hillsdale, NJ: Erlbaum, 1990.

―――. *Fighting for Liberty and Virtue: Political and Cultural Wars in Eighteenth-Century America.* Wheaton, IL: Crossway, 1995.

―――. *The Press and Abortion, 1838–1988.* Hillsdale, NJ: Erlbaum, 1988.

―――. *Prodigal Press: The Anti-Christian Bias of the American News Media.* Wheaton, IL: Crossway, 1988.

―――. *Standing for Christ in a Modern Babylon.* Wheaton, IL: Crossway, 2003.

―――. *Unmerited Mercy: A Memoir, 1968–1996.* Asheville, NC: World & Life, 2010.

―――. *World View: Seeking Grace and Truth in Our Common Life.* Greensboro, NC: New Growth, 2017.

―――, ed. *Salt [Not Sugar]: Twenty Years of World-Class Reporting.* Asheville, NC: World Magazine, 2006.

Pettigrew, Andrew. *Brand Luther: How an Unheralded Monk Turned His Small Town into a Center of Publishing, Made Himself the Most Famous Man in Europe—and Started the Protestant Reformation.* New York: Penguin, 2015.

Phillips, Jason. *The Looming Civil War: How Nineteenth-Century Americans Imagined the Future.* New York: Oxford University Press, 2018.

Piper, John. *Desiring God: Meditations of a Christian Hedonist.* Rev. ed. Colorado Springs, CO: Multnomah, 2011.

Ravitch, Diane. *The Language Police: How Pressure Groups Restrict What Students Learn.* New York: Knopf, 2003.

Reeves, Michael. *Delighting in the Trinity: An Introduction to the Christian Faith.* Downers Grove, IL: InterVarsity, 2012.

Robinson, Matthew. *Mobocracy: How the Media's Obsession with Polling Twists the News, Alters Elections, and Undermines Democracy.* Roseville, CA: Prima, 2002.

Rogers, Daniel T. *As a City on a Hill: The Story of America's Most Famous Lay Sermon*. Princeton, NJ: Princeton University Press, 2018.

Sandefur, Timothy. *The Permission Society: How the Ruling Class Turns Our Freedoms into Privileges and What We Can Do about It*. New York: Encounter, 2016.

Schmidt, Alvin J. *How Christianity Changed the World*. Grand Rapids, MI: Zondervan, 2001, 2004.

Schudson, Michael. *Discovering the News: A Social History of American Newspapers*. New York: Basic, 1978.

Selderhuis, Herman. *Martin Luther: A Spiritual Biography*. Wheaton, IL: Crossway, 2017.

Sexton, Jay. *A Nation Forged by Crisis: A New American History*. New York: Basic, 2018.

Siebert, Frederick Seaton. *Freedom of the Press in England, 1476–1776: The Rise and Decline of Government Control*. Urbana, IL: University of Illinois Press, 1965.

Slezkine, Yuri. *The House of Government: A Saga of the Russian Revolution*. Princeton, NJ: Princeton University Press, 2017.

Stark, Rodney. *The Victory of Reason: How Christianity Led to Freedom, Capitalism, and Western Success*. New York: Random House, 2005.

Steffens, Lincoln. *The Autobiography of Lincoln Steffens: The Life Story of America's Greatest Reporter*. New York: Harcourt, Brace, 1931.

Stephens, Mitchell. *Beyond News: The Future of Journalism*. New York: Columbia University Press, 2014.

———. *A History of News: From the Drum to the Satellite*. New York: Viking Penguin, 1988.

Stoll, Ira. *Samuel Adams: A Life*. New York: Free Press, 2009.

Stortz, Rodney. *Daniel: The Triumph of God's Kingdom*. Wheaton, IL: Crossway, 2004.

Strunk, William, Jr., and E. B. White. *The Elements of Style*. 4th ed. New York: Longman, 2000.

Taylor, S. J. *Stalin's Apologist: Walter Duranty: The New York Times's Man in Moscow*. New York: Oxford University Press, 1990.

Tocqueville, Alexis de. *Democracy in America*. Many editions available.

Van Til, Cornelius. *The Defense of the Faith*. Philadelphia: Presbyterian and Reformed, 1955.

Wayland-Smith, Ellen. *Oneida: From Free Love Utopia to the Well-Set Table*. New York: Picador, 2016.

West, John G. *Darwin Day in America: How Our Politics and Culture Have Been Dehumanized in the Name of Science*. Wilmington, DE: Intercollegiate Studies Institute, 2014.

White, James Emery. *Serious Times: Making Your Life Matter in an Urgent Day*. Downers Grove, IL: InterVarsity, 2004.

Wright, Christopher. *Hearing the Message of Daniel: Sustaining Faith in Today's World*. Grand Rapids, MI: Zondervan, 2017.

Xi, Lian. *Blood Letters: The Untold Story of Lin Zhao, a Martyr in Mao's China*. New York: Basic, 2018.

Zhao, Lin. *Blood Letters: The Untold Story of Lin Zhao, a Martyr in Mao's China*. New York, NY: Basic Books, 2018.

Zhu, Ying. *Two Billion Eyes: The Story of China's Central Television*. New York, NY: The New Press, 2014.

Index of Subjects and Names

Marvin Olasky is editor in chief of *World* and the author of twenty books, including *The Tragedy of American Compassion* and *Compassionate Conservatism*. He is also dean of the World Journalism Institute and an elder in the Presbyterian Church in America.

Olasky has a BA from Yale University and an MA and PhD from the University of Michigan. He was a *Boston Globe* correspondent, taught journalism for twenty-five years at the University of Texas, and has published articles in the *New York Times*, the *Washington Post*, *Fortune*, and many other newspapers and magazines. He has edited *World* since 1992.

As of 2019, Olasky had been married for forty-three years. He and his wife Susan co-authored four sons who have given them five grandchildren so far.

Did you find this book helpful?
Consider writing a review online.
The author appreciates your feedback!

Or write to P&R at editorial@prpbooks.com
with your comments. We'd love to hear from you.

ALSO FROM P&R PUBLISHING

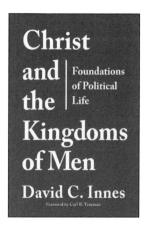

**Christure
and | Foundations
of Political
the | Life
Kingdoms
of Men**

David C. Innes

Foreword by Carl R. Trueman

What are a Christian's civic responsibilities, and why? David Innes provides a principled political theology for understanding our civic "life together" in God's world. God calls our human officeholders and their civic business to a high moral purpose. His involvement in earthly rule reveals the nobility of political life—a practice it rarely conforms to but to which we should aspire.

"*Christ and the Kingdoms of Men* shows that we have many ways to do things together: all who read it will learn which activities should involve government, and which should not."
   —**Marvin Olasky**, Editor-in-chief, *World* magazine

"At once learned and lucid, sophisticated and accessible. . . . The book is a formidable synthesis of deep scriptural and theological learning, on the one hand, and a broad and rich understanding of the history of political philosophy, on the other. We will long be in Professor Innes's debt."
   —**Joseph M. Knippenberg**, Professor of Politics, Oglethorpe University

"This book is long overdue and much needed. . . . Dr. Innes has given all of us, of whatever theological stripe, a critical work at a critical time."
   —**Kevin L. Clauson**, Director, Center for Faith, Freedom, and the Constitution, Bryan College